CONTEXTS OF
CANADIAN CRITICISM

CONTEXTS OF
CANADIAN CRITICISM

Edited and with
an Introduction by
ELI MANDEL

University of Toronto Press
Toronto and Buffalo

Published 1971
© The University of Chicago 1971. All rights reserved

Reprinted by University of Toronto Press 1977
Toronto and Buffalo
Printed in USA

ISBN 0-8020-1780-0 (paper)
LC 78-143280

CONTENTS

PREFACE

For a variety of reasons, it seems important to expand the notion of literary criticism in Canada to include the work of historians and philosophers. Not the least reason is that some of the best writing in the country is historical and philosophical. Moreover, Canadian literary criticism consistently seeks its organizing principles not only in theories of literature but in historical and social contexts. It may be that Canadian concern with historiography, social structure, and esthetics can be viewed best as an expression of an almost paranoiac self-consciousness or simply as part of an attempt to understand the importance of communication theories in a demanding physical setting. Whatever the explanation for this obsession with self-definition and theoretical configurations, this much is obvious: any collection of critical essays that aspires to represent Canadian critical writing fairly and accurately will obviously present selections concerned not only with traditional comments on patterns of literary development but with the history and form of Canadian society and with problems in poetic theory as well. And it is this threefold concern that the organization of this volume reflects.

The history of Canadian criticism remains to be written. We possess fragments, bright and sharp though they may be: introductions to anthologies, prefatory comments scattered throughout collections of essays, jottings on critical problems. In the introductions to A. J. M. Smith's *Masks of Poetry* and *Masks of Fiction*, in Dudek's and Gnarowski's *The Making of Modern Poetry in Canada*, in Woodcock's comments introducing his *Choice of Critics*, the beginnings of a history of criticism appear. The Introduction to this volume attempts to move one step further by mapping out the problems and patterns of that history and the contexts within which it takes its shape. It attempts, in addition, to indicate something of the richness of material and excitement that await the writer or student who will venture into a relatively unexplored domain.

ELI MANDEL

CONTEXTS OF
CANADIAN CRITICISM

INTRODUCTION

This volume intends to present some approaches to what could properly be called a Canadian literary criticism. It ought to be apparent at once that the approaches chosen here are in a certain sense extraordinarily oblique. Our attention diverts itself from criticism to the field around it. Or it may be that we discover Canadian criticism is only its fields or contexts. At one time, *contexts* referred to speech constructions, or to connections between parts of a discourse, or even to a continuous composition. Present usage, of course, takes the word to mean "framing devices" or "background." Matthew Arnold would have said, more simply, "an order of ideas" or "an intellectual situation of which the creative power can profitably avail itself."

If we intend to concentrate our attention on literary criticism as such, we will be concerned with questions about the extent to which formal, structural, and generic considerations enter into discussions of Canadian writing. We might also want to consider whether the literature itself coheres into a consistently developing form, the context for which is both its own body of images and that larger body of traditional literary patterns that extends beyond anything so narrow—some might say parochial—as a national boundary. For as soon as we add the word *Canadian* to criticism, we move the object of our concern into a particular space and time, a geographical and historical context, where what might normally remain simply an element of the background—the sociology of literature—becomes the foreground. Like much else in Canadian life, Canadian literary criticism suffers from a form of national schizophrenia. It tries to find its boundaries outside itself, in some imperial world of literary tradition beyond nationality, and it seeks, both in its origins and in its development, for an authentic identity—something that expresses itself as a sort of conceptual space between its works of literature. In other words, its major impulse has been to fill up an emptiness, or to create, as Marshall McLuhan would put it, an "anti-environment" that will enable us to perceive the environment—the art, poetry, and literature of an invisible country.[1] At its worst, this sort of "composition by

[1] Marshall McLuhan, *Understanding Media,* 2d ed. (Toronto, 1964), p. ix.

field" sounds more like heavy breathing than serious social, historical, or critical comment. At its best, it stands in relation to narrowly defined critical techniques as, say, the transistor to the vacuum tube: the latter throws some light, but the former allows for large-scale integration of materials of different characteristics.

Northrop Frye reads the *Literary History of Canada* (Toronto, 1965), that Royal Commission of Canadian critical writing, as "a collection of essays in cultural history" and remarks, somewhat pessimistically, that "of the general principles of cultural history we know relatively little."[2] Nothing elsewhere in Canadian criticism promises to relieve our ignorance. It seems important, then, to be not less but more rigorous in defining the contexts of Canadian criticism. Remarks on patterns of literary and critical development really do need to be framed by essays on historiography and on social, as well as cultural, history. Notions of tradition and interpretation need to be seen as part of a developing awareness of critical theory. For these reasons, this volume interprets *criticism* so broadly as to include whatever comes into the field of Canadian vision: in brief, all those contexts within which discussions of literature in this country take place.

For convenience it is possible to distinguish three major contexts. The first frames that sort of criticism for which environment is primary—what could be described roughly as sociological or perhaps historical criticism. The second provides the connections that articulate various kinds of structual and interpretative criticism. And the third, concerning itself with patterns of literary development, seeks to define literary tradition or whatever may be discussed as distinctive in a national literature.

I

For Canadians, George Grant remarks, "the primal . . . was the meeting of the alien and yet conquerable land with English-speaking Protestants."[3] Only a certain gloomy temperament, one is tempted to say, could find so fateful and positive a word

[2] Northrop Frye, "Conclusion," in *Literary History of Canada,* ed. Carl F. Klinck et al. (Toronto, 1965), p. 822.

[3] George Grant, *Technology and Empire* (Toronto, 1969), p. 19.

as *primal* to describe a beginning. Yet Grant's ponderousness, which reaches elegiac eloquence in his *Lament for a Nation* (Toronto, 1965), catches precisely the feeling that something outside Canadian literature (indeed, outside Canadian life) impinges on it in an enormously threatening way. The encounter with the land signifies that literature itself must obviously be small, a secondary, derived activity, its survival a miracle. The first, the major, the most persistent pattern of Canadian criticism thus appears.

As A. J. M. Smith points out in his collection of critical essays, *Masks of Poetry* (Toronto, 1962), the view that a particular environment—frontier and colonial—shapes Canadian writing is adumbrated early: in Edward Hartley Dewart's introductory essay to *Selections from Canadian Poets* (1864), for example, and in the poet Lampman's "Two Canadian Poets: A Lecture" (1891).[4] And though Smith reads W. D. Lighthall's introduction to *Songs of the Great Dominion* (1889) as a contrast to Dewart because of Lighthall's "enthusiastic and hopeful rationalism," Lighthall's major note is surely vulgar sociology, the identification of poetry with its environment, as in the Binksian passage in which Lighthall tells us that if we listen closely we will hear in his poets "something of great Niagara falling, of brown rivers rushing with foam, of the crack of the rifle in the haunts of the moose and caribou, the lament of vanishing races singing their death-song as they are swept on to the cataract of oblivion."[5]

It remained for the first attempts at an extensive account of Canadian writing—that is to say, excluding such enterprising though fundamentally uninteresting catalogs as Archibald MacMurchy's *Handbook of Canadian Literature* (Toronto, 1906), R. P. Baker's *History of English-Canadian Literature to the Confederation* (Cambridge, 1920), Archibald MacMechan's *Head-Waters of Canadian Literature* (Toronto, 1924), and even Lorne Pierce's *Outline of Canadian Literature* (Toronto, 1927)—to develop the notions first touched upon by Dewart, Lampman, and Lighthall. E. A. McCourt's *The Canadian West in Fiction* (Toronto, 1949), as one might expect, insists upon an

[4] A. J. M. Smith, ed., *Masks of Poetry* (Toronto, 1962). Dewart's "Introductory Essay" and Lampman's "Two Canadian Poets" are included in Smith's collection.
[5] Smith, *Masks of Poetry*, p. 17.

ELI MANDEL

environmental interpretation of regionalism.[6] R. A. Rashley's
Poetry in Canada: The First Three Steps (Toronto, 1958), reflects a Marxist orientation, and Desmond Pacey's *Creative
Writing in Canada*, revised edition (Toronto, 1961), presupposes throughout a social and physical context so pervasive as to
constitute a determinism. Like Wilfred Egglestone's *The
Frontier and Canadian Letters* (Toronto, 1957), whose title
tells us what we need know of its preoccupation, all these works
share E. K. Brown's conviction: "To one who takes careful
account of the difficulties which have steadily beset [Canadian
literature's] growth its survival as something interesting and
important seems a miracle."[7]

Brown's *On Canadian Poetry* (Toronto, 1943) stands as a
minor classic, not only because of its liberal and humane spirit
and its measured account of the literature itself, but precisely
for its uncanny sense of the forces which it chooses to take into
account: the big land, the rough people, divided allegiances,
puritanism, materialism, colonialism, regionalism, the French;
in short, the frontier theory or myth of the wilderness, qualified
by its special Canadian characteristics: the imperial demands
of Britain and America and the polarization of French-English
cultures. However much this might seem to be a caricature of
Brown's meticulous prose (though it is startling to notice that
his remarks on French minority culture sound what seems now
an unbelievably condescending note),[8] Brown's position involves two of the most widely held notions in Canadian criticism: the theoretical view that a "new" literature evolves from
some primitive beginning toward a more and more sophisticated
present ("A great literature is the flowering of a great society,
a mature and adequate society");[9] the sociological and historical notion that this evolution is hampered in Canada by a
variety of social and physical conditions, the single name for

[6] E. A. McCourt, *The Canadian West in Fiction* (Toronto, 1949), p.
55.
[7] E. K. Brown, *On Canadian Poetry* (Toronto, 1943), pp. 5–6.
[8] See, for example, Brown's remarks that the French "read little if at
all in any language except French," that "French Canada is almost without curiosity about the literature and culture of English Canada," and that
"most cultivated French Canadians do not know even the name of the
significant English Canadian creative writers, whether of the past or of
the present." Ibid. p. 7.
[9] Ibid., pp. 25–26.

6

which is the frontier or wilderness, that haunting and haunted place that breeds the crazy manitous of symbolic voyages.[10] Or as Northrop Frye puts it in a justly famous and influential review of A. J. M. Smith's anthology *The Book of Canadian Poetry* (Toronto, 1943): "The outstanding achievement of Canadian poetry is in the evocation of stark terror. Not a coward's terror, of course; but a controlled vision of the causes of cowardice. The immediate source of this is obviously the frightening loneliness of a huge and thinly-settled country."[11]

The frontier theory, of course, has its powerful supporters, notably, if we accept J. M. S. Careless's analysis in his essay "Frontierism, Metropolitanism, and Canadian History,"[12] such historians as W. B. Munro, F. H. Underhill, W. N. Sage, A. R. M. Lower, F. London, A. S. Morton, and A. L. Burt, and, with some qualifications, J. B. Brebner and W. L. Morton. "The key principle to be applied by Canadian environmentalist historians," according to Careless, is "that thanks to the continuous process of adaptation to the environment, an American content had steadily grown in Canada within external forms of government, society, or culture, inherited from Britain or France."[13] In its variations, environmentalism or frontierism involves oppositions between the "dynamic west" and "torpid east" or between "pioneer agrarian interests" and "exploitative urban centres" or pioneer virtues and effete civilization. "In brief," as Careless puts it, "the West was the true America."[14] But, of course, the Canadian version of the frontier theory is qualified in peculiar ways. For one thing, it is not the West but the North that constitutes the physical and psychic frontier.[15] W. L. Morton, for example, insists that the "relevance of Canadian

[10] Specifically, Douglas Le Pan's "Country without a Mythology," in *The Book of Canadian Poetry*, ed. A. J. M. Smith (Toronto, 1943), pp. 422, 423.

[11] Northrop Frye, "Canada and Its Poetry," in *The Making of Modern Poetry in Canada*, ed. Louis Dudek and Michael Gnarowski (Toronto, 1967), p. 93.

[12] J. M. S. Careless, "Frontierism, Metropolitanism, and Canadian History," in *Approaches to Canadian History*, ed. Carl Berger (Toronto, 1967), pp. 63–83.

[13] Ibid., p. 68.

[14] Ibid., p. 69 and passim.

[15] Compare Carl Berger, "The True North Strong and Free," in *Nationalism in Canada*, ed. Peter Russell (Toronto, 1966), pp. 3–26.

history," that is, its relation to all history, "takes its rise in the relations and orientations which result from four permanent factors," one of which is its northern character.[16] Not the least element of this character is an alternating rhythm of withdrawal and return:

> this alternate penetration of the wilderness and return of civilization is the basic rhythm of Canadian life, and forms the basic element of Canadian character whether French or English, the violence necessary to contend with the wilderness, the restraint necessary to preserve civilization from the wilderness violence, and the puritanism which is the offspring of the wedding of violence to restraint. Even in an industrial and urban society, the old rhythm continues, for the typical Canadian holiday is a wilderness holiday, whether among the lakes of the Shield or the peaks of the Rockies.[17]

Morton would have it that Canadian art and literature, then, do not simply reflect northern scenery (Lighthall's moose, caribou, and paddle) but instead tend to "northern" qualities, the heroic, the epic, and because "northern life is moral and puritanical . . . harsh," the satiric as well.[18] But the rhythmic alternation between city and wilderness, restraint and violence, begins to look more like a pastoral myth of the sort Leo Marx describes in his "Pastoral Ideals and City Troubles"[19] than northern epic. Indeed, all that is needed to complete the pattern is the garden or town, Mariposa, or Crocus, Saskatchewan.

It is at this point that the context of our discussion necessarily widens to include not simply literary criticism, but historiography. The distinction we need is rather more sharp than that provided by William Kilbourn's brilliant account of the differences between the Laurentian and Continentalist schools of history, though it is important to be reminded by Kilbourn that whereas the critic seeks to find informing or structural principles for his art in history, the historian seeks out his structures in story, Canadian history proving itself finally just an-

---

[16] W. L. Morton, *The Canadian Identity* (Madison, 1961), p. 89.

[17] Ibid., p. 5.

[18] Ibid., p. 109.

[19] Leo Marx, "Pastoral Ideals and City Troubles," in *The Quality of Man's Environment* (Washington, D.C.: Smithsonian Institution Press, 1968), pp. 121–44.

other "art of narration."[20] Where indeed do we locate the structural principles of the story that is Canada's history? As Carl Berger points out in a brief but extraordinarily suggestive introduction to a collection of essays on Canadian historiography, three matters at least need to be borne in mind in looking at theories of Canadian history. "The first is the question of why historical viewpoints change at all"; "The second . . . is the degree to which some of the central conceptions which have shaped the writing of history in Canada have been imported"; and "The third . . . is the way the various approaches to the past have become associated with particular views of the 'national character.' "[21] There is no reason to believe that Berger is unaware of the tautology implied by the sequence: imported conceptions become associated with particular views of the national character while these very views (that is, "the national character") provide the evidence to validate the historical truth of the imported concept. So it is that the frontier thesis borrows from Turner, Underhill's continentalism derives from Beard and Parrington, and Careless's metropolitanism "runs back at least to the work of Henri Pirenne."[22] This is by no means to say that origins determine value, but it does suggest that not only "national character" but the "wilderness" is a conceptual framework, and that far from being a determinism, an environment may be a human creation. McLuhan contends that "any technology gradually creates a totally new human environment," and "as our proliferating technologies have created a whole series of new environments, men have become aware of the arts as 'anti-environments' or 'counter-environments' that provide us with the means of perceiving the environment itself."[23]

The possibility that Canada exists not as a function of its physical environment but in the technologies that create a new human order was first explored by Harold Innis, notably, as J. M. S. Careless remarks, in *A History of the Canadian Pacific Railway* (1923) and *The Fur Trade in Canada* (1930), both of which as "studies of major Canadian economic enterprises,

[20] W. Kilbourn, "The Writing of Canadian History," in *Literary History of Canada*, p. 519.
[21] *Approaches to Canadian History*, pp. viii–ix.
[22] *Ibid.*, p. viii.
[23] *Understanding Media*, pp. viii–ix.

which were essentially great systems of continent-wide communications, pointed the way to a new general interpretation of Canadian history."[24] By identifying society with its dominant technology, Innis inverted the commonly held view that, because its natural geographical lines ran north and south, Canada's "real" affinities were North American rather than British. East-west connections, the so-called Laurentian view, now could be seen to be more integral to the country than the north-south lines, and since technologies moved not only goods, but cultures, Ontario was fundamentally closer to London than New York.[25]

Aside from its obvious importance to historians, Innis's argument sets out the terms for the discussion of another major theme in Canadian criticism, colonialism. "The Strategy of Culture" seeks to "point to the conditions which seem fatal to cultural interests,"[26] and is surely an early and somewhat surprising example of an attack on American imperialism. The surprise is to find in Innis a note so close to that sounded by George Grant in *Lament for a Nation* (Toronto, 1965), and even more sepulchrally in *Technology and Empire* (Toronto, 1969). For Grant, technology, Calvinism, and liberalism combine to produce that enterprise within whose forms and assumptions Canadians live entirely.[27] And that enterprise, which is the true America, permits only a hectic and shallow art.[28] What America destroys, then, is not "culture" but rather what Raymond Williams (or to take a Canadian example, Thelma McCormack) would call high culture as opposed to mass or popular culture.[29]

Grant and Innis speak from a profound sense that Canadian cultural life takes its character (or at least *once* took its character) from British institutions. Technology may be our own or America's disaster, but "we must remember that cultural strength comes from Europe."[30] The implied tension between culture and society we will consider later. What appears as

24 "Frontierism, Metropolitanism, and Canadian History," p. 76.
25 *Ibid.*, p. 78.
26 H. A. Innis, *The Strategy of Culture* (Toronto, 1952), p. 1.
27 *Technology and Empire*, p. 64.
28 *Ibid.*, p. 39.
29 See Raymond Williams, *Britain in the Sixties: Communications* (Penguin, 1962) and Thelma McCormack, "Writers and the Mass Media," *Canadian Literature* 20 (Spring 1964):27–40.
30 Innis, *The Strategy of Culture*, p. 2.

receding images on the horizon of Canadian life are the Greek gods and the Hebrew prophets and inspired German conductors blown away in a cloud of tobacco smoke. Yet cultural nationalism turns with equal skepticism (if not fury) on British as well as American models. If the present villain is American corporate power, it was not so very long ago that the British seemed productive only of what E. K. Brown calls "the butler mentality" of the true colonial. In fact, the dialectics of what we could term the branch-plant theory of Canadian writing are as dazzling and paradoxical as anything a neo-Marxist might desire. Part of the difficulty is that both theoretical and historical arguments are used without any attempt to sort out the confusion created by mixing the two. Part derives from a constant shifting of terms and meanings. What at one time appears as an example of the colonial mentality may very well be cited at another time as an example of unsullied nationalism. So it is that nationalism itself, in a paradox that would surely delight a historian of national movements, becomes colonial; originality and realism are opposed to imitation and symbolism; and both pairs are cited on both sides of the question about the connection between the derivative and the colonial, while nothing that could be called lucidity is added by conflicting and contradictory attempts to locate a specifically Canadian tradition in our literature itself.

Historically, at least, there seems to be some sort of double tradition in both poetry and fiction that proves to be a complicating factor in any discussion of colonialism in Canadian writing. The tension between the idyllic and the realistic in the novel has been described, by F. W. Watt, Desmond Pacey, F. P. Grove, Carlyle King, and others, but has scarcely been explained. And the sense that there are deep divisions between poetic traditions appears as early as Smith's introduction to his *Book of Canadian Poetry* (1943), occupies many of the writers in *The Making of Modern Poetry in Canada* (Toronto, 1967), edited by Louis Dudek and Mike Gnarowski, and is something close to an obsession with Dudek, who returns to it time and again in his frequent surveys of "The State of Canadian Poetry."

It seems clear enough that the major documents in the discussion are Smith's "Introduction," John Sutherland's "Introduction to *Other Canadians*" (a reply to Smith), Northrop

Frye's review of Smith's *Book of Canadian Poetry*, and Milton Wilson's "Other Canadians and After."[31] And whatever the convolutions of argument and theory, this much at least appears plain. Smith's praise of those poets who "made a heroic effort to transcend colonialism by entering into the universal civilizing culture of ideas"[32] implied that, as opposed to "cosmopolitan" poetry, native or national poetry remained colonial, presumably in its parochialism. Sutherland's reply simply identified "cosmopolitan" with British poetry and consequently with social reaction: "Our poetry is colonial because it is the product of a cultured English group who are out of touch with a people who long ago began adjusting themselves to life on this continent."[33] Noncolonial then implies North American, radical, proletarian, the "Brooklyn-bum self" who is the real Canadian self. If we now translate these oppositions into literary tradition, it becomes clear that for Smith the models are British, specifically Yeats and Eliot; whereas for Sutherland the models are American, specifically the Imagists, but also Sandburg, Fearing, Cummings, Marianne Moore—and, of course, Whitman. Smith is constructing a rationale for his own poetry and the poetry of A. M. Klein, F. R. Scott, and Leo Kennedy; Sutherland, for Irving Layton, Louis Dudek, and Raymond Souster.

In part, the issue between Smith and Sutherland is modernism; in part, it is the social function of poetry or literature. Neither critic, it is interesting to note, approaches the intensity with which Innis viewed the question of colonialism in the 1950s or Grant in the 1960s. What seems to be at stake is largely a question of whether one prefers the "cultivated" or the "uncultivated." Much of the confusion certainly involves what Warren Tallman speaks of as the crude-fine paradox of North American writing. Between these confusions, Frye looks for a ground that could be called Canadian and universal at the same time, but since that is a manifest absurdity, it is little wonder his

---

[31] A. J. M. Smith, Introduction to *The Book of Canadian Poetry* (Toronto, 1943); John Sutherland, "Mr. Smith and 'The Tradition,'" in *The Making of Modern Poetry in Canada*, pp. 47–59; Frye, "Canada and Its Poetry," pp. 86–93; Milton Wilson, "Other Canadians and After," in *Masks of Poetry*, pp. 123–38.

[32] Cited in *The Making of Modern Poetry in Canada*, p. 47.

[33] John Sutherland, "Mr. Smith and the Tradition," p. 57.

argument strikes one as confused, and that some years later, in *The Modern Century* (Toronto, 1967), he withdraws it as a version of folk romanticism. At least, he makes clear his distaste for regional quaintness, imperialism, the "Ferdinand the Bull theory of poetry" (that smelling flowers rates as more inspiring than reading books), and "Tarzanism," the preference for the aboriginal to the original, the primitive to the consciously literary. To all such mystification and breast-beating about identity, the enervating spirit of imported standards, and rousing calls to support the industry, Milton Wilson offers the ultimate answer by wondering whether just possibly "colonialism may not be, in theory at least, the most desirable poetic state,"[34] since it seems to be a kind of golden world, timeless and infinite, where all possibilities, but no real tests of virtue, exist. The position seems to be the result either of quiet desperation or of irony. But it has about it a familiar quality. Unlike the more strident nationalists, some of those represented in Peter Russell's edition of *Nationalism in Canada* (Toronto, 1966), for example, Wilson takes contradiction and tension to be the normal state of Canadian life and art.

Within the context of environmental criticism, then, the fundamental dualisms of Canadian art and society present themselves as the only possible explanation of the apparent contradiction of the local and international in Canadian writing. Contemporary art, which, as Frye argues in *The Modern Century*, is international in style, appears as the logical end toward which a consistently colonial art moves. Yet the difficulty in understanding the contemporary in Canada is surely that, like earlier cultural concerns, its focus also has been local and national in a world which, as Frye observes, "the nation is rapidly ceasing to be the real defining unit of society."[35] Contemporary primitivism is another matter: the Canadian writer's concern with a primitive past—simply so that he might claim a national memory—turns out to be a startlingly immediate contact with the present, both in art and in fact. One extreme limit of esthetic discussion then becomes apparent in the contradictions contained within environmental criticism. We may put it that the tension in Canadian life is between vulgarity and

---

[34] Wilson, "Other Canadians and After," p. 137.
[35] Northrop Frye, *The Modern Century* (Toronto, 1967), p. 18.

ELI MANDEL

gentility. Or we may choose other pairs: American as opposed to British influences on Canadian writing; colonialism as opposed to nationalism; social realism as contrasted with abstract design; originality as opposed to traditionalism. Whatever our terminology, dualism appears as a genuine rift in Canadian life, something that Malcolm Ross speaks of as "the broad design of our unique, inevitable, and precarious cultural pattern." And Ross goes on to say, "This pattern, by the force of historical and geographical circumstances, is a pattern of opposites in tension . . . the federal-regional tension . . . the American-British tension . . . the French-English tension."[36]

How pathetic it is that, confronting the gravest crisis the nation has endured, one of its most eloquent liberals can propose as a resolution to the deepest rift of all not the constitutionalism of the rationalists but only the vaguest hope, based on an illusion, and looking toward a mystery:

> What we should ask now of the spokesmen of Quebec is not so much a definition of what they claim for their province and for their racial group as of what they consider all of us still to have in common if their claims are granted. Nothing is so alarming in these French-Canadian speeches as the almost complete absence of any consideration of what French and English can still look forward to doing together through their common government in Ottawa, if Confederation is to continue for a second century. A nation is a body of men who have done great things together in the past and who hope to do great things together in the future. Confederation will not be saved by any new constitution-making between now and 1967 if the minds and hearts of men of both groups are not moved by dreams of the great things that we may yet do together in the future.[37]

Environmentalism ends here, either in the irony of disillusioned eclecticism or an illusion itself, literature appearing as a reflection of environment: detached, ironic, remote, or "the evocation of stark terror." But if environmentalism is one extreme, criticism itself offers another: the contexts of criticism provided by theories of form. And it is to these we now turn.

[36] Malcolm Ross, ed., *Poets of the Confederation* (Toronto, 1960), p. xi.

[37] F. H. Underhill, *The Image of Confederation* (Toronto, 1967), p. 58.

14

II

Presumably, in critical theory one looks for the sort of argument which will resolve the form-content dichotomy that comes into being when the material of art—the "Canadian" content —calls for special attention for either political or social purposes. But then "content" is not so simply disposed of. Orwell insisted that all art is propaganda and that every line he wrote he intended politically, to serve democratic socialism as he understood it. And Dostoevski was willing to sacrifice everything to the commands of his message in *The Possessed.* Lacking its Dostoevskis and Orwells, Canadian literary criticism nevertheless is not without its polemicists, and although official "academic" criticism tends toward a melancholy blandness of style, the consistency of custard, there has been, throughout the years, a sort of critical underground where, in the revolutionary cells of their little magazines, practicing poets and their editors talked of their craft and projected each year a whole New Jerusalem of poetic possibilities.

An odd fact about Canadian criticism is that so little of this material has been collected or even properly cataloged. A. J. M. Smith's *Masks of Poetry* (Toronto, 1962) and *Masks of Fiction* (Toronto, 1961) contain some pertinent essays and prefaces by poets and novelists; Robert Weaver's anthology *The First Five Years* (Toronto, 1962) collects a few interesting interviews and essays; George Woodcock's *A Choice of Critics* (Toronto, 1966), despite its significance as a critical collection, belongs in a different category; the most important single volume is certainly *The Making of Modern Poetry in Canada* (Toronto, 1967), in which the editors, Louis Dudek and Michael Gnarowski, bring together a wide range of materials, "essays and documents intimately involved in the literary history of the period, rather than exemplary or autotelic show pieces of criticism."[38] Perhaps even more odd is that what we do possess of writers on their own art seems so uninteresting. F. P. Grove, Hugh MacLennan, Ethel Wilson, and Morley Callaghan scarcely suggest

[38] *The Making of Modern Poetry in Canada,* preface. Two other collections which should be mentioned here are John Glassco, ed., *English Poetry in Quebec* (Montreal, 1965), and G. Whalley, ed., *Writing in Canada* (Toronto, 1956).

ELI MANDEL

the kind of excitement attached to the criticism of a D. H. Lawrence, Henry James, or E. M. Forster; although Grove's prefatory essay to his *In Search of Myself* evokes with considerable power the desolation of the writer's position in the early years of the twentieth century in Canada, and, as Douglas Spettigue's recent study of Grove suggests, his powers of invention surpass anything that previously had been granted to him.[39] Similarly, in poetics, although the essays of A. J. M. Smith, Earle Birney, and Louis Dudek, in particular, are important for historical reasons as well as for their own visions of craft and art, one would not want to place them for comparison in the company of Eliot's *Collected Essays*, Pound's criticism, or for that matter Charles Olson's *Human Universe* or Auden's *The Dyer's Hand*. At the same time, one would welcome a collection of Irving Layton's prefaces to his books of poetry, surely the single most important body of criticism of its kind in Canada; and although Dudek's and Gnarowski's anthology of contributions to modern criticism in *The Making of Modern Poetry in Canada* is equally valuable, there is clearly room for more volumes of this sort, particularly one which will pick up some of the fugitive pieces from little magazines. What particularly remain to be collected are important essays and manifestos from *Contemporary Verse*, *Alphabet*, *Northern Review*, *Delta*, *Contact*, *Civ/n*, *Combustion*, *Fiddlehead*, and *Canadian Forum* (the last suggesting through the work of its former poetry editor, Milton Wilson, that academic and "practicing" Canadian criticism are not always at odds, and reminding one of the importance of academic magazines like *Malahat Review*, *Canadian Literature*, *Tamarack Review*, and *Queen's Quarterly*). A simple list of some of the names in Michael Gnarowski's *Contact 1952–1954, Notes on the History and Background of the Periodical and an Index* (Montreal, 1966), tells more about the history of American-Canadian poetic interaction and about real lines of literary development than any historical essay could hope to do; for example: A. G. Bailey, Paul Blackburn, Cid Corman, Robert Creeley, Louis Dudek, Larry Eigner, Ralph Gustafson, Irving Layton, Denise Levertov, Charles Olson, Kenneth Patchen, Raymond Souster, and Phyllis Webb.

[39] Frederick Philip Grove, "In Search of Myself," in *Masks of Fiction*, ed. A. J. M. Smith (Toronto, 1961), pp. 14–22; Douglas O. Spettigue, *Frederick Philip Grove* (Toronto, 1969).

Whatever else one makes of catalogs, it is worth remembering that among the shambles of little magazines and their polemics can be found some of the major critical focuses in Canadian writing. A. J. M. Smith's "Contemporary Poetry" in the *McGill Fortnightly Review* (15 December 1926) and his "Wanted: Canadian Criticism" in the *Canadian Forum* (April 1928)[40] declared for modernism, for craft, for tradition, and began Smith's relentless campaign for clarity and integrity in Canadian poetry, with a reversal of perspective at once simple and profound: "Canadian poetry . . . is altogether too self-conscious of its environment, of its position in space, and scarcely conscious of its position in time."[41] And the journey in time that Smith begins comes to its climax in James Reaney's editorial to the first issue of his magazine *Alphabet* (no. 1, September 1960) in which Reaney, explicitly invoking Frye and Blake, called on his readers to "rouse their faculties" and to grasp the "secret alphabet or iconography or language of symbols and myths" of contemporary poetry.[42]

Reaney reminds us that a genuinely revolutionary alteration of perspective and perception occurs rarely and then only in the presence of a major poet or critic. Much Canadian criticism is thorough and competent, consistently professional. Some of it is of genuine historical interest. In the work of three writers, at least, it touches greatness; that is to say, it radically alters the context within which we can view ourselves, our society, and our literature; with the criticism of Northrop Frye, Marshall McLuhan, and Francis Sparshott, Canadian criticism properly can be said to have come to its senses so that finally it might perceive aright.

The paradox, of course, is that "to come to their senses," all three writers turn their attention away from the immediate present to a theoretical ground, their reflexiveness consisting in their attention to problems of criticism itself rather than problems of literature or society. That in the end they return to the local does not alter their essentially abstract concerns, which prove to be capable of gathering together or integrating surprisingly disparate materials. In the grossest terms, one could say Frye raises questions about design and structure; McLuhan

[40] *The Making of Modern Poetry in Canada*, pp. 27–33.
[41] *Ibid.*, p. 33.
[42] *Ibid.*, p. 197.

concerns himself with technology, environment, and art; and Sparshott deals with problems in description and evaluation. It would probably be more accurate to speak of three kinds of formalism or theories of critical contexts, and the fairest description of these would see them in a Borgesian way as variations on a theme of infinite regression in which the contexts they provide are contexts for further contexts. This is not to suggest that critical theory, like metaphysics, is the highest form of fantasy, but rather that it is on the question of regression or tautology that the possible solution to the form-content dualism rests. For other literatures, the question of dualism might seem arid; for Canadians, it has the poignancy of a dream that the diagnosis after all was wrong and schizophrenia is not the national illness.

Frye's version of literature that imitates literature—creativity that is criticism and vice versa—not only presents an autonomous world of words that detaches literature from society, but grants peculiar authority to the imagination and therefore resolves the duality of national content and international style by turning society itself into a series of literary conventions. One hardly need rehearse here either the nature of his argument or the objections that have been urged against it. These, after all, are internationally known. More to the point here is his insistence that the principles of literary structure are within literature, that mythology and the Bible or scriptures provide grammars of such symbolic language, and that although criticism can choose to pretend to enthusiasms, it really cannot participate in experience but can only draw diagrams which we can choose to call commentaries or archetypes. As Reaney puts it, the surprise about such diagrams is "their electrifying organizing effect with regard to the imagination." Some writers, like Louis Dudek, speak glumly about Frye's "Pharmacopoeia," but in fact the prescriptions seem to have had some effect. It is difficult, if not impossible, to know to what extent a critic moves poets, but, along with Frye's contribution to the "Letters in Canada" series of the *University of Toronto Quarterly* for a period of ten years, a mythopoeic poetry of some power, in fact, did develop; and without claiming them as Frye's disciples, one notices certain poets whose work takes shape around this time: Wilfred Watson, Douglas Le Pan, James Reaney, Anne Wilkinson, and Jay Macpherson. In criticism, an equally interesting development occurs. Where myth appears as a formal and therefore autonomous element in poetry, we seem to be remote from any possibility of cultural criticism; yet Frye's perception that with the Confederation poets, particularly Carman, myth developed out of romantic impressionism provides a central clue to a genuine cultural history. And it is this clue which seems to explain the structure of those mythic geographies we find in James Reaney's "The Canadian Poet's Predicament," D. G. Jones's "The Sleeping Giant," Eli Mandel's, "A Lack of Ghosts," and Milton Wilson's "Klein's Drowned Poet."[43] The shape of a pastoral emerges in biblical parallels and images in Canadian poetry (a myth of city, garden, wilderness) and in the figures of wanderers, voyageurs, boatmen, and mirrored selves. The meaning of that pattern, or patterns like it, for social and educational experience now seems increasingly to occupy Frye as he turns from criticism to the kind of educational and social theorizing that characterizes *The Modern Century* and the conclusion to the *Literary History of Canada*.

Normally Marshall McLuhan's thought is not associated with Frye's or William Blake's, but like Frye and Blake, McLuhan begins with an attempt to "rouse our faculties" and ends with an image of the human body filling (or becoming) the universe. Like Blake's giant Albion, the environmentalist critic who sees an overwhelming physical landscape around him has splintered his senses and speaks with eyes rather than with tongues. The duality of form and content, in other words, or of "figure" and "ground," or of self and landscape, exists as a perceptual flaw and can be resolved as soon as the single or framing perspective becomes multiple or mosaic. This, McLuhan's organizing image, means simply that the content of any one medium (form or technology) is another medium, and that the development of a new form turns its content into a work of art, and art "is a

[43] James Reaney, "The Canadian Poet's Predicament," in *Masks of Poetry*, pp. 110–22; D. G. Jones, "The Sleeping Giant," in *A Choice of Critics*, ed. G. Woodcock (Toronto, 1966), pp. 3–24; E. W. Mandel, "A Lack of Ghosts: Canadian Poets and Poetry," in *Of Several Branches: Essays from the Humanities Association Bulletin*, ed. Gerald McCaughey and Maurice Legris (Toronto, 1968), pp. 176–87; Milton Wilson, "Klein's Drowned Poet: Canadian Variations on an Old Theme," *Canadian Literature* 6 (Autumn 1960):5–17. Frye's own approach, of course, is most fully developed in his *Fearful Symmetry* (Princeton, 1947) and *Anatomy of Criticism* (Princeton, 1957) though *The Educated Imagination* (Toronto, 1963) is a useful introduction.

means of perceiving the environment itself." The image for the process by which one form alters another is the inter-face.

Something George Grant says in *Technology and Empire* may serve as a summary of the position so baldly stated above: "Technique is ourselves [and] comes forth from and is sustained in our vision of ourselves as creative freedom, making ourselves, and conquering the chances of an indifferent world."[44] Yet to be in technological society seems to Grant a deprivation wherein even the possibility of articulating the nature of the loss seems to have disappeared. Presumably what is lost is "the something that is *not* ourselves"; but to mistake our own creations for eternal verities would be, in McLuhan's terms, equally grievous. As for Frye, so for McLuhan: society is a series of conventions, a form of art. To see it otherwise is to fall into the maelstrom or, like Narcissus, to drown in an image of oneself as the other. To see it as art is to see it theatrically, as the possibility of ritual and therefore of grace.

It may be no more than coincidence that McLuhan's image of the vortex and drowned poet is one of the major recurrent images of Canadian poetry, most fully articulated in Margaret Atwood's "Progressive Insanities of a Pioneer," while a title like Lionel Kearns's *By the Light of the Silvery McLune* tells us that, for better or worse, another Canadian critic has bemused the poets. Between them, Atwood and Kearns suggest the polarities of Canadian poetry and criticism: the wilderness as the radically alien "other," and society as a convention, form, or theater of the absurd.

If environmentalism threatens to dissolve both poetry and criticism into the dualities of space and time (Canadian history and geography), formalism threatens another kind of dissolution: it may suppose, suggests F. E. Sparshott, "that the critic's work is somehow more vital than the work he is writing about" and the critic will then become "prophet or necromancer, making (as Wilamowitz said) the ghosts speak by feeding them on blood."[45] Sparshott, then, seeks some point of balance be-

[44] *Technology and Empire*, p. 137. Probably the best approach to McLuhan still remains *The Gutenberg Galaxy* (Toronto, 1962) but *Understanding Media* must also be regarded as essential.

[45] F. E. Sparshott, *The Concept of Criticism* (Toronto, 1967), pp. 105–206.

tween the autotelic and the sociohistorical. The methodology to achieve this turns out to be surprisingly elaborate, an explicative study that proceeds "by unpacking the main concepts . . . used in defining criticism, and unfolding their implications."[46] Oddly enough, for a critic whose main argument develops the view that criticism must refer, that by definition, usage, and in its logically defined "causes" and "functions" criticism proves to be always "about" something, Sparshott remains determinedly self-referring in his discussion: it is, after all, criticism about criticism, and indeed is not so much "about" itself as about whether it can be about itself. A further problem presents itself in Sparshott's definition of criticism as performance, for performance is "anything whatever . . . regarded as a performance" but particularly "something that is . . . an unmistakable manifestation of human agency and . . . self-contained to the point of isolation."[47] This is, according to Sparshott, a framing concept, one of those "physical or conceptual devices that mark a work of art off from its surroundings and isolate it for attention."[48] But having come so close to an autotelic position, Sparshott immediately veers off by the simple device of considering criticism itself as an institution and criticism as a marketable commodity for "the mass-medium market," "the academic-scholarly market," "the academic-instructional market," and "the market for quasi-permanent literature."[49] It is not likely then that Sparshott will treat kindly either the suggestion that criticism and art are identical or what would seem to him mere mystification: the view that one new work of art alters the whole existing order of art; a notion, oddly enough, common to Eliot and McLuhan.

Sparshott's purpose, of course, is not simply to sneer. If the fate of societies and cultures does not seem to him to depend on theories of criticism, that is because, one suspects, neither concepts of the wilderness nor the theater of the absurd mean more than interesting, if exaggerated, poeticisms. Criticism is evaluation grounded in reasoned discourse. Its "proper province . . . remains that marked out by the terminology appropriated to complex structures of formal speech: evaluation, appraisal, ex-

---

[46] *Ibid.*, p. 213.
[47] *Ibid.*, p. 183.
[48] *Ibid.*, pp. 183–84.
[49] *Ibid.*, p. 194.

planation, interpretation."[50] Obviously, that definition intends to preserve critical integrity, "a complex structure of formal speech," while at the same time insisting on a secondary derived position for criticism with respect both to art and to theories of value.

Sparshott's analysis thus reintroduces the form-content dualism, specifically in criticism itself, under the guise of criticism as evaluation of particular works (general theories of poetry, art, society, and the world are anathema).[51] For evaluation implies standards of value and these must be derived from theories of value. In turn, value theories impose themselves as social content or, if one so chooses, as metaphysical content.

It may very well be true that no literature or criticism can attain the wholeness it seeks solely on its own terms and that to think of complex social structures as literary conventions both vulgarizes and brutalizes society. It may be equally true that, as Frye says, "there is no division, though there may be a distinction, between the creative power of shaping the form and the critical power of seeing the world it belongs to" and that "any division instantly makes art barbaric and the knowledge of it pedantic."[52] The context of literature is human civilization; the context of evaluative criticism is society and physical nature. It now appears that the perennial choice for criticism is between those two contexts and that the Canadian dilemma is only a local version of the endlessly recurrent demands of imagination and reason.

III

Accounts of the character and development of Canadian writing are marked by the struggle to avoid talking about national identity or local politics as much as by the desire to find distinctive national characteristics. And presumably one must pay tribute to those critics who, finding themselves faced with an almost impossible task, manage to maintain balance, tact, and coherence. Of course, it has been suggested more than once that it is precisely this precarious, mannered control that marks out the "Canadian" part of the critic, particularly when

[50] *Ibid.,* p. 213.

[51] *Ibid.,* p. 208.

[52] Northrop Frye, "The Road of Excess," in *Myth and Symbol,* ed. Bernice Slote (Lincoln, Nebraska, 1963), p. 20.

such balance suggests an utter madness within. Not for nothing is one prime minister, known for his manic cautiousness in public and secret preference for Gothic ruins and mediums in private, symbolic of the typical Canadian: one who, in F. R. Scott's words, never let his "on the one hand" know what his "on the other hand" was doing.

Ways to avoid talking about the "geographical fallacy," as Milton Wilson terms it, become as interesting as ways of talking about it. Wilson's own suggestion is that one might busy oneself by observing "how certain problems of diction, imagery and form recur in . . . Canadian poetry."[53] Paul West concerns himself with matters of tone and voice, remarking somewhat skeptically on the slightly fey lists one can construct of imaginative landscapes. His own list ranges delightfully from "sleazy beer-parlours, desolate plains, blue lakes, plaid shirts" to "dead moose and pure cold."[54] The catch is that the negatives (as in film-making) contain their opposites: like Dorothy Livesay, West feels that only a form as huge as an epic will be adequate to a huge place, even though he is not certain whether the place is a mythic whale, "a coy colossus," or a country. So it is, too, that Robert McDougall advances the startling and important thesis that the almost complete blindness of our literature to class struggle and social structure results from its genteel, academic bias. He might easily have added, from the evidence he himself adduces, that a literature so ignorant of manners and morals must be primitive.

To any reader of Northrop Frye, the identification of the academic and the primitive will come as no surprise, even if the route to it is by way of McDougall's negations. In brief, aside from questions of the sort that would interest a critic like Sparshott (that is, how certain value judgments manage to manifest themselves in rigorously structuralist criticism), the curious fact about attempts to define or characterize a tradition of Canadian writing is the inevitable, obsessive concern with physical landscape:

> There is only old mother North America with her snow hair, her mountain forehead, her prairie eyes, and her wolf teeth,

[53] Milton Wilson, ed., *Recent Canadian Verse* (Kingston, [n.d.]), p. 6.
[54] Paul West, "Ethos and Epic: Aspects of Contemporary Canadian Poetry," *Canadian Literature* 4 (Spring 1960):14.

> her wind songs and her vague head of old Indian memories . . .
> when the house is repossessed the gods come back—snow gods,
> dust gods, wind gods, wolf gods.[55]

It is possible to say that in the crudities or mannerisms of the north, criticism has lost its balance, though whether it is more balanced elsewhere remains in question. It is possible to accuse Canadian criticism of monomania or, the opposite, an almost inhuman eclecticism. There are curious, disturbing lapses: so little to the point about the regional, the idyllic, the nostalgic, the grotesque, all major modes and tonalities of our literature and of the myth of the wilderness or completed pastoral; and so little of seriousness about fiction, about the craft of the novel or its concern. But perhaps what prevails, after all, is what we would on all grounds—theoretical, logical, historical, cultural, political, social—want to reject: the image with which we began.

Recently a gifted young poet published a volume of poems derived, worked out, from, as she says, a "personality . . . which reflects many of the obsessions still with us." In an afterword to her *The Journals of Susanna Moodie* (Toronto, 1970), Margaret Atwood writes:

> If the national illness of the United States is megalomania, that of Canada is paranoid schizophrenia. Mrs. Moodie is divided down the middle: she praises the Canadian landscape but accuses it of destroying her; she dislikes the people in Canada but finds in the people her only refuge from the land itself; she preaches progress and the march of civilization while brooding elegiacally upon the destruction of the wilderness; she delivers optimistic sermons while showing herself to be fascinated with deaths, murders, the criminals in the Kingston Penitentiary and the incurably insane in the Toronto lunatic asylum. She claims to be an ardent Canadian patriot while at all times she is standing back from her country and criticizing it as though she were a detached observer, a stranger. Perhaps that is the way we still live. We are all immigrants to this place even if we were born here: the country is too big for anyone to inhabit completely, and in parts unknown to us we move in fear, exiles and invaders. This country is somthing that must be chosen— it is so easy to leave—and if we do choose it we are still choosing a violent duality.[56]

[55] Warren Tallman, "Wolf in the Snow," in *A Choice of Critics*, p. 76.

[56] Margaret Atwood, *The Journals of Susanna Moodie* (Toronto: Oxford University Press, 1970), p. 62. With the permission of Oxford University Press.

That may be bad criticism, but it does connect 1832 with 1970 in Canada; Upper Canada with Edmonton; Moodie's *Roughing It in the Bush* with the University of Alberta, English Department. It may be anything but the truth and yet "the only form of knowledge that does not date and continues to hold its interest for future generations."[57] Like poetry, criticism may tell lies and yet provide us with the only memory we can have and which, if we are to survive, we must possess. Whether we should ask more of it—or of ourselves—remains as always the most difficult question.

[57] Northrop Frye, "Preface to an Uncollected Anthology," in *Studia Varia: Royal Society of Canada Literary and Scientific Papers,* ed. E. G. D. Murray (Toronto, 1957), p. 36.

I

THE SOCIAL
AND HISTORICAL CONTEXT

I

E. K. BROWN

Canadian Poetry

There is a Canadian literature, often rising to effects of great beauty, but it has stirred little interest outside Canada. A few of our authors, a very few, have made for themselves a large and even enthusiastic audience in Britain or in the United States or in both. Among these the first in time was Thomas Chandler Haliburton, a Nova Scotian judge, who would not have relished the claim that he was a Canadian. A curious blend of the provincial and the imperialist, he ended his days in England, where long before he himself arrived his humorous sketches were widely read, so widely that Justin McCarthy has reported that for a time the sayings of his most ingenious creation, Sam Slick, were as well known as those of the more durably amusing Sam Weller. Haliburton's papers were also popular in the United States, and their dialectal humor and local color have left a perceptible stamp upon New England writing. At the mid century, when Sam Slick was already a big figure in English humor, *Saul*, a huge poetic drama by a Montreal poet, Charles Heavysege, had a passing vogue in Britain and in the United States, impressing Emerson and Hawthorne and inducing Coventry Patmore to describe it as "indubitably one of the most remarkable English poems ever written out of Great Britain." Its vogue was lasting enough for W. D. Lighthall, a Montreal poet of a later generation, to recall that "it became the fashion among tourists to Montreal to buy a copy of *Saul*." Today, along with Heavysege's other works, his *Count Filippo* and his *Jephthah's Daughter*, it is unknown within Canada and without. Even the songs and sonnets of Heavysege are absent from recent Canadian anthologies. At the turn of the century the animal stories of C. G. D. Roberts extended the range of North American writing in a direction it might naturally have

Reprinted from E. K. Brown, *On Canadian Poetry*, 1943, by permission of the Ryerson Press, Toronto.

been expected to take with equal success somewhat sooner—the imaginative presentation of the forms of wild life characteristic of this continent in their relationship to the frontiers of settlement. These tales, simple and at times powerful, continue to hold a high place in the rather isolated and minor kind of literature to which they belong; but there is no doubt that in our time they are more talked of than opened except by youthful readers. There is little need for comment upon the writings of a handful of Canadians who at about this same time began to make their huge and ephemeral reputations as best-selling writers. Gilbert Parker soon left Canada to establish himself in Britain, and it is to English literature, to that group of British novelists who followed in the wake of Stevenson's romantic fiction, that his work belongs. Preeminent among the others, Ralph Connor, L. M. Montgomery and Robert Service continued to live in Canada, the first two until they died, Service till middle age. They were all more or less aggressively unliterary; and the only significance for our inquiry is the proof they offered that for the author who was satisfied to truckle to mediocre taste, living in Canada and writing about Canadian subjects, was perfectly compatible with making an abundant living by one's pen. The lesson they taught has not been forgotten: fortunately it has not been widely effective.

More recently Canadian work of value comparable with that of Haliburton's sketches and Roberts's animal tales has become known outside the country. There were the humorous papers of Stephen Leacock, the best of which have delighted not only Americans and Englishmen, and the peoples of other parts of the British Commonwealth, but also some Europeans. I can remember hearing M. André Maurois read to a group of students at the Sorbonne the charming study called "Boarding House Geometry"; and I never heard merrier laughter in Paris. The endless Jalna chronicles of Miss Mazo de la Roche maintain a large audience in Britain, and a sizable one in the United States; and in a more restricted group in the latter country the short stories and, to a less degree, the novels of Morley Callaghan are valued. I think that I have mentioned all the Canadians who have acquired considerable popularity or reputation as imaginative authors, either in the United States or in Great Britain. To the reader outside Canada such works as have been mentioned have not been important as reflections of phases in a national culture;

the interest in the work has not spread to become an interest in the movements and the traditions in the national life from which the work emerged. Canadian books may occasionally have had a mild impact outside Canada; Canadian literature has had none.

I

Even within the national borders the impact of Canadian books and of Canadian literature has been relatively superficial. The almost feverish concern with its growth on the part of a small minority is no substitute for eager general sympathy or excitement. To one who takes careful account of the difficulties which have steadily beset its growth its survival as something interesting and important seems a miracle.

Some of these difficulties, those of an economic kind, may be easily and briefly stated. Economically the situation of our literature is, and always has been, unsound. No writer can live by the Canadian sales of his books. The president of one of our most active publishing companies, the late Hugh Eayrs, estimated that over a period of many years his profit on the sales of Canadian books was one per cent.; and I should be surprised to learn that any other Canadian publisher could tell a much more cheerful tale, unless, of course, the production of text-books was the staple of his firm's business. Text-books make money in any country. In general the Canadian market for books is a thin one, for a variety of important reasons. The Canadian population is in the main a fringe along the American border: nine out of ten Canadians live within two hundred miles of it, more than half within a hundred miles. The one important publishing center is Toronto; and a bookseller in Vancouver, Winnipeg or Halifax must feel reasonably sure that a book will be bought before he orders a number of copies which must be transported across thousands of miles. Books like *Gone with the Wind* and *The White Cliffs*—to keep to recent successes—he will order in quantity with confidence; but the distinguished work, the experimental novel, the collection of austere verse, the volume of strenuous criticism is for him a luxury. The population of Canada is less than that of the State of New York; if our population were confined within an area of the same size the problem of distributing books would be soluble. Even if our fewer than twelve million people were confined within the huge triangle whose points are Montreal, North Bay and Windsor—enclosing an area comparable with that of the region of New England—the problem might be soluble. But it is hard to see how the cultivated minority is to be served when its centers are separated by hundreds and often thousands of miles in which not a single creditable bookstore exists.

Of the less than twelve million Canadians who are strung along the American border in a long thin fringe, almost a third are French-speaking. These read little if at all in any language except French, apart from a small, highly conservative minority which studies the classics and scholastic philosophy, and a rather larger minority which keeps abreast of books in English that treat of political and economic subjects. In French Canada the sense of cultural nationality is much stronger than in English Canada, but the nationality is French Canadian, not Canadian *tout court*. French Canada is almost without curiosity about the literature and culture of English Canada; most cultivated French Canadians do not know even the names of the significant English Canadian creative writers, whether of the past or of the present. Occasionally an important Canadian book is translated from the original into the other official language; but it is much more likely that the work of a French Canadian will be translated into English than that the work of an English Canadian will be translated into French. Louis Hémon was a *français de France*, but it was because *Maria Chapdelaine* dealt with French Canada that a distinguished Ontario lawyer translated the novel into English, making one of the most beautiful versions of our time. W. H. Blake's translation of Hémon's book is a masterpiece in its own right; no French Canadian has as yet labored with such loving skill to translate any book that deals with English Canada. A symbol of the fissure in our cultural life is to be found in the definition of sections in The Royal Society of Canada. Three sections are assigned to the sciences, one to mathematics, physics and chemistry, another to the biological sciences, and the third to geology and allied subjects; in these sections French and English fellows sit side by side. But in the two sections assigned to the humanities the French and English fellows are severely separate: in each the subjects run the impossible gamut from the classics to anthropology. It is not too much to say that the maximum Canadian audience that an English Canadian imaginative author can hope for is less than eight million people.

To write in the English language is to incur the competition of the best authors of Britain and of the United States. Every Canadian publisher acts as agent for American and British houses; and it is as an agent that he does the larger and by far the more lucrative part of his business. Every Canadian reviewer devotes a large part of his sadly limited space to comment on British or American books. Every Canadian reader devotes a large part of the time and money that he can allow for books to those which come from Britain and the United States. Some angry critics have contrasted the plight of Canadian literature with the eager interest that Norwegians take in the work of their own authors. It is obvious that the accident by which Canadians speak and read one of the main literary languages of the world is a reason why they are less likely to read native books than a Norwegian is, speaking and reading a language peculiar to his own country.

Our great distances, the presence among us of a large minority which is prevailingly indifferent to the currents of culture that run among the majority, the accident of our common speech with Britain and the United States—here are three facts with enormous economic importance for literature. The sum of their effect is the exceedingly thin market for the author who depends on Canadian sales. Unless an author gives all or most of his time to writing for popular magazines he can make very little indeed; and even the resort of the popular magazines is a precarious solution. There are few of these—they, too, are affected by the factors that have been mentioned. They are in almost ruinous competition with American magazines, they cannot pay very much, they print a good deal written outside Canada, and they live so dangerous an existence they commonly defer slavishly to the standards of their average readers.

The serious Canadian writer has a choice among three modes of combining the pursuit of literature with success in keeping alive and fed. He may emigrate: that was the solution of Bliss Carman, and many have followed in his train. He may earn his living by some non-literary pursuit: that was the solution of Archibald Lampman, and it has been widely followed. He may while continuing to reside in Canada become, economically at least, a member of another nation and civilization: that is the solution of Mr. Morley Callaghan. Each of these solutions is open to danger and objection.

The author who emigrates becomes an almost complete loss

to our literature. It is probable that in the end, like Henry James or Joseph Conrad or Mr. T. S. Eliot, he will take out papers of citizenship in the country where he has found his economic security and to which he has transferred his spiritual allegiance. If he goes to Britain, the choice will not arise in this form, but he will be at best simply a citizen of the Empire, ceasing to be an authentic Canadian. No one thinks of Grant Allen as a Canadian author nor did he so consider himself though he was born in Ontario. How the creative powers of a writer are affected by expatriation is much too vast a problem to receive adequate consideration here. Only this I should like to say: the expatriate will find it more and more difficult to deal vigorously and vividly with the life of the country he has left. Joseph Conrad did not write about Poland. When toward the end of his career Henry James read some of the early tales of Edith Wharton, before he had come to know her, he urged that she should be tethered in her own New York backyard. His own experience persuaded him that exile disqualified one from treating the life of one's own country without admitting one to the center of the life in the country to which one had fled. If one compares the later novels of Edith Wharton, written after she had lost contact with New York, with the earlier ones which rose out of strong impacts that New York made upon her sensibilities, it is immediately evident that the colors and shapes are less vivid and definite, and that the works of her elder years are less significant. I should argue that Bliss Carman, our most notable exile, suffered a grave loss by passing his middle years in the United States, that he did not become an American writer, but merely a *déraciné*, a nomad in his imaginary and not very rich kingdom of vagabondia.

People often ask why an author cannot satisfy himself with the solution of Archibald Lampman. Lampman, after graduating from Trinity College, Toronto, entered the employ of the federal government as a clerk in the Dominion Post Office at Ottawa. Why, people inquire, cannot a writer earn his living as a clerk, or a teacher, or a lighthouse keeper and devote his leisure to literature? The answer to this question must be an appeal to experience. One of our most gifted novelists, Mr. Philip Child, once remarked to me that a writer must be the obsequious servant of his demon, must rush to write when the demon stirs, and let other things fall where they may. If you fob off the demon with an excuse, telling him to wait till you can leave the office, he will sulk, his visits will become rarer and finally he will not return at all. Temperaments differ; and some writers may, like Anthony Trollope, give fixed hours to authorship and the rest of the day to business and pleasure. Even the Trollopes of this world would prefer to be free from their unliterary employments, since it is not to manage a post-office that a Trollope came into this world. Temperaments less phlegmatic than Trollope's find even the mild yoke of the post-office too heavy for them. Lampman did. He had easy hours, from ten to four-thirty, work which did not exhaust, and long holidays; but he was irked by his employment and made desperate and always unsuccessful efforts to escape from it. One has only to read his letters to realize that he believed that his task-work was fatal to his full development, and one has only to read his poems to believe that there was something in Lampman that never did come to full fruition, something that would have led to deeper and wiser poetry than he did write except in snatches. It appears to me so obvious as to require no argument that whatever success a particular writer may have had in combining the practice of his art with the business of earning a living by work which is remote from letters, the notion that a whole literature can develop out of the happy employment of the odd moments of rather busy men is an unrealistic notion, and one that shows an alarming ignorance of the process by which great works are normally written. I suggest that the richness of Canadian poetry in the lyric and its poverty in longer and more complicated pieces, in epic, or dramatic composition, is related to the need of Canadians to be something else than writers in most of their time through their best creative years. Some of them have, like Matthew Arnold—also as a poet the victim of his unliterary employment—left unfinished their main poetic atempt.

There remains a third solution, Mr. Callaghan's solution. It is possible to write primarily for an American or a British audience. Most of Mr. Callaghan's novels and shorter tales are about the city in which he lives, Toronto; but it seems to me, and I speak as one who was born and brought up in that city, that Mr. Callaghan's Toronto is not an individualized city but simply a representative one. I mean that in reading Mr. Callaghan one has the sense that Toronto is being used not to bring out what will have the most original flavor, but what will remind people

who live in Cleveland, or Detroit, or Buffalo, or any other city
on the Great Lakes, of the general quality of their own milieu.
If one compares Mr. Callaghan's Toronto with Mr. Farrell's
Chicago, the point becomes very plain. When I pass through
Mr. Farrell's Chicago, that part of the South Side which has
been deserted by the Irish to be seized by the Negroes, the
memory of what he has written of a life which has ceased to
exist becomes very moving. When I walk through the parts of
Toronto that Mr. Callaghan has primarily dealt with, the poor
areas toward the center and a little to the north-west of the
center, or the dingy respectability of the near east end, it is
only with an effort that I remember that he has written of them
at all. It is a notable fact that never once in all his novels does
he use the city's name. Just as Mr. Callaghan uses his Canadian
setting for its interest for a larger North American audience, so
Miss Mazo de la Roche sets her emphasis on those exceedingly
rare aspects of rural Ontario life which would remind an English
reader of his own countryside and the kind of life that goes on in
it. In the work of both writers an alien audience has shaped the
treatment of Canadian life. Whether this peculiarity has injured
the novelists's art as art, whether the characters and the setting
are less alive and moving than the characters and setting in, let
us say, Mr. Farrell's novels or Arnold Bennett's is not the immediate question; but there is not a scrap of doubt that the
methods of Mr. Callaghan and Miss de la Roche have interfered
with their presentation of Canadian life in the terms most stimu-
lating and informing to Canadian readers. One of the forces that
can help a civilization to come of age is the presentation of its
surfaces and depths in works of imagination in such a fashion
that the reader says: "I now understand myself and my milieu
with a fullness and a clearness greater than before." Many a
Russian must have said so after reading *Fathers and Sons* or
War and Peace. It is difficult to believe that a Canadian will say
this or anything of the sort after reading the work of Miss de la
Roche or Mr. Callaghan.

I should like to turn for a moment to the question momentarily put aside, the question whether the solution adopted by
such writers as Mr. Callaghan and Miss de la Roche is injurious
to their art, whether it reduces the worth of their fiction for
readers who are not Canadians, and not interested in the problems peculiar to Canada as the ideal Canadian reader must be.

A great opportunity has been refused by Mr. Callaghan—the opportunity of drawing the peculiarities of Toronto in full vividness and force. This is a subject that no writer has yet treated. Most Canadians who are not born and bred in Toronto emphasize that there is a quality in the life of that city which is to them mysterious, and obnoxious. To make plain what that quality is, perhaps to satirize it as Mr. Marquand satirized something peculiar to Boston in *The Late George Apley*, perhaps to give it a sympathetic interpretation as Arnold Bennett interpreted the Five Towns in *The Old Wives' Tale*—here was a great theme calling aloud for imaginative treatment. Had Mr. Callaghan not been essentially a part of American civilization, it would have forced itself upon his perceptive and completely realistic mind. There is also something unique in the life of rural Ontario, something that no novelist has succeeded in catching, and Miss de la Roche has refused an opportunity perhaps no less golden than Toronto offers.

II

The difficulties that have so far appeared, unlike as they are, all have economic roots. It is time to turn to the psychological factors, implied in much that has been said, against which the growth of a Canadian literature must struggle.

Among these the most obvious, the most discussed, although *not* the most potent, is the colonial spirit. Long ago Harvard's President Felton doubted that Canada would come to much since a colony was doomed to be second-rate. In a later generation an American who knew us much better than Felton and who wished us well, William Dean Howells, used almost the same language. In *Their Wedding Journey* he conducts his couple from Niagara Falls by way of Kingston and Montreal to the east coast, giving sharp little pictures of the Canadian towns; he concludes that in comparison with the free nation to which they belong this colony is second-rate in the very quality of its life. Just a year or so ago the Halifax novelist, Mr. Hugh Mac-Lennan, gave to one of the colonially minded characters in *Barometer Rising* the same thought: "I've wasted a whole lifetime in this hole of a town. Everything in this country is second-rate. It always is in a colony." These are probably independent judgments. What do they mean? That a colony lacks the spiritual energy to rise above routine, and that it lacks this energy because it does not adequately believe in itself. It applies to what it has standards which are imported, and therefore artificial and distorting. It sets the great good place not in its present, nor in its past nor in its future, but somewhere outside its own borders, somewhere beyond its own possibilities.

The charge that English Canada is colonial in spirit is the most serious of all the many charges that French Canada brings against us. Speaking in the 1942 session of the Canadian House of Commons, Mr. Louis Saint Laurent, the leading French member of the government, illustrated what he meant by our colonialism when he cited an interchange that is supposed to have occurred within the last few years between the two living ex-prime ministers of Canada. One said to the other, on the eve of his departure to live in England: "I am glad to be going *home*," and the other replied: "How I envy you!" For these two men—if the interchange did occur—Canada was not the great good place; and every French Canadian would regard their sentiments as justifying his practice of referring to us not as *Canadiens Anglais,* but merely as *Anglais,* or when his blood is up, as *maudits Anglais!* Colonialism of this kind is natural to emigrants. One can easily forgive Sir Daniel Wilson, although he spent almost his entire active career in Canada, for wishing to lie in Scottish earth; and yet for a Canadian who knows what Scotland is like in November it is an awe-inspiring thought that Sir Daniel on one of our autumn days, full of the crashing scarlet glories of the Canadian forests or the benign radiance of our Indian summers, wished to be amid the "sleety east winds" of his native land. What is odd, and unsatisfactory, is the perpetuation of this kind of colonialism in the descendants of emigrants even to the third and fourth generation. It is clear that those who are content with this attitude will seek the best in literature, where they seek the best in jam and toffee, from beyond the ocean. That anything Canadian could be supremely good would never enter their heads.

It is important to distinguish this attitude of pure colonialism from another, which is steadily confused with it by all French Canadians, and combined with it by a good number of English Canadians. As the nineteenth century drew on and the concept of empire in Britain herself assumed a new color, the Kipling color, some Canadians spoke and wrote of a Canada which would be a partner in the destinies of a great undertaking in which Britain would not be the master, but simply the senior partner. Charles Mair, our first important political poet, expressed the view I have in mind when he wrote, in 1888:

> First feel throughout the throbbing land
>   A nation's pulse, a nation's pride—
> The independent life—then stand
>   Erect, unbound, at Britain's side.

Another poet, Wilfred Campbell, coined an impressive phrase for Canada's destiny: Canada was to be a part of "Vaster Britain." "Stronger even than the so-called Canadian spirit," he wrote, "is the voice of Vaster Britain." It is unjust to speak of this version of the imperialist ideal as showing the "butler's mind": it contemplated not serving Britain, but sharing Britain's glories. The psychological source of this intoxicating imperialism was not perhaps so much loyalty to Britain, but rather discontent with the dimensions of the Canadian scene. Canada was at the close of the last century a poor country, mainly concerned with material problems, and steadily losing many of her people to the large, rich, exultant land to the south. Imperialism was a kind of beneficent magic which would cover our nakedness and feed our starving spirits. The imperialist dream still lingers, but it is only a dream, for the mode in which the empire has evolved has been centrifugal—away from the concept of imperial federation—and there is nothing sufficiently rich and various to which the loyalty the dream evokes can attach itself. In practice the imperialist has drifted unconsciously into a colonial attitude of mind.

As the idea of imperial federation receded—and it was an idea that we may well judge impractical since French Canada could never have shared it, nor the Dutch in South Africa, nor the Southern Irish—Canada entered upon a period in which thinking was extremely confused. I cannot attempt to provide here any account of the extraordinary political evolution of the Dominions within the past generation. But the confusion is obvious if one notes merely a few significant political facts. Canada has no distinct flag, and no single distinct anthem although Mr. Mackenzie King paused on the very brink of asserting the latter; the relations between Canadian Provinces and the federal government are subject to review in London; and the Judicial Committee of the Privy Council, also in London, is our highest court.

But Canada has her own ministers in foreign countries, makes treaties without reference to Britain, and declares, or refuses to declare, war by the instrument of her own Parliament. Is it any wonder that Canadian thinking about Canada is confused, that one set of clear-thinking men demands that we cease sending ministers and signing treaties and declaring war for ourselves, and that another set of clear-thinking men demands that we provide ourselves with a distinct flag and anthem and end the ingestion of the British Parliament and the British Privy Council in our affairs? The average English Canadian would still like to have it both ways and is irritated, or nonplussed, by the demand that he make a resolute choice; at heart he does not know whether Canada or the Empire is his supreme political value.

In the contemporary world autonomy is the most luxurious of privileges, one which this anxious country cannot now afford and will not be able to afford in any measurable future. It is not an unmixed good. Autonomy almost always breeds chauvinism, and usually brings as an immediate consequence an unwholesome delight in the local second-rate. Its advent opposes strong obstacles to international currents of art and thought. This is to be set firmly against the notion that out of autonomy all good things soon issue. Still it must be appreciated just as clearly that dependence breeds a state of mind no less unwholesome, a state of mind in which great art is most unlikely to emerge or to be widely recognized if it did. A great art is fostered by artists and audience possessing in common a passionate and peculiar interest in the kind of life that exists in the country where they live. If this interest exists in the artist he will try to give it adequate expression; if it exists in the audience they will be alert for any imaginative work which expresses it from a new angle and with a new clearness. From what was said a moment ago it will be obvious that in a colonial or semi-colonial community neither artist nor audience will have the passionate and peculiar interest in their immediate surroundings that is required. Canada is a state in which such an interest exists only among a few. I have pointed out how Mr. Callaghan and Miss de la Roche have written as they could not have written if they had possessed such interest. It is the same with Canadian readers. A novel which presents the farms of the prairie, or the industrial towns of south-western Ontario, or the fishing villages in the Maritime

Provinces will arouse no more interest in the general reader than a novel which is set in Surrey or in the suburbs of Chicago. Canadian undergraduates are much less likely than Americans to write stories about their immediate environment: their fancies take them to nightclubs in Vienna (rather than Montreal), islands in the South Seas (rather than the St. Lawrence), foggy nights in London (rather than Halifax). It is almost impossible to persuade Canadians that an imaginative representation of the group in which they live could clarify for the reader his own nature and those of his associates. To the typical Canadian reader such a notion is arty folly. I give this as a fact; and I offer as a partial interpretation, at least, that most Canadians continue to be culturally colonial, that they set their great good place somewhere beyond their own borders.

Somewhere beyond their borders—not necessarily beyond the seas. Canada is colonial not only in its attitude toward Britain, but often in its attitude toward the United States. It is true that the imprint of a London publisher, or of a British university press, is a more impressive guarantee of a book or an author than any Canadian sponsorship, even a Governor-General's. When the late Lord Tweedsmuir remarked that a Canadian's first loyalty should be toward Canada (rather than toward Britain or toward the Empire) it was believed in some circles, and these not the least cultivated, that he had been guilty, as one journalist phrased it in cynical fun, of "disloyalty towards himself." It was inevitable that a Scottish man of letters should think in such terms, Scotland being almost wholly free from the spirit of colonialism. Pleas that we should seek to free ourselves from our colonial feelings toward Britain are met with cries of "ingrate!" or "traitor!" There can, of course, be no question of such open and violent objection against efforts to free us from a colonial attitude toward the United States. Our colonialism in relation to the United States is unavowed, but it is deep. The praise of a couple of New York reviewers will outweigh the unanimous enthusiasm of Canadian journals from coast to coast. There is every reason to suppose that as Canadian feeling becomes more and more friendly toward the United States, as it has done during the past quarter century, our cultural dependence on the Americans will grow. If it does, our literature may be expected to become emphatically regionalist; of the dangers of regionalism something will be said a little later.

III

A more powerful obstacle at present to the growth of a great literature is the spirit of the frontier, or its afterglow. Most Canadians live at some distance from anything that could even in the loosest terms be known as a material frontier; but the standards which the frontier-life applied are still current, if disguised. Books are a luxury on the frontier; and writers are an anomaly. On the frontier a man is mainly judged by what he can do to bring his immediate environment quickly and visibly under the control of society. No nation is more practical than ours; admiration is readily stirred, even more readily than south of the border, by the man who can run a factory or invent a gadget or save a life by surgical genius. This kind of admiration is a disguised form of the frontier's set of values. No such admiration goes out to any form of the esthetic or contemplative life. The uneasiness in the presence of the contemplative or esthetic is to be ascribed to the frontier feeling that these are luxuries which should not be sought at a time when there is a tacit contract that everyone should be doing his share in the common effort to build the material structure of a nation. That a poem or a statue or a metaphysic could contribute to the fabric of a nation is not believed. In a gathering of ruminative historians and economists, speaking their mind one evening in Winnipeg years before the war was imminent, the unanimous opinion was that a destroyer or two would do more than a whole corpus of literature to establish a Canadian nationality. The dissent of two students of literature was heard in awkward silence. If there were any belief in the national value of art or pure thought, the strong desire of the frontiersman that what is being built should eclipse all that was ever built before would make a milieu for art and thought that would at the root be propitious.

In a disguised form of frontier life what function can the arts hold? They are at best recreative. They may be alternatives to the hockey match, or the whiskey bottle, or the frivolous sexual adventure as means of clearing the mind from the worries of business and enabling it to go back to business refreshed. The arts' value as interpretation is lost in the exclusive emphasis on their value as diversion, and even their value as diversion is simplified to the lowest possible form—a work of art must divert strongly and completely. It must divert as a thriller or a smashing jest diverts, not as an elaborate and subtle romance or a complicated argument diverts. In a word, Canada is a nation where the best-seller is king, as it is on the frontier.

A third factor telling against the appreciation of art is our strong Puritanism. Every foreign observer notes with amazement, both in our French and in our English books, the avoidance of the themes that irk the Puritan, or the language that now irks him more. Canada has never produced a major man of letters whose work gave a violent shock to the sensibilities of Puritans. There was some worry about Carman, who had certain qualities of the *fin de siècle* poet, but how mildly he expressed his queer longings! Mr. Callaghan has fallen foul of the censors of morals in some of our more conservative cities, and even among those of his own Roman Catholic faith a novel as *Such Is My Beloved* has had an uneasy path; but how cautious in the description of sordor and how chastened in language he has always been! Imagination boggles at the vista of a Canadian Whitman, or Canadian Dos Passos. The prevailing literary standards demand a high degree of moral and social orthodoxy; and popular writers accept these standards without even such a rueful complaint as Thackeray made in warning that he could not draw his Pendennis as a full man, since no hero of an English novel intended for the general public had been drawn in full since Fielding went to his grave.

Even our Canadian Puritanism, however, has not been proof against the international currents of moral relaxation which have coursed so strongly during the past quarter century. In the poetry of those who are now approaching their fortieth year, there is a broad range of emotion, which does not stop short of carnality, and an equally broad range of speech for which nothing in the Canadian literary past gave a precedent. This poetry does not yet circulate at all widely, most of it is still locked away in periodicals read by few, and it is not possible to be sure whether it could even yet pass the moral test of the general reading public.

If Puritanism operated simply to restrain the arts within the bonds of moral orthodoxy, its effects, though regrettable, would be much less grave than they now are. Puritanism goes beyond the demand for severe morality: it disbelieves in the importance of art. It allows to the artist no function except watering down moral ideas of an orthodox kind into a solution attractive to minds not keen enough to study the ideas in more abstract presentations. At its most liberal Puritanism will tolerate, a little uneasily, the provision through the arts of an innocent passing amusement which is expected to leave no deep trace on character. To popularize orthodox morality and to provide light, clean fun—that is the very limit of what the arts can be allowed to do without alarming the Puritan mind. For the Puritan a life devoted to one of the arts is a life misused: the esthetic life is not a form of the good life. That profane art, both for artist and for audience, may provide the contemplation of being, may offer an insight into the life of things, is for the Puritan mist and moonshine.

Puritanism is a dwindling force, and the time is not far off when it will no longer exercise its ruinous restraint upon the themes or language of a Canadian writer who is addressing the general public. Regionalism, another force which tells against the immediate growth of a national literature, cannot be expected to dwindle so fast. Canada is not an integrated whole. The Maritime Provinces recall the days—only seventy-five years in the past—when they were separate colonies; Nova Scotia, for instance, has re-established its colonial flag, dating from the eighteenth century and flying now from the Province House at Halifax; French Canada is a civilization apart; Ontario unconsciously accepts itself as the norm of Canadian life; the Prairie Provinces are steeped in their special vivid western past; and British Columbia has a strong sense of its pre-confederation life and of its continuing separate identity. Geography confirms the influence of history. Ontario is separated from the Maritime Provinces by the solid enclave of Quebec; between the populous southern part of Ontario and the prairies the Laurentian shield interposes another huge barrier; and this barrier is no stronger, if broader, than the Rocky Mountains create between the prairies and the coastal province of British Columbia. There is little doubt that the Fathers of Confederation, or the majority of the leaders among them, expected and planned for a much more unified whole than has so far come into being. In time of war the tendency to self-aggrandizement on the part of the Provinces is arrested, even reversed; but there is ground for fearing that the return to peace will start it into vigorous being once more. Among most Canadians there is little eagerness to explore the varieties of Canadian life, little awareness how much variety exists, or what a peril that variety is, in time of crisis, to national unity. It may be that the next important stage of Canadian literature will be strongly particularist and regionalist: one remembers what a force regionalism was in American literature in the years after the Civil War.

Regionalist art may be expected to possess certain admirable virtues. One of these is accuracy, not merely accuracy of fact, but accuracy of tone; and throughout our literature there has been a disposition to force the note, to make life appear nobler or gayer or more intense than Canadian life really is in its typical expressions. It would help us toward cultural maturity if we had a set of novels, or sketches, or memoirs that described the life of Canadian towns and cities as it really is, works in which nothing would be presented that the author had not encountered in his own experience. It should also be acknowledged that a warm emotion for one's *petit pays* can lead to very charming art, as in Stephen Leacock's humorous transposition of an Ontario town in his *Sunshine Sketches*. In the end, however, regionalist art will fail because it stresses the superficial and the peculiar at the expense, at least, if not to the exclusion, of the fundamental and universal. The advent of regionalism may be welcomed with reservations as a stage through which it may be well for us to pass, as a discipline and a purgation. But if we are to pass through it, the coming of great books will be delayed beyond the lifetime of anyone now living.

IV

What I have been attempting to suggest with as little heat or bitterness as possible is that in this country the plight of literature is a painful one. People who dislike to face this truth—and most Canadians do—have many easy answers. One is that Canadians have been so busy making a new world that it is harsh and unrealistic to expect that they might have written a large number of important books, read them with strong and general interest, and set a distinctive literary tone for their civilization. To this answer one may retort by pointing to what had been achieved in the United States a century ago, calling the roll of the names of those Americans who had written works of the first order, of national and international importance, by 1843—Edwards, Franklin, Jefferson, Irving, Cooper, Poe, Hawthorne and Emerson. In certain other ways the American environment up to 1843 was more hospitable to literature than ours has been up to the present time; but there can, I think, be no doubt that Americans were in the century and a half preceding 1843 just as busy building the material structure of a nation as we have ever been. Another easy answer is often put in such terms as these: "If a Dickens begins to write in Canada we shall greet him with a cheer, we shall buy his books by the scores of thousands, get him appointed to the Senate of Canada, and request the Crown to give him an O.M. Meanwhile, don't bother us, with your complaints. You can't point to a single man of anything approaching the caliber of Dickens who has written in this country. We have neglected no one of great importance. Wait till our Dickens comes along, and then we'll prove to you that we know how to honor a great writer." The line taken here depends on the belief that literature is an autonomous thing, a succession of single great men, each arising accidentally, each sufficient to himself. On this view you will get your great literature when you get your great men of letters, and meanwhile there is no problem worth discussing.

Thinking of this sort ignores a fundamental fact: that literature develops in close association with society. I should not deny that a single man of genius might emerge and express himself more or less fully in a society which was inhospitable to literature; but I find it significant that the most original of our poets, E. J. Pratt, has maintained:

> The lonely brooding spirit, generating his own steam in silence and abstraction, is a rare spirit, if indeed he ever existed, and as far as one may gather from scientific discussions on the point, there is no biological analogy for this kind of incubation. Rather, the mountains come to birth out of the foothills, and the climbing lesser ranges. The occasional instance cited in literary history, of personal isolation ignores the context of spiritual companionship with books and causes and movements.

The ways of genius cannot be fully predicted; but the "occasional instance," the single man of genius, is not a literature and does not bring a literature into being. No doubt if a Browning or a Yeats were to write in Canada and to make himself felt in Canada, the effect on Canadian literature would be considerable. But the stimulus such a writer could give, great though it would be, and much as it may be wished for by all who hope for the growth of a great literature in this country, would be a passing stimulus, unless it were assisted by social conditions friendly to creative composition. A great literature is the flowering of a great society, a mature and adequate society. Here I must reluctantly take leave of this subject, for it is not in the province of a student of letters to say how a society becomes mature and adequate.

In the observations I have offered it will be thought by many Canadians that the note of pessimism, or at least of rigor, is too strong. On the side of hope and faith it should be said that the future of Canada is almost singularly incalculable: none of the factors that now tell so strongly against the growth of our literature is necessarily eternal and many of them are likely to diminish in force. Every reflective Canadian must feel a mixture of disturbance and delight in our inability to foresee even the main stresses of the Canada that will exist a hundred years from now.

W. L. MORTON

The Relevance of Canadian History

THE CHARACTERISTICS OF CANADIAN HISTORY

Relevance, for the purpose of this chapter, may be understood to mean the relations between the history of Canada and the histories of other communities. It also means the orientation given to Canadian history by the interaction of those relations with the environment and historical development of Canada. How those relations and that orientation are defined will in turn suggest the interpretation of Canadian history embodied in a work approaching completion. Relevance, finally, means what universal or philosophic significance belongs to the Canadian historical experience.

By Canadian history also is to be understood one history, not one French and one British, but the entire history of all Canada. There are not two histories, but one history, as there are not two Canadas, or any greater number, but one only. Nor are there two ways of life,[1] but one common response to land and history expressed in many strong variants of the one, it is true, but still one in central substance. The reason for this is that the history of Canada after 1760 is only a continuation and extension of the history of Canada before 1760. There is but one narrative line in Canadian history.

The argument of this chapter is equally simple. It is that the relevance of Canadian history takes its rise in the relations and orientations which result from four permanent factors in that

Reprinted from W. L. Morton, *The Canadian Identity*, by permission of the University of Wisconsin Press. Copyright 1961 by the Regents of the University of Wisconsin. Originally, presidential address read before the Canadian Historical Association, Queen's University, Kingston, Ontario, 11 June 1960.

[1] A. R. M. Lower, "Two Ways of Life: the Primary Antithesis of Canadian Life," *Report of the Canadian Historical Association, 1943*.

history. These are a northern character, a historical dependence, a monarchical government, and a committed national destiny, committed, that is, to special relations with other states.

THE FACTOR OF NORTHERN ORIENTATION

The northern character springs not only from geographical location, but from ancient origins in the northern and maritime frontier of Europe. That frontier extends from Norway by Scotland and the North Atlantic islands to Greenland and Canada. Within that area from medieval to modern times there is discernible a frontier of European culture developing across the northern latitudes in which the forward movement was largely by sea. It was not a Turnerian frontier, but it was a frontier in every sense, and it was this frontier which began the exploitation and settlement of Canada. Many of its characteristics survive in Canada to this day, and presumably will continue to do so indefinitely.

The historical characteristics of this northern and maritime frontier are clear and definite. The most evident was that of coastal and riverine settlement. The largely Precambrian geology of the region afforded few extensive or fertile plains. The shelves in the fjords, the estuaries of seasonal rivers, the terraces around bays, these were the foothold and the baseland the northern frontier afforded to settlement. Even the Laurentian trench in America simply raised the foothold to continental proportions but did not change its character. Moreover, the maritime character of the frontier tended to settlement by the sea, even when extension of the economy inland was possible.

The settlements sometimes consisted of small port towns, but the characteristic mode was the family farmstead. This was the center of a complex of arable land, pasture, fuel land, and hunting ground much more delicate in its relationships than those of a farmstead in a more favorable climate and a more fertile soil. Land near the stead yielded vegetable and cereal foods, if climate permitted. The outfields and hill pastures gave pasture and hay. The adjoining forests or bogs furnished firewood or peat. The summer was a season of sowing, herding and gathering in, the winter a season of concentration in house and byre, or relaxation or rationing according to the summer's yield.

The winter was also the season of hunting, whether for food

or fur. The northern frontiersman in this lull penetrated the wilderness and used it to supplement the returns of the farmstead. The dependence of any one farmstead or settlement on the hunt varied from place to place, but hunting as a seasonal occupation was always one characteristic of the northern frontier.

Fishing was equally a supplementary occupation to a degree also varying with locality. It too furnished an addition to the diet, and even forage for the cattle. The run of the fish in the rivers was seasonal, and curing by smoking or drying made fish, for example the eel fishery of the St. Lawrence, an indispensable part of the diet of the northerner. The sea fisheries were summer fisheries, but tended to equal cattle raising in importance, to take the men away for the season and thus to demand co-operative effort and specialization. They might also yield a staple for trade.

The fisheries, it may be supposed, were the origin of the seafaring that made possible both the migration of the frontier across the North Atlantic and also the amount of trading which took place between it and the central lands of the European metropolis. Certain it is that the northern frontier was much more a maritime than a land frontier, a character which to a curious degree Canada retains even yet, and which will increase again as arctic navigation develops. The pioneers of that frontier were not long hunters or the *voortrekkers*, but fishermen seeking new fishing grounds, seamen-farmers in quest of new island pastures, Viking voyagers who sought in new lands whatever fell to them of plunder, trade, or homestead.[2]

The northern and maritime frontier had its own northern economy with characteristics equally explicit. It was an extensive and a gathering economy, dependent on new lands, new seaways, and the transport the seas and rivers afforded. It required a base of arable soil and habitable climate for the farmstead settlements. The farmstead was a highly self-subsistent unit, but it was the base of an economy which as a whole was an exchange economy to a high degree. The surplus staples of fish, fur, and timber, with exotics like arctic ivory and oil, falcons, and Polar bears, earned the funds with which to buy the metals,

[2] A. W. Brøgger, *Norse Emigrants* (Oxford, 1929).

the cereals, the church goods, and the luxuries the northern settlements needed or desired. Some of the traffic was inter-regional; it was, for example, its timber that made Vinland of primary interest to the Greenlanders.

That the Canadian economy historically has been an economy of this kind requires no demonstration. The great staple trades have been extensive, in-gathering trades. The population which carried them on lived in and worked from relatively narrow bases of good land in the sea inlets and river valleys; most of Canada is simply a hinterland extensively exploited from the soil base of the St. Lawrence and Saskatchewan valleys, and from the delta of the Fraser. The Canadian economy has also largely bought its external supplies by the sale of surplus staples.

The first discovery and early exploration of the lands which were finally to be united in Canada were the outcome of the advance westward of the northern and maritime frontier of Europe and the extension of the northern economy to America. These discoveries and the first occupation of Canadian shores were made by way of the northern approach. Somehow, by methods yet only guessed at, the Viking frontiersmen, the Bristol traders, and Norman fishermen made their way across the North Atlantic. Their sea skill and navigational science were so far developed that they could use the brief and uncertain easterlies of late spring and early summer which blow as the belt of the westerlies shifts north with summer to make their way across by a northern route.[3] They did not, like the Spaniards and the Elizabethan English, use the long but certain southern route of the trade winds. The discovery and occupation of Canada was separate and distinct from the discovery and occupation of the Americas.

Nor was it the result of high-pitched, scientific exploration aimed at the trade of Asia. It was the outcome of the piecemeal ventures of Norse seamen-farmers probing the northern seas for new harbors and fisheries, new hay meadows and timber stands. The process is scantily documented. Government archives record it scarcely at all; it can now be understood and comprehended only by an understanding of the character of

[3] D. W. Waters, *The Art of Navigation in England in Elizabethan and Early Stuart Times* (London, 1958), p. 577.

the northern frontier and economy, an understanding which is as bold an extension of the hints of the sagas as were the original voyages themselves.

The evidence, however, is slowly accumulating to suggest that between the last connections with Greenland and the voyages of the Bristol seamen there was no break in sea knowledge or experience.[4] The Bristol men, with the knowledge of the Azoreans and, presumably, of the Normans and Bretons, were taking over the western half of the old Norse sea empire, and were being caught in the western tug of the northern frontier. It is scarcely to be doubted that their own efforts would have discovered the Newfoundland fisheries if John Cabot and Henry VII had not imposed on their limited and practical efforts the scientific concepts of the Italian navigators and the first imperial impulse of Tudor England. In any event, the outcome was the same. Asia was not discovered, nor was the English empire founded in the fifteenth century, but the Newfoundland fishery of the English west country, and of Normandy and Brittany, was in being by the opening of the sixteenth.

This, then, is the first orientation of Canadian historiography. Canadian history is not a parody of American, as Canada is not a second-rate United States, still less a United States that failed. Canadian history is rather an important chapter in a distinct and even an unique human endeavor, the civilization of the northern and arctic lands. From its deepest origins and remotest beginnings, Canadian history has been separate and distinct in America. The existence of large areas of common experience and territorial overlap no one would deny. History is neither neat nor categorical; it defines by what is central, not by what is peripheral. And because of this separate origin in the northern frontier, economy, and approach, Canadian life to this day is marked by a northern quality, the strong seasonal rhythm which still governs even academic sessions; the wilderness venture now sublimated for most of us to the summer holiday or the autumn shoot; the greatest of joys, the return from the lonely savagery of the wilderness to the peace of the home; the puritanical restraint which masks the psychological tension set up by the contrast of wilderness roughness and home discipline. The line which marks off the frontier from the farmstead, the wilderness

[4] Vilhjalmur Stefansson, *North West to Fortune* (New York, 1958).

from the baseland, the hinterland from the metropolis, runs through every Canadian psyche.

THE FACTORS OF DEPENDENCE: THE ECONOMIC

We come now to the second factor, that of dependence, of the external ties and background of Canadian history. Canada throughout its history has in varying degrees been dependent economically, strategically, and politically. The northern economy, for example, was self-subsistent only at the base. Even there it was not necessarily so, as the extinction of the Greenland colonies grimly demonstrated, and as the plight of the prairie provinces in the 1930s re-emphasized. As a whole, however, the northern economy was a highly dependent one. It was a hinterland economy dependent on the sale of a few basic staples and a few exotics in a metropolitan market.

That is, the whole culture of the northern and maritime frontier, to succeed as well as survive, required from outside a high religion, a great literature, and the best available science and technology to overcome its inherent limitations. These very limitations of climate and of material and human resources made the frontier dependent on a metropolitan culture for those essentials. The alternatives were extinction or complete adaptation to the lowest level of survival in northern conditions. Was not the basic difference between the north European and the Eskimo that the former had a central and metropolitan economy and culture on which to draw, while the latter had none until very recent times and lived in a wholly and wonderfully self-subsistent culture?[5]

The northern economy, then, was a dependent one, both for the markets which absorbed its staples and exotics, and for the supply of the needs of mind and body which raised life on the northern frontier above the level of subsistence and enabled it to produce in Iceland the literature of the sagas and in modern

---

[5] And is not the extraordinary readiness with which the Eskimo adopts the techniques and implements of modern culture an indication of how necessary such a metropolitan culture is for a life of more than survival in arctic conditions? Surely contemporary anthropology has no more fascinating study than that of the fusion of the Eskimo culture with that of the Canadian frontier which is proceeding in the far north today. One may hope that Canada is at least giving those wonderful people the central base they lacked for so many unrecorded centuries.

Canada the political fabric which unites the technology of a highly civilized and industrialized baseland with the exploitation of the resources of a harsh and enormous hinterland.

THE FACTORS OF DEPENDENCE: THE STRATEGIC

If the northern and maritime has been economically dependent, it has been even more so strategically. Down to the fifteenth century it was defended more by remoteness and poverty than power. Its own population and resources were too slight for the task of defense. The decline of Danish sea power and the rise of the Hanseatic League left it entirely defenseless, as the English raids on Iceland in the fifteenth century revealed. And with the development of the ocean-going sailing ship in the same century, the northern frontier became explicitly dependent on sea power. "Empire of the North Atlantic" would be naval empire.

It was not, however, until the end of the seventeenth century, when the use of naval power became systematic after the Dutch conquest of the Spanish power at sea and the balance of power in Europe was extended to include the Americas, that the northern frontier in its Canadian extension actually came into the strategic pattern of European empire. The capture of Port Royal in 1710 and the Hill-Walker expedition against Quebec in 1711, though a failure, may be taken as marking the beginning of the operation of European strategy through sea power upon the northern frontier.

The result was, because French sea power had declined relatively to the British since 1692, that New France had to develop a holding policy and count on victory in Europe to regulate the Euro-American balance. This policy succeeded until the Anglo-American conquest of Canada in 1760. Canada then became wholly dependent on British sea power, if indeed one may refer to Canada when for the first and only time the northern frontier was politically united with the developing agricultural and industrial power to the south. That transient union was, however, to be broken in part by the Quebec Act, in part by the American War of Independence. The Anglo-American empire had failed to absorb the northern frontier with its primitive economy and Indian tribes, and the break-up of the empire in America was preliminary to the larger disruption caused by American independence. The sea power of Britain was then the decisive factor in the survival of Canada, but it did not operate alone. Conscious and deliberate choice by Canadians and Nova Scotians made their survival a complex historical process by which the northern community resumed its identity in the North Atlantic system.

The situation after 1783 of course remained fluid and uncertain. Canada and the maritime colonies remained part of the northern economy and strategically dependent on Britain. The new balance achieved in 1814 was registered in the boundary convention of 1818 and completed by the Oregon Treaty. These diplomatic achievements and their military backing revealed how firmly a part of British policy was the defense of Canada and the retention of a strategic check on the United States. Until the rise of the iron warship, the timber of the northern frontier, whether in the Baltic or on the St. John and the St. Lawrence, was a necessary element in British sea power. But after the emergence of the United States from the Civil War as a great military power and the gradual British withdrawal from the Americas, Canadian military strength by no means rose in correspondence with the decline of British power. Canada, in fact, as Laurier remarked to Lord Dundonald in 1902, was henceforth defended by the Monroe Doctrine.[6] Canadian dependence had taken a new, an American, form.

The dependence was by no means complete, nor was it ever to prevent Canada as a member of the Empire from making war abroad. The situation did, however, make it clear that the resources of the northern economy had proved insufficient to create a military power of significant stature except in alliance with one or other of the great powers. What had been accomplished, however, had been the transformation of dependence into free association and free alliance by the development of national self-government in the Empire and America.

THE FACTORS OF DEPENDENCE: THE POLITICAL

The factors of economic and strategic dependence were until the end of the nineteenth century also expressed in terms of political dependence. The French exploitation of the fisheries and the fur trade, with the zeal of French missionaries and an intermittent interest in a trade route to the Far East, had led to

[6] G. F. G. Stanley, *Canada's Soldiers* (Toronto, 1960), p. 294.

the development of the French empire in America. On the private commerce of the fishery and fur trade, with their need of defense and regulation, the French Crown imposed its own interests in the conversion of the native people and the colonization of Acadia and Canada. Underlying these interests was the strategic purpose of establishing in New France a base for commerce with the new lands and, if possible, with the Far East.

This partnership of royal power with the northern economy was often an uneasy and a fretful one, as when the *coureurs de bois* after 1672 defied the royal policy of limiting the fur trade and carried their enterprise westward. Yet in the end the two were reconciled in the imperial purpose after 1700, when France began to use its northern base and its continental spread to confine the English colonies to the seaboard.[7] The primitive northern economy had penetrated the continent by the great river systems, as the Swedish Vikings had Russia, and the rivers, the canoes, the fur traders, and the Indians were the means used to check the advance of the English settlers. The union of the primitive and the sophisticated, of war and trade, of small means and ranging enterprise which characterized the northern culture was never better exemplified than in Canadian captains like Iberville, or in the French empire in America in the eighteenth century.

The first British Empire had developed similar characteristics in the north. The Hudson's Bay Company was the outcome, and a continuation of, the search for the Northwest Passage. It too needed metropolitan protection, and only escaped absorption into the French empire by Marlborough's victories in Europe. On the New York frontier in the days of William Johnson the English developed the same alliance with the Indian and the northern economy of the fur trade that the French had done. And in Nova Scotia the same factors of colonial dependence and imperial purpose produced Halifax. When the British empire in America broke up in the War of Independence, it was in part because the differences between the old northern empire of France and the old colonies of England had not been reconciled.

[7] How serious this purpose was is revealed by the annual payments made by the French Crown for the government and defense of New France from 1661 to 1760.

And when the disruption was complete, the union of northern dependence with imperial strategy ensured that Nova Scotia and Canada, the northern elements of the fishery and the fur trade, should remain within the British Empire.

British America had the same northern character as French America, a base for the fisheries and the fur trade, for trade by the St. Lawrence with the continental interior, and for naval power and Northwest exploration. How true this was is apparent if a glance is taken at what Imperial policy actually did in British North America between 1783 and 1871. It not only paid much of the cost of government and defense; it preserved the territorial claims to which the Dominion was to be heir. From 1818 to 1854 it employed Franklin and his fellow explorers in the same scientific exploration that under Cook's genius had led to the opening of the Pacific and the colonization of Australia and New Zealand. At the same time it halted Russia in Alaska by diplomacy, and forestalled it in the arctic archipelago[8] by the great feats of naval exploration of Ross, Parry, and M'Clintock. By so doing, it laid the groundwork for the Canadian occupation and development of the Arctic. This Imperial policy was not only a major element in Confederation, in ensuring its achievement, but also in delivering to it, as to a new metropolitan base, the whole of northwestern and arctic hinterland. By this stroke, the northern and maritime frontier of the empire of the North Atlantic became a northern and a continental one in the Dominion of Canada.

The new Dominion was meant to be a new nation. Yet its northern character, the limitation imposed by its situation and climate, meant that in fact the new nation was to remain still dependent on other states, the United Kingdom and the United States, for capital, technology, and defense. The continued support of the United Kingdom was needed to discourage the intermittent continental stirrings of the United States. American engineers were needed to build Canadian railways, and British capital to finance them. Anything like instant and full-blown independence was neither possible nor desirable. The two factors of national aspiration and external support were slowly reconciled by the gradual transformation of continued dependence

[8] L. P. Kirwan, *A History of Polar Exploration* (New York, 1959), pp. 77–78.

in a free association which ensured the needed support while affording the desired independence. The character of Canada's association with both the Commonwealth and the United States is thus the outcome of its historical development as a northern frontier.

The Factor of Monarchical Institutions

That association derives also from another aspect of the northern frontier, the form of its political dependence. Although its remoteness and the separation of communities created a spirit of local independence, the limitations of its economy made for political dependence. That dependence found the most ready historical and the most satisfying psychological expression in allegiance to a monarchy. Until the rise of modern communication it was difficult to maintain unity in states based on popular sovereignty. Moreover, in Canada two historic factors combined to make monarchical allegiance a particularly satisfying political tie.

One was the French monarchical tradition of the old regime. The royal government of France, and particularly in New France, was largely military in organization and combined much personal independence in its subject with a regular hierarchy of rank and subordination. It was also paternalistic in that all ranks looked to the higher for the defense of rights and the grant of help. The exercise of the power conferred on the king and his officers by the system was extraordinarily humane, and the bureaucracy remained a surprisingly serviceable one, partly because the personal royal will might always be invoked to correct hardship or bestow favor, partly because it was suffused with the religious principle that royal authority was a trust to be exercised for the doing of justice and the granting of mercy. The failure of the early British regime to capture and perpetuate some of this spirit is to be explained not so much by the fact of conquest as by the pressure of the "old subjects" and loyalists for government favors and by the fears aroused by the French Revolution. Nonetheless, much of the old attitude to government and public service survived in French Canada.

The second factor was the great strengthening in the bond of allegiance in British America caused by the American Revolution. The decisive act of the Revolution was of course the throwing off of allegiance by the Declaration of Independence.

Equally decisive was the resolution of the loyalists to maintain their allegiance. How clearly the matter was understood is shown by the declaration required of settlers in British America after 1783, in which they were required to acknowledge "the Authority of the King in his Parliament as the Supreme Legislature of this Province."[9] Not only allegiance was required, that is, but an acknowledgment of that theoretically unqualified supremacy of the Crown in Parliament against which the thirteen colonies had revolted. The second British Empire was founded explicitly on allegiance and the legislative supremacy of the King in Parliament.[10]

In the British American colonies after 1783, however, an essentially democratic or popular spirit, fed by the practices of the Protestant churches and by local needs, operated to turn the constitutional development of the colonies away from the monarchical ideal affirmed after the Revolution toward popular and American practices. The local democracies from time to time and in varying degrees used the assemblies to express and assert interests in conflict with Imperial policies or the outlook of the colonial administrations. The assemblies made the Speaker their leader, and sometimes, especially in Lower Canada, a tribune of the people and the leader of a popular opposition. By the use of committees and commissioners to administer expenditures of money voted by the legislature, they assumed executive powers and of course strengthened their own hands by the distribution of patronage. The recurrent clashes which led up to the rebellions of 1837 in the Canadas were thus not only political struggles between the assemblies and the entrenched councillors and governors; they were a constitutional conflict between an ideal of government essentially republican and one essentially monarchical.

The former was the "elective system" of Papineau and the republic of Mackenzie, the latter was the "responsible government" of W. W. Baldwin and Etienne Parent. The effect of the latter, the application of the concept of ministerial responsibility to a colonial constitution, was quite clear. It was the preservation of a British, hereditary, and monarchical executive acting on the

---

[9] A. G. Doughty and D. A. McArthur, *Documents Relating to the Constitutional History of Canada, 1791–1818* (Ottawa, 1914), p. 22, Instructions to Dorchester, Sept. 16, 1791, no. 35.

[10] Except in the matter of taxation.

advice of local ministers. By the application, the democracy of the colonies was reconciled with the allegiance of the colonists. Political sovereignty in Canada could become democratic, as democratic as in a republic, while legal sovereignty remained unaffected and not less powerful in its ancient form, the monarchy. British America might walk in its own political paths, but never lose contact with its constitutional heritage of political and civil liberty upheld by law declared in the Queen's courts and made by the Queen in Parliament.

While responsible government was a Canadian concept amplified by Joseph Howe and sanctioned by Durham, there can be little doubt that in Canada the compromise its adoption embodied was made possible in large and perhaps decisive measure by the great British migration that began after Waterloo and was at flood tide when responsible government finally became a basic convention of Canadian government at mid-century. English Canada had until 1812 become largely American in population and in the functioning of its institutions. After 1815 the old American stock, both loyalist refugee and mere immigrant, was swamped by the new British immigrants. Political power in the English Canada was taken from the native-born by the British-born by the eighteen fifties, a process which happened, to a less degree and much more slowly, in the Atlantic provinces. The names tell the story, Baldwin, Hincks, Gowan, Draper, Harrison, Macdonald, Brown—all were British born.[11] Only the French remained to represent the native-born in the first exercise of the new powers of self-government.[12]

It is also to be noted that while the governors ceased to be active executives with the adoption of the principles and practices of cabinet government, and became in theory constitutional or limited monarchs, they by the change also became the guardians of the conventions of responsible government.[13] These indeed had, if not to be evolved, as they were still evolv-

[11] J. M. S. Careless "Mid-Victorian Liberalism in Canadian Newspapers, 1850–67," *Canadian Historical Review*, Sept. 1950.

[12] This of course partly explains why self-government was used in Canada to reform the institutions of English Canada and to confirm those of French, with the one great exception of the abolition of seigneurial tenure.

[13] W. M. Whitelaw, "Responsible Government and the Irresponsible Governor," *Canadian Historical Review*, Dec. 1932, pp. 364–86, reveals how freely the governors exercised their power after 1848.

ing in the United Kingdom, at least to be adapted to Canadian conditions. The governors became, from the glimpses our present knowledge affords us, the mentors of politicians who themselves had to learn the manifold and often subtle applications of the conventions. In turn, because the succession of governors was periodic and on the average much more frequent than the succession of hereditary monarchs, no doubt the experienced politicians and permanent clerks often became the instructors of the governor. The immediate point is, however, that all these men were of British birth before Confederation, with the single exception of Sir Fenwick Williams. None of them had parliamentary experience approaching that of Sydenham, but only two, Williams and Sir Charles Hastings Doyle, were soldiers, and all came from the British governing class and knew the traditions and nuances of parliamentary government and no doubt, even before Bagehot, had a very clear idea of the limitations which hedged a constitutional monarch.

Certain it is that by Confederation in Canada and Nova Scotia the politicians who achieved cabinet rank from time to time had learned and were at home in the mixture of traditional form and business-like dispatch with which the prerogatives of monarchy were exercised in the service of democracy. It was this familiar and valued working system that British American politicians thought infinitely preferable to the democratic presidency and the government of separated powers of the United States. The belief was not a mere provincial prejudice, but the sober judgment of mature and experienced men who had learned their art in one of the most difficult of all schools, a democracy of diverse ethnic groups. For it is to be remembered that there were not only French and English in British America; there were Highland Scots, Catholic Irish, and Lunenburg and loyalist Germans, all of whom had had small experience of parliamentary government, though as quick as the French to learn all the tricks of the game. In such a society responsible government had been made to work so that local communities and special interests could get done what they wanted done, if it were not blatantly contrary to the public interest.

Extraordinarily little republican sentiment, always to a degree endemic in Canada as in the United Kingdom, seems, moreover, to have survived in the last years of the generation after the rebellions. There was therefore a great consensus of opinion in both French and English British America that in any future union the basic institution of responsible cabinet government in the Queen's name should be embodied in the new general government and continued in the continuing local ones. "The Executive Government and authority of and over Canada continues and is vested in the Queen," was to be the most significant, as it is the most simple and direct of all the sections of the British North America Act. On that basic principle there was neither hesitation nor complexity to blur the simple, positive affirmation. The language is lucid, the intent unquestionable. Canada was to continue a constitutional monarchy.[14]

So insistent is the emphasis on monarchy in the Confederation debates and in the speeches made throughout the provinces that it is necessary to ask just what was meant by it. No one spelled it out. By inference from the whole of what was said and from the historical context in which it was said, it is legitimate to suppose that it meant on one hand the retention of personal allegiance to the Crown with responsible and parliamentary government, and on the other the avoidance of popular sovereignty (or democracy) and a federal union.

The desire to continue personal allegiance to the Crown, after liberal principles had triumphed in British America with the grant of responsible government, and at a time when British America was about, by uniting, to take a great and conscious step towards nationhood, calls for explanation. Responsible government, of course, had been a compromise in which parliamentary democracy had been combined with constitutional monarchy on the British model. The monarchical element was in fact central to the compromise. By it a number of things were accomplished, over and above the essential matter of maintaining the personal bond of allegiance between the Queen and her subjects in British America. One was the maintenance of the Imperial connection. The material bonds of empire, it is true, had ended with the commercial revolution of 1846–49. There was, moreover, no good reason, commercial or financial, still less military, why the connection between the United Kingdom

---

[14] I trust it is unnecessary to point out that in speaking of monarchy in this context I have in mind only a set of constitutional principles, and neither a sentimental royalism nor the regrettable Edwardian pomp which alienated the affections of so many Canadians from the outward expression of what is the core of the Canadian political tradition.

and the colonies should be kept up. And there were those who looked to a speedy end of the connection. But there were other reasons, important to British America, for maintaining the tie. The main and central one was that the Imperial connection sustained the whole constitutional heritage of the colonies. Without the connection, the allegiance to the Crown would have ended and the monarchical principle would have been lost. With it would have gone the compromise of responsible government and all the gains made since 1837. The ending of the connection would have thrown the control of events into the hands of the extremists, *les rouges*, the Clear Grits, and, so do extremes meet, the old Compact Tories, none of whom valued responsible government, and all of whom would have plumped for republican institutions and annexation.[15]

With parliamentary and cabinet government would have gone other matters of value to the moderates and conservatives of that day, a few of which are still of value to most Canadians. One was the limited franchise and the idea that the franchise was a trust. Another was the British system of justice, challenged at the time of course by the principle of election applied to the selection of judges by the Jacksonian democrats across the border. Yet another was the sense of public rank and personal honor, then still strong in British as in French Canada. Finally, there was the instinctive feeling, an articulate perception in French Canada, that monarchical allegiance allowed a diversity of customs and rights under law in a way that the rational scheme and abstract principles of republican democracy did not. The monarchy, in short, subsumed a heterogeneous and conservative society governed in freedom under law, law upheld by monarchy, where the republic would have leveled the diversities and made uniform the various groups by breaking them down into individuals, free indeed, but bound by social conformity and regimented by an inherent social intolerance.

Such a leveling and uniformity was the work of the principle of popular sovereignty, of French Jacobins and American Jacksonians. The diffusion of power among the people gave rise inevitably to the demand that it be diffused equally, and Canadian radicals used the Benthamite formula of one man, one vote. The demand for representation by population was of course

[15] As some of all of the three groups did in the crisis of 1849.

another application of the same ideal of political equality in a society of equals. What excesses that principle had led to in France and the United States all liberal and conservative Canadians at Confederation knew, and in their view Canada had been saved from it only by the repression of the rebellions of 1837. In a republic, it was felt, such a principle could lead only to anarchy or a Caesarian dictatorship, as it had done in France, as perhaps it had done in the United States at civil war under Lincoln. Again, the monarchy by ensuring that legal sovereignty rested on foundations independent of the results of the last election, ensured also, however political sovereignty might be diffused through the electorate, that the last essential of government, the maintenance of peace and order, would be independent of popular impulse.

Finally, the emphasis on monarchy by the Fathers of Confederation arose from their conviction that monarchical institutions had enabled them to avoid the necessity of resorting to a federal union in their scheme of union for British America. It was true that they had left the provincial governments in being. It was true that the scheme could be described and defended as a federal one. But they were persuaded that they had not recognized the principle of co-ordinate sovereignty, as they were convinced they had avoided those weaknesses of federal union which had plunged the United States into civil war. They thought in fact that, under the supremacy of the Imperial Crown in Parliament, they had created a Canadian Crown in Parliament which would be actively supreme in the union as the Imperial power was supreme, if with a supremacy mostly latent, in the Empire. The union, to their minds, was a legislative union, not a federal or a quasi-federal one, and the anomalies of the special rights of French Canada, or provincial legislatures which possessed all the potent apparatus of responsible government, were no more striking than the many which the Empire in the amplitude of its constitutional variety had nourished from the covenant of Plymouth Colony to the latest experiment in Western Australia.[16]

[16] I am indebted to Mr. Peter B. Waite, "Ideas and Politics in British North America, 1864–1866" (Unpublished Ph.D. Thesis, University of Toronto, 1953) for the substance of this paragraph.

THE FACTOR OF COMMITMENT

The monarchical emphasis of the Confederation debates was unusual in Canadian politics, a response both to the profounder than usual reflections of the nature of Canadian government prompted by the work on constitution making and also to the collapse of the American scheme of government in the Civil War. But as a consequence, the monarchy continued in its central place in the Canadian political tradition to become after 1931 the symbol of association with the Commonwealth, and that association is one part of the commitment of Canada. The second part is the new and unfamiliar alliance with the United States. The association with the Commonwealth expresses exactly the Canadian desire for an association compatible with independence. The alliance with the United States, however, raises the question of whether an alliance between states so unequal in power and so intimately linked by economy, language, and culture can in fact be compatible with independence. The point made here is that the preservation of Canadian integrity in that alliance will depend upon the relevance of Canadian history, on its cultural and moral significance in universal history, and on American recognition of that relevance.

THE MAINTENANCE OF THE NORTHERN NATIONALITY

The relevance of Canadian history lies, then, in the morally defensible character of Canadian purpose in maintaining a northern nation in independence and vigor in the circumstances of the second half of the twentieth century. The first element of that purpose is to be found in the realization of the northern economy. For that Canada possesses the necessary land bases in the great river valleys of the south. It possesses also in ever-increasing measure the industrial power by which to bring to bear on the Canadian Shield and the Arctic the technological skill and power to conquer the north. It possesses in its scientists and its universities the knowledge and the capabilities in research to fathom the deep secrets of the north and to measure the hair's-breadth difference between disaster and success in northern development.

In this, there need be no thought of turning the Canadian back on the south. The northern economy has never been self-sufficient, nor can it ever be. But it is manifest from Canadian history that every time that Canada has sought a destiny in the south, disaster has threatened. Every time that impulse came from outside, from the imperial aims of the House of Bourbon in 1701, from the European strategy of La Galissonnière in 1749, from the desire of Great Britain to tap the commerce of the Mississippi valley between 1783 and 1846. The effort was beyond the resources of a northern economy and a northern people, and every time Canada was thrown back upon the Shield and the Northwest.

That is not to say that ordinary, or even special, ties to southward need be harmful; on the contrary. Reciprocity, on Canadian terms, as in 1854 and 1936, strengthened the northern economy. The great areas of overlap in the Atlantic provinces, the Eastern townships, the Ontario peninsula, in Michigan, Wisconsin, Minnesota, and the prairies, and on the Gulf of Georgia, reveal how rough the division between the northern and the continental economies has been. But the division was made and remains, and the areas of overlap have been areas of exchange in which the two economies mingle and strengthen one another by a traffic in raw materials, goods, and skills which, however, is the exchange that arises from difference, not from uniformity.

The northern economy is a clear and evident thing, explicit in history. Not so definite, but still discernible, is what may be called the northern outlook of Canadian arts and letters. The mere reflection in art of northern scenery, or northern life, important though that is, is not what is meant. What is meant is the existence in Canadian art and literature of distinctive qualities engendered by the experience of northern life. These are a tendency to the heroic and the epic, to the art which deals with violence, a tendency not only realized in the work of E. J. Pratt, but also indicated in that of Louis Fréchette, and in the much less successful writings of Charles Heavysege and William Wilfred Campbell. The later canvases of Lawren Harris and those of Emily Carr have this same heroic quality stylized.

That is the art of the hinterland. The art of the baseland is the lyric of Archibald Lampman, of Octave Crémazie, and the landscape of Cornelius Krieghoff and W. J. Phillips. The great cities of the baselands have their sophisticated art, of course, and that eludes the generalization attempted here, as it should. The reference is only to what is characteristically Canadian, not to what is universal as well as Canadian.

To the heroic and the lyric, the satiric is to be added. For northern life is moral or puritanical, being so harsh that life can allow little laxity in convention. But the moral affords the substance and creates the disposition for satire. Canadian literature has been comparatively rich in satire, from the parody of Sam Slick's Yankee sharpness by a Tory loyalist to the extravaganzas on small town life of Stephen Leacock, or prairie rural life of Paul Hiebert. For satire feeds upon the gap between profession and performance, and the puritan both displays the gap more and sees it in other men's performance more readily than those of less rigid standards. The excellence of Canadian political and social caricature stands on the same satiric footing. In all these qualities, Canadian literature has of course affinities with both Scottish and Icelandic literature. They give promise of a literature, and an art, as idiomatic as it is significant universally.

Finally, the northern quality of Canadian life is maintained by a factor of deliberate choice and natural selection. As the American frontier has always been open, absolutely or comparatively, to Canadians, Canadians have always been free to live as Canadians or to become Americans. Many who make the latter choice do it with reluctance, but the choice is nearly always made on the grounds of greater reward or wider opportunity. That is, they have rejected the harder life and smaller material rewards of Canada. The result is that Canadians to an extraordinary degree are Canadians by choice. In consequence, Canadians become generation by generation more and more a northern people, either because northern origins have fitted them for northern life, or because they have become adapted to it.[17]

THE CHARACTER OF CANADIAN NATIONALITY

One element in that choice has often, perhaps usually, been the desire to maintain the Canadian allegiance. Here, perhaps,

[17] Lest this seem harsh, as it is not meant to be, let a well-known Canadian-American speak: "So far as Canadian academic migration is concerned, this means an awareness of the growth of a North American nationality in which the old loyalties are cherished, not for provincial exclusiveness but for the maintenance of the enduring virtues which embody the ideals of human rights and freedom as expressed in the history and the institutions of both Canada and the United States." H. T. Shotwell, in *Canadian Historical Review*, March 1947, pp. 42–43.

it will be permissible to elaborate something touched on in the preceding chapter. Canada has never been a country royalist in sentiment any more than Canadian society has remained formally hierarchical in structure. Canadian manners have always tended to be simple, and Canadian society has steadily become a society of social equals. But for many reasons it has been a monarchical country, and not a country of the social compact like its great neighbor. The reasons for this have been historic rather than sentimental. Allegiance means that the law and the state have an objective reality embodied in the succession of persons designated by Parliament and hereditary right. They do not rest on contemporary assent, although the policies and acts of government do. In Canada, therefore, government possesses an objective life of its own. It moves in all its parts at popular impulse, but if there were no impulse, it would still move. In the United States government is subjective. It is designed to move on popular impulse, and if there is no impulse, the movement soon flags and falters. The republican government, massive as are its institutions, historic as is its momentum, in a very real sense rests upon assent periodically renewed. Such a government requires as basis a society of great intrinsic unity and conformity in which a consensus works to a common end. In Canada, a country of economic hazard, external dependence, and plural culture, only the objective reality of a monarchy and the permanent force of monarchical institutions could form the center and pivot of unity. Allegiance was a social and political necessity of national existence and prevailed over the manifest and insistent attraction of republican institutions and republican liberty.

Not life, liberty, and the pursuit of happiness, but peace, order, and good government are what the national government of Canada guarantees. Under these, it is assumed, life, liberty, and happiness may be achieved, but by each according to his taste. For the society of allegiance admits of a diversity the society of compact does not, and one of the blessings of Canadian life is that there is no Canadian way of life, much less two, but a unity under the Crown admitting of a thousand diversities.

For this reason it is not a matter of political concern that Canada has two major cultures and many smaller ones. It would be foolish to deny that the dual culture is one of history's many harsh gifts to Canada, that the duality arose from the ordeal of conquest and suppression and that it has given rise to friction and to weakness. But it is manifest that it is a gift which admits of transmutation into something rich and strange, into a political order as liberal as those which Lord Acton, by way of example, thought approached nearest the ideal.[18] The transmutation can be wrought when the two cultures are seen as variations on a common experience of the land and history of Canada, and of the common allegiance in law and spirit to the traditions and the Crown of that land.

That common experience has created a common psychology, the psychology of endurance and survival. Canadian experience teaches two clear lessons. One is that the only real victories are the victories over defeat. We have been beaten many times, defeat has been our national portion in America, but we survive and we go on in strength. And our experience teaches also that what is important is not to have triumphed, but to have endured. The pride of victory passes, but a people may survive and have its way if it abides by the traditions which have fostered its growth and clarified its purpose.

The common experience extends also to the Canadian achievement of the secret of Commonwealth, that free association in self-government is a bond of union which may yet outlast the controls and authority of empires, however strong. That achievement was the work of Canadians of both the major stocks, it is the outward expression of our domestic institutions, and its spirit informs Canadians of all other origins with an equal pride in free institutions elaborated by the Canadian political genius. We must bring to the working out of the American alliance the same persistence in freedom and the same stubborn ingenuity, recognizing always that this special relationship with the United States is different in kind from the historic associations of Canada and can in no sense take their place.

In the end, that common experience extends to a common

---

[18] "If we take the establishment of liberty for the realization of moral duties to be the end of civil society, we must conclude that those states are substantially the most perfect which, like the British and Austrian empires, include various distinct nationalities without oppressing them."— *Home and Foreign Review*, II, 25, quoted in David Mathew, *Action: the Formative Years* (London, 1946), p. 180. Acton's instances seem somewhat unfortunate now, but his point that the state ought not to be identified with society is more valid than ever as the instances of totalitarian regimes multiply.

affirmation of moral purpose, the purpose which makes Canadian history relevant to universal history. Canadians, if one may judge by their history, believe that society cannot live by the state alone. Society has its own autonomous life, which is sustained by sources which may enrich the life of the state, but over which the state has neither authority nor control. Those sources are religious or moral, and flow into society only through persons. The personality of the individual citizen, then, is the object of the justice the state exists to provide and of the welfare society exists to ensure. The individual thus possesses the ultimate autonomy, since he is the end to which both state and society are means. But that autonomy carries with it a sovereign obligation to respect and safeguard the autonomy of his fellows, primarily by manners, which are the dealings of man with man, and secondarily through the social and political order. So reciprocal and delicate a complex of justice, welfare, and good manners may function only in an organic unity of state, society, and individual. It was such a unity of king, church, and people Canadians, both French and English, inherited from their remoter past and have elaborated in their history as a monarchical and democratic nation.[19]

The preservation of such a national society is not the unique mission of Canada, but it is the central fact of Canadian history that it has been preserved and elaborated by Canadians in one of the largest, harshest, and most intimidating countries on earth. Canada, that is, has preserved and confirmed the essentials of the greatest of civilizations in the grimmest of environments. It is an accomplishment worthy of a better end than absorption in another and an alien society, however friendly and however strong in its own ideals. In that accomplishment and its continuance lies the relevance of Canadian history.

[19] K. C. Wheare, *Modern Constitutions* (London, 1951), pp. 43–45 N. Mansergh, *Survey of British Commonwealth Affairs, 1939–1952* (London, 1958), pp. 369–75.

III

H. A. INNIS

The Strategy of Culture

With Special Reference to Canadian Literature: A Footnote to the Massey Report

Pay them well; where there is a Maecenas there will be a Horace and a Virgil also. *Martial*
Complaints are made that we have no literature; this is the fault of the Minister of the Interior. *Napoleon*.

The title of this article may be regarded as an illustration of the remark of Julien Benda concerning "the *intellectual organization of political hatreds*"[1] and as a further effort to exploit Canadian nationalism. "Political passions rendered universal, coherent, homogeneous, permanent, preponderant—everyone can recognize there to a great extent the work of the cheap daily political newspaper."[2] Whistler[3] and others have contended that art is not to be induced by artificial tactics. They have pointed to Switzerland as a country without art and it has interesting parallels with Canada, a country of more than one language, a federation, and dependent on the tourist trade. A distinguished Canadian painter has remarked: "I am not sure that future opinion of the contemporary art of our day will not consider the advertising poster, the window and counter card as most representative."[4]

Printers' ink threatens to submerge even the literary arts in Canada and it may seem futile to raise the question of cultural

Reprinted from H. A. Innis, *The Strategy of Culture*, 1952, by permission of The University of Toronto Press.

[1] Julien Benda, *The Great Betrayal* (London, 1928), p. 21.

[2] Ibid., p. 7.

[3] J. M. Whistler, *The Gentle Art of Making Enemies* (New York, 1904).

[4] William Colgate, *C. W. Jeffreys* (Toronto, n.d.), p. 28.

possibilities. The power of nationalism, parochialism, bigotry, and industrialism may seem too great. Cheap supplies of paper produce pulp and paper schools of writing, and literature is provided in series, sold by subscription, and used as an article of furniture. Almost alone Stephen Leacock, by virtue of his mastery of language, escaped into artistic freedom and was recognized universally and even he, as Peter McArthur pointed out, never attacked a publisher.

But we can at least point to the conditions which seem fatal to cultural interests. We can appraise the cultural level of the United States and appreciate the importance of New York as a center for the publication of books and periodicals, the effects of the higher costs of commercial printing in Chicago, and the dangers to literature and the drama of reliance on the authoritative finality of New York newspaper critics. We should be able to escape the influence of a western American news agency which advised that if you want it to sell "put a New York date line on it."

We can point to the dangers of exploitation through nationalism, our own and that of others. To be destructive under these circumstances is to be constructive. Not to be British or American but Canadian is not necessarily to be parochial. We must rely on our own efforts and we must remember that cultural strength comes from Europe.[5] We can point to our limitations in literature and to the consequent distortions incidental to the impact of mechanization, notably in photography. The story has been compelled to recognize the demands of the illustration and has become dominated by it.[6] The impact of the machine has been evident in the dependence of Edgar Wallace and

[5] "Until the English visitor to America comprehends that he is in the midst of a civilization totally different from anything he has known on our side of the Atlantic, he is exposed to countless shocks." Sir John Pollock, Bt., *Time's Chariot* (London, 1950), pp. 184–85. Sir John regards the great difference as having developed since 1880 as a result of the Civil War and foreign immigration. In England, with a background of feudalism, it seems possible to keep political differences and personal relationships in separate departments.

[6] Whistler's complaint that painting was subordinate to literature must be offset by the account of Newman Flower of Cassell & Co. He resorted to a *cliché* department or "bank" of illustrations built up since 1870, selected a promising illustration, and asked a young writer to write around it. *Just As It Happened* (London, 1951), p. 27.

Phillips Oppenheim and dictators of the quick action novel on the dictaphone.[7] An emphasis on speed and action essential to books produced for individual reading weakens the position of poetry and the drama particularly in new countries swamped by print.

Burckhardt[8] in his studies of Western civilization held that religion and the state were stable powers striving to maintain themselves and that civilized culture did not coincide with these two powers, that in its true nature it was actually opposed to them. "Artists, poets and philosophers have just two functions, i.e., to bring the inner significance of the period and the world to ideal vision and to transmit this as an imperishable record to posterity." In the words of Sir Douglas Copland, summarizing the philosophy of P. H. Roxby, "A cultural heritage is a more enduring foundation for national prestige than political power or commercial gain."[9] "It is the cultural approach of one nation to another, which in the long run is the best guarantee for real understanding and friendship and for good commercial and political relations. In the past, it has been, on the whole, sadly neglected, and especially as between western Europe and China." (Roxby.)[10] It has been scarcely less neglected as between Canada and the United States. In the long list of volumes of "The Relations of Canada and the United States" series, little interest is shown in cultural relations and the omission is ominous.

Inter-relations between American and Canadian publishing in the nineteenth century had significant implications for Canadian literature in the present century. In the nineteenth century the tyranny of the novel in England had been built up in part because of inadequate protection to English playwrights from transla-

---

[7] Ibid., p. 40. On the other hand Edgar Wallace protested that dictaphone stuff was "good Wallace publicity. I write my best stuff with a pen." Reginald Pound, *Their Moods and Mine* (London, 1939), p. 233. "Dictation always is rubbish" (George Moore). Ibid., p. 112. As a result of the influence of the newspaper on reading, novels have been written to be read rapidly and consequently emphasize length and description. "I do not want literature in a newspaper" (E. L. Godkin).

[8] See Jacob Burckhardt, *Force and Freedom: Reflections on History* (New York, 1943).

[9] D. B. Copland, "Culture versus Power in International Relations" in *Liberty and Learning: Essays in Honour of Sir James Hight* (Christchurch, 1950), p. 155.

[10] Ibid., p. 154.

tions of French plays, production of which had been systematically encouraged in France,[11] and by a monopoly of circulating
libraries protected by the high price of the three-volume novel
which made it, therefore, cheaper to rent than to buy books.[12]
Restrictive effects of high prices on exports of books from Great
Britain, absence of circulating libraries in the United States, lack
of protection to foreign, especially English, books before the
enactment of copyright legislation in America in 1891, and
section 5 of the American Copyright Act, May 31, 1790, which
was "an invitation to reprint the work of English authors," were
factors responsible for large-scale reprinting of English works
in the United States and for the publication of English works
first in the United States.[13]

In 1874 legislation in the United States reduced postage on
newspapers issued weekly or oftener to two cents a pound without regard to the distance carried. Under an act of March 3,
1879 (par. 14), second-class mail matter "must be regularly
issued at stated intervals as frequently as four times a year, and
bear a date of issue, and be numbered consecutively." Again, on
July 1, 1885, postal charges on paper-covered books were reduced from two cents per pound to one cent and cloth-bound
books were carried at eight cents per pound. The legislation
reflected the demands of a vigorous cheap book publishing period, concentrating on English or foreign books for which a
market had been created by established publishers.

In the ultimate development of the publication of English
books previous to the Copyright Act in 1891, Canadians, emigrants to the United States and undisciplined by the demands of
its distributing machinery, played an important role. George
Munro, a mathematics teacher in the Free Church College,
Halifax, who had emigrated to New York and acquired experience in the handling of dime novels in the firm of Beadle and

[11] In France the Théâtre Français was subsidized by the government,
and the Society of Dramatic Authors founded by Beaumarchais and
reorganized by Scribe in the nineteenth century fostered an interest in
plays rather than novels. See Brander Matthews, *Gateways to Literature
and Other Essays* (New York, 1912), p. 41 and also H. A. Innis, *Political
Economy in the Modern State* (Toronto, 1946), pp. 35–55.

[12] See introduction by Graham Pollard to I. R. Brussel, *Anglo-American First Editions, 1826–1900* (New York, 1935), p. 10.

[13] Ibid., p. 11. See also H. A. Innis, *The Bias of Communication* (Toronto, 1951), pp. 171–2.

Adams and in the publishing of the *Fireside Companion,* a family newspaper started in 1867, launched the "Seaside Library," a quarto, two or three columns to the page with cheap paper, on May 28, 1877. It was estimated that 645 pages in a regular edition could be printed in 152 pages quarto. As a result of saturation of the market for quartos in the latter part of 1883, Munro started a pocket-size edition in spite of the higher costs of manufacturing. In 1887 he cut wholesale prices from twenty and twenty-five cents to ten cents and from ten cents to five cents, and in 1889 sought protection by publishing a monthly "Library of American Authors," cheap cloth-bound twelvemos, "sold by the ton." In 1890 Munro sold the "Seaside Library" to J. W. Lovell,[14] on a three-year option to repurchase arrangement, for $50,000 plus $4,500 monthly. It was estimated that, by 1890, 30,000,000 volumes of the "Seaside Library" had been sold, chiefly through the American News Company.

J. W. Lovell was the son of John Lovell, who in 1872 had a printing shop on the American side near Montreal at which he printed British copyright works, free of copyright, and imported them into Canada under 12½ per cent duty to be sold at a lower price than editions imported from Great Britain.[15] The son moved to New York in 1875 and engaged in the sale of cheap unauthorized editions. After a failure in 1881 he followed the German plan of producing cheap handy books with neat covers and, in 1882, started publication of handy twelvemos in "Lovell's Library," paper-covered books selling at twenty cents, and "Lovell's Standard Library," cloth-bound at one dollar. In 1885 he concentrated on "Lovell's Library" and sold the remainder of his business to Belford and Clarke. This became a most popular series selling about seven million volumes annually. As a result of the reduction of prices by George Munro in 1887 competition became more intense and in 1888 Lovell bought the "Munro Library"[16] from Norman W. Munro, the brother of George Munro. The "Munro Library" in pocket-size books had been started in 1884 when the owner had returned to the business after

[14] The funds became the basis of a substantial gift to Dalhousie University.

[15] R. H. Shove, *Cheap Book Production in the United States, 1870 to 1891* (Urbana, 1937), p. 75. This book is a mine of information.

[16] This included 855 sets of plates and 1,500,000 copies of books for which $250,000 was paid.

failing with the "Riverside Library," sold between 1877 and 1879. With control over the "Seaside Library," acquired in 1890, and over the plates and stock of other cheap books publishers by purchase or rental to the extent of over half the titles of cloth-bound books and over three-fourths of the titles of paper-covered books, and supported by the Trow Printing Company, Lovell organized the United States Book Company with a reported capital of $3,500,000.

Alexander Belford and James Clarke, members of a firm of Belford brothers in Toronto, moved to Chicago and organized Rose, Belford and Company; it was reorganized in 1879 after a failure as Belford Clarke and Company. They became publishers of "railroad literature" and built up an elaborate retail system developing a policy of selling to the book trade at artificially high prices, first to jobbers, and then to the regular trade, and later at extremely low prices through drygoods and department stores. Showy bindings contrasted with the woodpulp, clay, and straw paper inside the books. In 1885 they acquired "Lovell's Standard Library" and became the largest producers of cheap cloth-bound twelvemos. As a result of the intensive price cutting after 1887 they failed in 1889.

In the absence of copyright on foreign books, publishers were compelled to rely on their only means of protection, namely, cheapness based on mass production. With efficient systems of distribution through the American News Company and the post office, equipment was steadily improved; cylinder presses were first installed in 1882 and in 1886 three cheap library publishers had their own typesetting, printing, and binding plants. The cheapest variety of paper was used and slight attention was given to proof reading and corrections. Paper manufacturers were compelled to sell their fine book papers chiefly to the large printing houses and the periodical publishers. Stereotype establishments or "sawmills" began to sell plates to publishers who then issued their own editions. Typographical unions[17] complained, and, following the sharp reduction in prices, recognized the importance of copyright. With lower postal rates on paper-covered editions, and prices from one-sixth to one-tenth those of cloth-bound volumes, it was estimated that almost two-thirds

[17] The unions were at first opposed to the Copyright Act but became active in its support; see G. A. Tracy, *History of the Typographical Union* (Indianapolis, 1913), p. 450.

of a total of 1,022 books published in 1887 were issued in the cheap libraries. Demands for new titles led to the publication of poorer classes of fiction.[18] The technological changes which lowered the prices of paper[19] and of printing widened the gap between the supply of written material and the demand of readers and intensified the need for non-copyright foreign books. Yet the supply of foreign material was limited, the market for lower grade fiction was saturated, it was no longer possible to increase sales by changing formats from quarto to twelvemo, deterioration of paper was not sufficiently rapid, and finally newspapers expanded to absorb supplies of newsprint. Publishers were now compelled to emphasize American writers, to whom copyright was paid. The basis was laid for the supremacy of the periodical, with significant consequences for American and Canadian literature. National advertising steadily advanced to impose its demands on the reading material of the periodical. The discrepancy between prices of books in England and in the United States gradually lessened. The three-volume novel disappeared in England as prices were leveled with those in the United States after the Coypright Act of 1891. To secure copyright it was necessary to print books in the United States.[20]

In the last decade of the nineteenth century the advantages of cheap newsprint, of cheap composition following the invention of the Linotype, and of the fast press as the basis of large circulations were being fully exploited by newspapers. Every conceivable device to increase circulation was pressed into service, notably in the newspaper war between Pulitzer and Hearst in the late nineties in New York City, including sensational headlines, the comics, and the Spanish American War. Crusades were started in every direction to enhance goodwill for newspapers.

The sudden improvement in technology in the production of newspapers was accompanied by an increase in magazine readers. The weekly was replaced by the monthly, which became a lead-

[18] Brussel, *Anglo-American First Editions*, p. 19.

[19] In 1871, newsprint straw paper was twelve cents per pound, fine book paper sixteen to seventeen cents; in 1875 newsprint was nine cents, machine-finish book paper ten to eleven cents; in 1889 newsprint was three and one-quarter cents and calendared book paper six and one-half to seven and one-half cents. Shove, *Cheap Book Production*, p. 4.

[20] Cheap unauthorized editions disappeared and the works of authors such as Kipling, which had sold widely in pirated editions, were sold at higher prices and in smaller numbers.

ing factor in modern publishing. The Copyright Act of 1891, in itself a recognition of the problem of creating a supply of American writers,[21] was followed by the training of an army of fiction writers who by 1900 met the demands of magazines. Muckraking magazines[22] were supported by experienced newspapermen such as Lincoln Steffens (who wrote a series on "The Shame of the Cities"). They followed the tactics particularly of the Hearst newspapers in the struggle for circulation.[23] McClure, for instance, applied the sensational methods of the cheap newspaper to the cheap and new magazine. He sponsored a reform wave which was effectively exploited by Theodore Roosevelt. He built up circulation by paying enormous sums to famous writers and trying to corner a market in them. As a former peddler of coffee pots, he knew the demands of people on farms and in small towns.[24] Munsey,[25] in the all-fiction magazine which followed the Sunday magazine section of the newspaper with smooth paper and clearer half-tones, made fiction the basis of circulation and earning power by 1896.[26]

The position of women as purchasers of goods led to concentration on women's magazines and on advertising. In Philadelphia, Curtis developed the great discovery that reading matter trailed through a periodical compelled readers to turn the pages and to look at the advertising which made up most of the page into an extensive magazine business.[27] Through the national magazine,[28] advertisers such as the manufacturers of pianos, high cost two-wheeled bicycles, and other commodities were able to reach a large market at less cost than through the daily

[21] The suit brought against the *New York World* by Harriet Monroe for printing her ode presented at the opening of the Chicago World's Fair and the award of $5,000 damages strengthened the position of authors. Harriet Monroe, *A Poet's Life: Seventy Years in a Changing World* (New York, 1938), pp. 139–43.

[22] C. C. Regier, *The Era of the Muckrakers* (Chapel Hill, N.C., 1932).

[23] H. L. Mencken, *Prejudices, First Series* (New York, 1929), p. 175.

[24] S. S. McClure, *My Autobiography* (New York, 1914).

[25] F. A. Munsey, *The Founding of the Munsey Publishing-House* (New York, 1907); also George Britt, *Forty Years—Forty Millions: The Career of Frank A. Munsey* (New York, 1935).

[26] Algernon Tassin, *The Magazine in America* (New York, 1916), pp. 342–43.

[27] Arthur Train, *My Day in Court* (New York, 1939), p. 419.

[28] Frank Presbrey, *The History and Development of Advertising* (New York, 1929), p. 339.

newspaper and to concentrate on more attractive layouts appealing to people in higher income brackets. The national magazine made a systematic attack on older advertising media. Religious papers dependent on patent medicine advertising felt the effects of a crusade of the *Ladies' Home Journal* which in 1892[29] refused to handle medical advertising and exposed widely advertised preperations by printing chemical analyses. With the growth of large-scale printing, the printer assumed the direction of advertising and displaced the single advertiser and agency. Specialization of printing and increased pressure of overhead costs necessitated effective control of publications. Lorimer, an able writer of advertisements, became editor of the *Saturday Evening Post* and gave advertisements the personality of articles.[30] A four-color printing press costing $800,000 and a new building in 1910 led the Curtis publications to add a third magazine to cover agriculture.[31]

The average circulations of magazines increased from 500,000 to 1,400,000 in the period from 1905 to 1915 and following the boom beginning in 1922 reached 3,000,000 by 1937.[32] *The Reader's Digest* was started in 1922, *Time* in 1923, and the *New Yorker* in 1925. Extension of education and increased use of text-books conditioned youth to acceptance of the printed word and to magazine consumption. The demand for writers exceeded the supply. After the First World War, women's magazines, which had begun as pattern makers in the *Delineator* and other Butterick papers, gained conspicuously in circulation. Women's magazines reached the largest circulations, paid most highly for

[29] Ibid., pp. 531–2. See *The Americanization of Edward Bok: The Autobiography of a Dutch Boy Fifty Years After* (New York, 1937). Also Edward W. Bok, *A Man from Maine* (New York, 1923). The campaign against patent medicines provoked the announcement by Eugene Field of the engagement of the grand-daughter of Lydia W. Pinkham to Edward W. Bok, the editor of the *Ladies' Home Journal*.

[30] Bok, *A Man from Maine*, p. 171. "The secrets of success as an editor were easily learned; the highest was that of getting advertisements. Ten pages of advertising made an editor a success; five marked him as a failure." *The Education of Henry Adams: An Autobiography* (Boston, 1918), p. 308. "The art of advertising has outgrown the art of creative writing. . . . Three-fourths of the income of the magazines comes from their advertisers. . . . just take the advertising and rewrite it." W. E. Woodward, *Bunk* (New York, 1923), p. 51.

[31] Bok, *A Man from Maine*, p. 183.

[32] Train, *My Day in Court*, p. 421.

articles, and were the chief market for writers. Competition between magazines for writers with an established reputation brought sky-rocket prices.[33] The sale of film rights to popular novels brought even more than that of serial rights. An average best-seller in "the slicks" with serial rights, movie, book, and other rights brought returns varying between $70,000 and $125,000. Writers concentrated on magazines rather than books.[34]

Writing for the great popular magazines built up on advertising implied assiduous attention to their requirements on the part of writers and editors. Dullness was absolutely abhorrent. Serial installments involved consideration of appropriate terminal points at which intense interest might be sustained for the next number. Magazines with the largest circulation were able to carry longer fiction by writers with an established reputation but tended to reduce installments and stories from 12,000 to 5,000 or 4,500 words.[35] Since dependence on advertising meant that the magazine "expands and contracts with the activity of the factory chimney"[36] writers were particularly affected by fluctuations of the business cycle. The reputations of authors were built up through advertising by editors of magazines who were thus enabled to sell advertising material, and stories[37] became commercialistic. George Ade could write "I guess I can now sell anything I write, even if it's good."[38]

The influence of the newspaper and advertising on the magazine was developed to a sophisticated level in the twenties when magazines such as the *New Yorker* playfully exposed the foibles of its advertisers and advertisers exploited the foibles of the

[33] Fairfax Downey, *Richard Harding Davis, His Day* (New York, 1933), p. 219.

[34] Ibid., pp. 430–1, 433.

[35] Train, *My Day in Court*, pp. 423–25. In England Gilbert Frankau held that the serial market was disappearing because readers of monthly magazines would not wait and newspapers preferred the short story "in these days of so much front-page excitement." Pound, *Their Moods and Mine*, p. 241.

[36] Train, *My Day in Court*, p. 420. The limited circulation of Canadian magazines makes for a seasonal expansion. Advertising is sufficient only during the period of the two or three months before Christmas to warrant a full-fledged interest in features, especially short features. Longer features appear after the holiday season.

[37] Train, *My Day in Court*, p. 440.

[38] F. W. Wile, *News Is Where You Find It* (Indianapolis, 1939), p. 36.

magazine. More recently the campaign of the *New Yorker* against loud speaker advertising in public buildings has not been unrelated to competition for advertising—all of course in the spirit of good clean fun. The rigid limitations in style of advertising copy enabled the *New Yorker* to succeed by emphasizing the independence of the editor from the business office, and by developing a new style of writing which in turn led to a revolution in the style of advertising copy. In the *Smart Set* and the *American Mercury* H. L. Mencken, a Baltimore newspaperman, was successful in building up circulation in a direct attack on the limitations of a society dependent on advertising. In reviewing books for newspapers he had become familiar with trends in literature and he attracted to the *Smart Set* new authors unable to secure publication with old firms and willing to acquire prestige in lieu of high rates of pay. As a columnist Mencken had also gained an intimate knowledge of libel laws. Of German descent, he had suffered from the frenzied propaganda of the First World War. The *American Mercury* was started in 1924 as a fifty-cent magazine and practically doubled its average monthly circulation from 38,694 to 77,921 by 1926.[39] Debunking became a new word and a profitable activity. In developing the *American Mercury* as a quality magazine designed to make the common man respectable,[40] Mencken pursued his attacks on the puritanical and on the English book to the point of recognizing in a powerful fashion the new language of the newspaper and the magazine in his *American Language*.

The women's magazines began to feel the restraining influence of puritanism and its effects on advertising. Bok became concerned with the importance of sex education. Theodore Dreiser, editor of *Delineator*, came into conflict with censorship regulations in his novels and triumphantly conquered in *An American Tragedy*. Mencken, in the tradition of Mark Twain and Ambrose Bierce, secured the support of the Author's League for Dreiser's position.[41] The Calvinistic obsession of hypocritical people with the subject of sex[42] became the center of attack by Dreiser as chief artist and Mencken as high priest, determined

[39] W. Manchester, *Disturber of the Peace: The Life of H. L. Mencken* (New York, 1951), p. 15.
[40] Ibid., p. 155.
[41] Ibid., pp. 93–94.
[42] Ibid., p. 101.

to defeat "the iron madonna who strangles in her fond embrace the American novelist" (H. H. Boyesen). With a shrewd appreciation of the advertising value of censorship regulations Mencken seized upon the occasion of the banning of a copy of the *American Mercury* to attack the Boston Watch and Ward Society as the stronghold of Catholic and Protestant puritanism.[43] His active interest in the Scopes trial, following a law enacted in Tennessee on March 21, 1925, against the teaching of evolution was a part of the general strategy against religious bigotry.

Decline of the practice of reading aloud led to a decline in the importance of censorship. The individual was taken over by the printing industry and his interest developed in material not suited to general conversation. George Moore in England and H. L. Mencken in the United States exploited the change in their attacks on censorship. Censorship could no longer be relied upon to secure publicity. Significantly the advertiser had contributed to a change of atmosphere and women no longer feared to smoke cigarettes in public.

Even before the Copyright Act, the effects of advertising, as reflected in the newspaper and the magazine, on the writer had important implications for the book. "Most people now do not read books, but read magazines and newspapers" (H. C. Baird).[44] Limited distributing facilities for books evident in the high costs of book agents and subscription publishing[45] in the nineties, and the development of special publishers of text-books in the early part of the century were gradually being offset by department stores. Small retail stores for books could not compete with rents paid by diamonds, furs, and bonds. Mail order

[43] Ibid., p. 207. See an account of the failure of attempts by Covici, Friede to secure suppression of Radclyffe Hall's *Well of Loneliness* by the Boston Watch and Ward Society. Donald Friede, *The Mechanical Angel* (New York, 1948), p. 94.

[44] J. C. Derby, *Fifty Years among Authors, Books and Publishers* (New York, 1884), p. 559.

[45] Subscription selling was accompanied by a development of techniques of salesmanship and depended for its success to an important extent on snob appeal, particularly the prestige attached to owning a large book among the relatively illiterate. Estes and Lauriat of Boston, prominent subscription book agents, who came under the control of Walter Jackson and Harry E. Hooper after 1900, were active in developing schemes for the sale of the *Encyclopaedia Britannica* in connection with the London *Times*.

business in books expanded in the early 1900's but the results were perhaps evident in the remark of a publisher's reader, "this novel is bad enough to succeed."[46] W. D. Howells wrote in 1902: "Most of the best literature now sees the light in the magazines, and most of the second best appears first in book form." The increasing importance of apartment buildings and lack of space for shelves supported the rapid development of the lending library in the twenties. Book clubs increased rapidly[47] after 1926 as a means of securing the economies of mass production. Nevertheless, the inadequacy of book distributing machinery and dependence on British and Continental devices[48] showed the limitations of the book in contrast with the newspaper and the magazine. Publishing firms such as Doubleday, Page and Company entered on policies of direct vigorous advertising, which built up, for instance, the success of O. Henry,[49] but their most significant results were in less obvious directions.

The experience of the prominent publishing firm of Scribner's illustrates directly the impact of advertising on the newspaper and the magazine and in turn on the book. Roger Burlingame,[50] trained in a newspaper office, and M. E. Perkins, a reporter on the *New York Times,* exercised a powerful influence on publications of the firm. Perkins was concerned to arouse a consciousness of the value and importance of the native note in opposition to the imitation of English and European models and "the cynical disparagement of American materialism."[51] To him great books were those which appealed to both the literati and the masses. The book-buying public was made up of fairly successful people but to Perkins the reading of Thomas Wolfe's books "to pieces" in the libraries reflected the truer sense of life of people in the lower economic level.[52] While he condemned the mad pursuit of best-sellers which developed during the boom period of the twenties and the newspaper policy of playing up the work of

[46] W. H. Page, *A Publisher's Confession* (New York, 1905), p. 27.

[47] E. H. Dodd, *The First Hundred Years: A History of the House of Dodd, Mead, 1839–1939* (New York, 1939), p. 36.

[48] O. M. Sayer, *Revolt in the Arts* (New York, 1930).

[49] Train, *My Day in Court*, p. 439.

[50] Roger Burlingame, *Of Making Many Books* (New York, 1946), p. 221.

[51] J. H. Wheelock, *Editor to Author: The Letters of Maxwell E. Perkins* (New York, 1950), p. 8.

[52] Ibid., p. 184.

authors of best-sellers and criticized the Book of the Month Club for concentrating the attention of the public on one book a month,[53] he was concerned primarily with the newspaper public. Writers from the newspaper field included Hemingway, Edmund Wilson, Stanley Pennell, Stephen Crane, and Dreiser. It was his opinion that the teaching of literature and writing in the colleges compelled students to see things through a film of past literature and not with their own eyes. Two years with a newspaper were better than two years in college.[54] He favored what Irving Babbitt called "art without selection." The demands of commercialism were evident more directly in the avoidance of controversy. "The sales department always want a novel. They want to turn everything into a novel."[55] The public and the trade preferred books of 100,000 words and works of 25,000 to 30,000 words were padded to give the appearance of books of a larger size.

An orderly revolt against commercialism was significantly delayed and frustrated in literature possibly more than in any other art. Henry James had escaped to England and in the period after the First World War Ezra Pound and T. S. Eliot followed. "The historians of Wolfe's era ... all record this strange phase of our cultural adolescence; the same sad and distraught search for foreign roots."[56] "You could always come back" (Hemingway). But in the words of Pound: "We want a better grade of work than present systems of publishing are willing to pay for."[57] "The problem is *how*, how in hell to exist without over-production."[58] "The book-trade, accursed of god, man and nature, makes no provision for *any* publication that is not one of a series. . . ."[59] "The American law as it stands or stood is all

[53] Ibid., p. 128.

[54] Ibid., p. 267. "What the eighteenth century thought simply vulgar, and the nineteenth gathered data from, has now become literary material; even the annals of the poor are to be short and simple no longer." H. W. Boynton, *Journalism and Literature and Other Essays* (Boston, 1904), p. 164.

[55] Wheelock, *Editor to Author*, p. 84.

[56] Maxwell Geismar, *Writers in Crisis: The American Novel between Two Wars* (Boston, 1942), p. 214 and *passim*.

[57] *The Letters of Ezra Pound, 1907–1941*, ed. D. D. Paige (New York, 1950), p. 175.

[58] Ibid., p. viii.

[59] Ibid., p. 319.

for the publisher and the printer and all against the author, and more and more against him just in such proportion as he is before or against his time."[60] Books by living authors were, he claimed, kept out of the United States and "the tariff, which is iniquitous and stupid in principle, is made an excuse."[61] Even in Great Britain from about 1912 to 1932 booksellers did "their utmost to keep anything worth reading out of print and out of ordinary distribution." "Four old bigots" of Fleet Street practically controlled the distribution of printed matter in England.[62] Criticism was related to publishers' advertising.[63]

The distorting effects of industrialism and advertising on culture in the United States have been evident on every hand. Architecture as a sort of tyrant of the arts had the advantage of the utilitarian demands of commerce. Painting and sculpture as allied to it had the support of collectors, private and public, and the encouragement of awards and prizes.[64] Poetry was the subject of paragraphers' jokes, a space filler for magazines[65] and "must appeal to the barber's wife of the Middle West."[66] Poetry had no one to speak for it."[67] In the drama the lack of interest of actors in modern art[68] and the support of tradition involved reliance on Shakespeare and a terrific handicap to playwrights.[69] The commercial theater manager and the newspaper critic have been reluctant to recognize the vitality of a demand for the imaginative artistic work of the little theater[70] particularly in competition with the cinema. In the words of George Jean Nathan the talking picture may be "the drama of a machine age

[60] Ibid., p. 52.

[61] Ibid., p. 53. See J. L. May, *John Lane and the Nineties* (London, 1936), p. 159.

[62] *Letters of Pound*, pp. 239–40.

[63] Ibid., p. 337.

[64] Harriet Monroe, *A Poet's Life*, p. 241.

[65] Ibid., p. 247. A study of the demands of space on Bliss Carman's poetry might prove rewarding.

[66] Ibid., p. 288.

[67] Ibid., p. 242.

[68] Nathan refers to "the mean capacity of the overwhelming number of them, whatever their nationality. . . . the downright ignorance, often made so conspicuously manifest." *The Intimate Note-books of George Jean Nathan* (New York, 1932), p. 144.

[69] See a letter from Mrs. Fiske in Harriet Monroe, *A Poet's Life*, pp. 176–77.

[70] Ibid., p. 419.

designed for the consumption of robots" and the theater may
have gained enormously by the withdrawal of "shallow and
imbecile audiences," but the change has been costly and
painful.[71]

The overwhelming pressure of mechanization evident in the
newspaper and the magazine has led to the creation of vast monopolies of communication. Their entrenched positions involve
a continuous, systematic, ruthless destruction of elements of
permanence essential to cultural activity. The emphasis on change
is the only permanent characteristic. Thomas Hardy complained
that narrative and verse were losing organic form and symmetry,
the force of reserve, and the emphasis on understatement, and
becoming structureless and conglomerate.[72]

The guarantee of freedom of the press under the Bill of Rights
in the United States and its encouragement by postal regulations
has meant an unrestricted operation of commercial forces and
an impact of technology on communication tempered only by
commercialism itself.[73] Vast monopolies of communication have

[71] See St. John Ervine, *The Alleged Art of the Cinema* (n.p., March
15, 1934). "Actors and actresses were certainly regarded with far greater
interest than they are nowadays. The outstanding ones inspired something
deeper than interest. It was with excitement, with wonder and with rever-
ence, with something akin even to hysteria, that they were gazed upon.
Some of the younger of you listeners would, no doubt, if they could, inter-
rupt me at this point by asking, 'But surely you don't mean, do you, that
our parents and grandparents were affected by them as we are by cinema
stars?' I would assure you that those idols were even more ardently
worshipped than are yours. Yours after all, are but images of idols, mere
shadows of glory. Those others were their own selves, creatures of flesh
and blood, there, before our eyes. They were performing in our presence.
And of our presence they were aware. Even we, in all our humility, acted
as stimulants to them. The magnetism diffused by them across the foot-
lights was in some degree our own doing. You, on the other hand, have
nothing to do with the performances of which you witness the result.
Those performances—or rather those innumerable rehearsals—took place
in some far-away gaunt studio in Hollywood or elsewhere, months ago.
Those moving shadows will be making identically the same movements
at the next performance or rather at the next record; and in the inflexions
of those voices enlarged and preserved for you there by machinery not
one cadence will be altered. Thus the theatre has certain advantages over
the cinema, and in virtue of them will continue to survive." Sir Max
Beerbohm in *The Listener*, Oct. 11, 1945, p. 397.
[72] May, *John Lane and the Nineties*, p. 177.
[73] See Upton Sinclair, *Money Writes! A Study of American Literature*
(Long Beach, Calif., 1927).

shown their power in securing a removal of tariffs on imports of pulp and paper from Canada though their full influence has been checked by provincial governments especially through control over pulpwood cut on Crown lands. The finished product in the form of advertisments and reading material is imported into Canada with a lack of restraint from the federal government which reflects American influence in an adherence to the principle of freedom of the press and its encouragement of monopoly. Sporadic attempts have been made to check this influence in Canada, as in the case of the banning of the Hearst papers in the First World War and in the imposition by the Bennett administration of a tariff based on advertising content in American periodicals. Protests are made by institutions against specific articles in American periodicals but without significant results other than that of advertising the periodical. To offset possible handicaps Canadian editions of *Time, Reader's Digest* and the like are published. Canadians are persistently bombarded with subscription blanks soliciting subscriptions to American magazines, and their conversation shifts with regularity following the appearance of new jokes in American periodicals. Canadian publications supported by the advertising of products of American branch plants and forced to compete with American publications imitate them in format, style and content. Canadian writers must adapt themseves to American standards.[74] Our poets and painters are reduced to the status of sandwich men. The ludicrous character of the problem may be shown by stating that the only effective means of sponsoring Canadian literature involves a rigid prohibition against all American periodicals with any written material and free admission to all periodicals with advertising only. In this way trade might be fostered and Canadian writers left free to work out their own solutions to the problems of Canadian literature. Indeed they would have the advantage of having access to the highly skilled examples of advertiser's copy.

Publishers' lists in Canada are revealing in showing the position of American branches or American agencies in the publication of books. Advertising rates for a wide range of commodities,

---

[74] One Canadian writer has complained of writing an article of 60,000 words for an American woman's magazine, cutting it to about 40,000 words to make two instalments, and expanding it to 80,000 for the English market. Canadian writers should become efficient concertina players.

determined by newspapers and magazines particularly in relation to circulation, are such as to make it extremely difficult for publishers to compete for advertising space, particularly as book advertising is largely deprived of the powerful force of repetition.[75] Moreover, the demands of a wide range of industries for advertising compete directly and effectively for raw materials, paper, capital, and labor entering into the production of books, and restrict the possibility of advertising them. American devices such as book clubs and the mass production of pocket books to be sold on news-stands and in cigar stores and drug stores have immediate repercussions in Canada. The extreme importance of book titles—perhaps the most vital element in American literature—evident in the changing of titles of English books in the United States and of American books in Great Britain and in the interest of the movie industry in the publishing field,[76] is felt in Canada also. In the field of the newspaper, dependence on the Associated Press and other agencies, on the *New York Times,*[77] and other media needs no elaboration. In radio and in television accessibility to American stations means a constant bombardment of Canadians.

The impact of commercialism from the United States has been enormously accentuated by war. Prior to the First World War the development of advertising[78] stimulated the establishment

[75] Wheelock, *Editor to Author*, p. 138.

[76] See J. T. Farrell, *The Fate of Writing in America* (n.p., n.d.); also W. T. Miller, *The Book Industry* (New York, 1949). "Before the war British publishers were often told by friends in the Canadian book trade that their public preferred the bigger, handsomer American book. They wanted value for money, and had been accustomed to measure value by size and weight. The story has often been told of the Canadian agent who handed one of his travellers an advance copy of a new book from a British publisher and asked, 'How many can you sell of that?' The traveller, without opening the book, handed it back and said, 'None.' The agent, somewhat nettled, said, "None? But you haven't even looked at it.' The traveller replied, 'I don't need to. It doesn't weigh enough.'" Michael Joseph, *The Adventure of Publishing* (London, 1949), p. 131.

[77] It "set out to be dull and ponderous and it has achieved its purpose with a fidelity and thoroughness justly commanding the admiration of all lovers of bulk and solidity." G. M. Fuller, "The Paralysis of the Press," *American Mercury*, Feb. 1926, p. 160.

[78] Will Irwin, *Propaganda and the News* (New York, 1936). For an account of the influence of an advertising agent of a Canadian department store on advertising and journalistic ideas in England, see *Autobiography of a Journalist* edited with an introduction by Michael Joseph (London,

of schools of commerce and the production of text-books on the psychology of advertising. European countries were influenced by the effectiveness of American propaganda. Young Germans were placed with American newspaper chains and advertising and publishing agencies to learn the art of making and slanting news. American treatises on advertising and publicity were imported and translated. American graduate students were attracted to Germany by scholarships and experiments in municipal government. In turn, German exchange professorships were established, especially with South American universities. The Hamburg-American Lines became an effective propagandist organization. But German experience[79] proved much too short in contrast with that of American[80] and English propagandists,[81] though their effectiveness is difficult to appraise since the estimates have been provided chiefly by those responsible for the propaganda.

American propaganda[82] after the First World War became more intense in the domestic field. Its effectiveness was evident in the emergence of organizations representing industry, labor, agriculture, and other groups. The Anti-Saloon League pressed its activities to success in prohibition legislation. In the depression the American government[83] learned much of the art of propaganda from business and exploited new technological devices such as the radio. With the entry of the United States into the

---

n.d), pp. 45, 50. The author, advised by the agent to begin journalism by writing advertisements for shopkeepers, used samples of full-page advertisements of the Canadian store (p. 66). Advertising methods were then introduced effectively in political campaigns.

[79] G. S. Viereck, *Spreading Germs of Hate* (New York, 1930).

[80] James R. Mock and Cedric Larson, *Words That Won the War: The Story of the Committee on Public Information, 1917–1919* (Princeton, N.J., 1939).

[81] See Neville Lytton, *The Press and the General Staff* (London, 1921); Sir Campbell Stuart, *Secrets of Crewe House: The Story of a Famous Campaign* (London, 1920); Walter Millis, *Road to War: America 1914–1917* (Boston, 1935); James Squires, *British Propaganda at Home and in the United States from 1914 to 1917* (Cambridge, Mass., 1935); H. D. Lasswell, *Propaganda Technique in the World War* (London, 1927).

[82] See O. W. Riegel, *Mobilizing for Chaos: The Story of the New Propaganda* (New Haven, Conn., 1939).

[83] See George Michael, *Handout* (New York, 1935); L. C. Rosten, *The Washington Correspondents* (New York, 1937).

Second World War instruments of propaganda[84] were enormously extended.

The effects of these developments on Canadian culture have been disastrous. Indeed they threaten Canadian national life. The cultural life of English-speaking Canadians subjected to constant hammering from American commercialism is increasingly separated from the cultural life of French-speaking Canadians. American influence on the latter is checked by the barrier of the French language but is much less hampered by visual media. In the period from 1915 to 1920 the theater in French Canada was replaced by the movie or French influence by American. With the development of the radio, protection of language enabled French Canadians to take an active part in the preparation of script and in the presentation of plays. During the Second World War the revue and the French-Canadian novel received fresh stimulus. The effects of American technological change on Canadian cultural life have been finally evident in the numerous suggestions of American periodicals that Canada should join the United States. It should be said that this would result in greater consideration of Canadian sentiment by American periodicals than is at present the case when it probably counts for less than that of a religious sect.

The dangers to national existence warrant an energetic program to offset them. In the new technological developments Canadians can escape American influence in communication media other than those affected by appeals to the "freedom of the press." The Canadian Press has emphasized Canadian news but American influence is powerful.[85] In the radio, on the other hand, the Canadian government in the Canadian Broadcasting Corporation has undertaken an active role in offsetting the influence of American broadcasters. It may be hoped that its role will be even more active in television. The Film Board has been set up and designed to weaken the pressure of American films.

---

[84] See *Propaganda by Short Wave* ed. H. L. Childs and J. R. Whitton (Princeton, N.J., 1943); C. J. Rolo, *Radio Goes to War: The "Fourth Front"* (New York, 1940).

[85] "I am sceptical about the value of 90 per cent of press reports. Most of them tend to say enough to be misleading and not enough to be in any sense informative." Interview with a veteran Vancouver journalist. See M. L. Ernst, *The First Freedom* (New York, 1946) and Herbert Brucker, *Freedom of Information* (New York, 1949).

The appointment and the report of the Royal Commission on National Development in the Arts and Sciences imply a determination to strengthen our position. The reluctance of American branch plants to support research in Canadian educational institutions has been met by taxation and federal grants to universities. Universities have taken a zealous interest in Canadian literature but a far greater interest is needed in the whole field of the fine arts. Organizations such as the Canadian Authors' Association have attempted to sponsor Canadian literature by the use of medals and other devices. The resentment of English and French Canadians over the treatment of a French-Canadian play on Broadway points to powerful latent support for Canadian cultural activity.

We are indeed fighting for our lives. The pernicious influence of American advertising reflected especially in the periodical press and the powerful persistent impact of commercialism have been evident in all the ramifications of Canadian life. The jackals of communication systems are constantly on the alert to destroy every vestige of sentiment toward Great Britain, holding it of no advantage if it threatens the omnipotence of American commercialism. This is to strike at the heart of cultural life in Canada. The pride taken in improving our status in the British Commonwealth of Nations has made it difficult for us to realize that our status on the North American continent is on the verge of disappearing. Continentalism assisted in the achievement of autonomy and has consequently become more dangerous. We can only survive by taking persistent action at strategic points against American imperialism in all its attractive guises. By attempting constructive efforts to explore the cultural possibilities of various media[86] of communication and to develop them

[86] The problem to an important extent centers around the confusion as to the distinct possibilities of each medium. Literary agents deliberately exploit the demands of technological innovations, adapting the same artistic piece of work to the book, the magazine, and the film. See Curtis Brown, *Contacts* (London, 1935). Shaw refused to allow a play to be filmed, stating that no one would go to see it after seeing it on the screen and that the author suffered because the play became dull with the dialogue left out (ibid., p. 51). The studios wanted "a big kick" at the end of every sequence of the film (ibid., p. 33). Mechanization demands uniformity. The newspapers are concerned with news and contemporary topics, and books, plays, films, and novels center around newspaper owners. The book has been subordinated to the demands of advertising for the movies,

along lines free from commercialism, Canadians might make a contribution to the cultural life of the United States by releasing it from dependence on the sale of tobacco and other commodities which would in some way compensate for the damage it did before the enactment of the American Copyright Act.

---

business firms in centennial volumes, radio broadcasts, and articles from magazines. Bible scenes are exploited for plays and movies. Shakespeare's plays for actors are primarily studied in print as texts. Newspaper serials and radio scripts differ from novels and emphasize topics of the widest general interest. Any fresh idea is immediately pounced on and mauled to death. Irvin Cobb remarked concerning the dull conversation of Hollywood that the phrase coiners preserved silence until they had sold the wheeze themselves.

IV

WILLIAM KILBOURN

The Writing of Canadian History

"The phrase 'literary historian' . . . does not mean a historian with a talent for turning an occasional pleasing trope to decorate the collected facts" but rather "the historian who saw the body of his subject while still it lay scattered in unorganized source materials; who re-created the body by reanimating the form it required." In these words, from *The American Adam*, R. W. B. Lewis might easily have been describing Donald Creighton. In his three most important works, *The Commercial Empire of the St. Lawrence* (1937), *Dominion of the North* (1944), and his two-volume biography of Sir John A. Macdonald (1952, 1955), Creighton's subject forms itself around the central image of the river—the river of Canada—and the hero who grasped its meaning and embarked upon the immense journey to possess and subdue the inland kingdom to which the river was the key.

> It was the one great river which led from the eastern shore into the heart of the continent. It possessed a geographical monopoly; and it shouted its uniqueness to adventurers. The river meant mobility and distance; it invited journeyings; it promised immense expanses, unfolding, flowing away into remote and changing horizons. The whole west, with all its riches, was the dominion of the river. To the unfettered and ambitious, it offered a pathway to the central mysteries of the continent . . . from the river there rose, like an exhalation, the dream of western commercial empire. . . . The dream . . .runs like an obsession through the whole of Canadian history; and men followed each other through life, planning and toiling to achieve it. The river was not only a great actuality: it was the central truth of a religion. Men lived by it, at once consoled and inspired by its promises, its whispered suggestions, and its shouted commands; and it was a force in history, not merely because of its accom-

Reprinted from W. Kilbourn, "The Writing of Canadian History," in *Literary History of Canada*, ed. C. Klinck et al., 1965, by permission of The University of Toronto Press.

plishments, but because of its shining, ever-receding possibilities. [*The Commercial Empire of the St. Lawrence*]

Whether the hero's name was Cartier or Mackenzie, Champlain or Simon McTavish, some half-remembered merchant or nameless *coureur de bois*, whether his journey and his mastery were mainly one of stout limb and heart or one of the willing imagination, it mattered little; in the hero's act of penetration and possession of the land of the St. Lawrence there lay the central secret of Canadian history.

The first Canadian statesman to be caught in the Laurentian spell was the great seventeenth-century Intendant of New France, Jean Talon.

Talon began it. No doubt he had gone out to Canada with his head full of neat, orderly Colbertian assumptions about the future of New France. His first term was almost exemplary. He planned some model villages at Charlesbourg. He built a brewery. He was busy encouraging shipbuilding, hemp production, and manufacture. And yet, almost from the beginning, something began to happen to him. He started writing the oddest letters back to Colbert. He dilated upon the vast extent of the country. He urged the capture of New York. He assured the King that "nothing can prevent us from carrying the name and arms of his Majesty as far as Florida. . . ." These curious effusions, with their hints of suppressed excitement and their sudden vistas of gigantic empires, surprised and perplexed the minister at home. . . . Colbert made the prudent comment "Wait" on the margin of one of Talon's most intemperate suggestions. . . . Talon ought to have been impressed by it, but he was scarcely aware of the rebuke. He had suddenly become conscious of the river and of the enormous continent into which it led. He had yielded to that instinct for grandeur, that vertigo of ambition, that was part of the enchantment of the St. Lawrence. [*Dominion of the North*, pp. 68–69.]

The St. Lawrence had a rival, however, and in the end it did not bring its heroes the possession of the entire continent. "Something stood between the design and its fullfilment." "Two worlds lay over against each other in North America. . . . Of their essence, the St. Lawrence and the seaboard denied each other. Riverways against seaways, rock against farm land, trading posts against ports and towns and cities, *habitants* against farmers and fur traders against frontiersmen—they combined, geography and humanity, in one prime contradiction." Creighton's first book was the story of the frustration of the original grand design. By his choice of a beginning and end date for his subject (one of the few choices that the historian as artist possesses), Creighton managed to suggest the pattern of tragedy in the story of the empire of the St. Lawrence between the Conquest and the end of the Second British Empire in 1850. His *Dominion of the North* told in longer perspective of the three centuries of rivalry between the rich seaboard colonies, who rebelled and made a nation of the southern temperate zone of the continent, and the proud Judah of the north, which stubbornly held to its original Laurentian and imperial destiny. Creighton's masterpiece, the biography of Sir John A. Macdonald, celebrated the greatest but also the most practical of the Laurentian heroes, the statesman who gave to the northern kingdom the political frame which its nature and economy and history had so long demanded.

Creighton's was a tale of vast dimensions, and he did not shrink from telling it in the grand manner. But rarely after his first book was there the least sign of rhetorical overwriting. He had the natural gifts of the story-teller. He could change the pace and mood of his narrative without losing any of its power. He deliberately prepared his climaxes, and he made it a rule never to cast ahead in analysing the aspects of a given moment in time and so lose both the suspense of the story and the feel of the actual historical moment. He had a poignant sense of the place and an ability to describe in loving sensual detail the homely pastoral landscape of picnic and country fair or the most formal of state occasions. Rarely, but with telling effect, would he break away from the quiet clear development of the details of a political story to illuminate it with some stark dramatic juxtaposition of natural to human catastrophe: "On a night in early September, 1883, a black and killing frost descended out of a still, autumnal sky on the wheat crop of the north-west . . . before the autumn was out, the depression, like a sinister grey familiar, returned to haunt the Dominion." (*The Story of Canada*, p. 173.)

Creighton varied with great care the construction and length of sentences and paragraphs. He was particularly fond of the spare simple sentence at the beginning of a chapter ("In those days they came usually by boat." "It was his day if it was anybody's"), followed by a longer sentence describing, explaining, carrying forward the narrative. These openings always made some precise historical point, but, more important, they were his own unmistakable way of casting a spell, his manner of saying "Once upon a time."

Creighton's brief history *The Story of Canada* (1959) is a fine example of his narrative style. Cartier's departure from St. Malo, Champlain's first encounter with the Iroquois, the capture of Quebec, the rebellions of Mackenzie and Riel are all succinctly and dramatically recreated. The book is a gallery of character sketches, a *commedia* of persons captured in the description of a telling gesture or feature. One powerful sentence brings together two of the central actions of modern Canadian history, and evokes the whole struggle of a dominion linking two oceans and encompassing two cultures in its farflung diversity:

> On November 7th [1885], far out in the mountains, at a spot which Stephen determined must be called Craigellachie in memory of his clan's meeting-place and battle slogan, the bearded Donald Smith drove home the last spike in the railway's transcontinental line; and nine days later, on November 16th, while the autumnal sun rose late over plains which were white with hoar frost, the sprung trap in the Regina prison gave and Riel dropped to his extinction. [p. 180].

In spite of his achievement, there is a sense in which Creighton has appeared somewhat isolated from his contemporaries and from the life of contemporary Canada. Even his narratives tend to gray and sadden a little as they approach the present. On occasion he has wrapped himself in the mantle of Don Quixote to go tilting at Americans, Establishment Liberals, and the Fabians he took for something far worse. In the face of a philistine world of journalist-historians, and the confident, successful, efficient professionals of the learned societies and graduate schools, he has sometimes responded with Eeyore's gloom and baleful eye.

Yet if anyone has reshaped the tradition of Canadian historical writing it has been Donald Creighton. It is difficult to think of a narrative on a nineteenth-century subject by any of his younger contemporaries in the past decade whose style or structure does not owe him some debt. There are times when one could wish it otherwise. One tires of rather patronizing gestures of consideration for the general reader, of earnest and embarrassing attempts at poetic prose, and of clumsy, inappropriate insertions of little Creightonesque tableaux in the midst of dry recitals of facts. None of Creighton's followers, even at their best, quite show his ability to make use of a broad general culture in their writing. But it is a revealing measure of a writer's true stature if the only major fault to be found in him is that he has too many disciples.

In a sense, it is difficult to conceive of a man whose thinking and writing, whose life style and very being, would stand in sharper contrast to Donald Creighton than Canada's other pre-eminent historian of the mid-twentieth century, Frank Underhill. Born in 1889, thirteen years before Creighton, a Clear Grit from that North York farm country beyond the ridges which supplied the Mackenzie rebellion with its best recruits, he has been for almost forty years the chief gadfly of the Family Compact's spiritual descendants and of any and all Canadian Establishments, including that liberal-intellectual one which has embraced but never quite smothered or tamed him with its honors and applause. Where Creighton was a scholar and an artist, the bardic singer celebrating and creating a nation by giving it a past, Underhill was an intellectual, a Socratic teacher, and a Shavian wit. Creighton's chief medium has been the prose narrative of epic dimensions, Underhill's the lecture and the informal essay or review; Underhill has never written a book, although his work has been collected in books. Creighton uses several different modes of expression, from that of the ruminative academic to the incantation and the lyric. Underhill's voice never strays far from that of conversation, of clear, simple, brilliant talk.

Creighton's sympathies have been not so much conservative as with the living past itself, and with those great scholars like Harold Innis whom he admired for their refusal to be caught up in intellectual fashions of the day or to turn their history into present politics. Underhill on the other hand attacked the majority of his Canadian academic colleagues "who lived blameless intellectual lives, cultivated the golden mean and never stuck their necks out." His historical writing is alive with insights which might never have been gained but for his involvement in the present.

Trained as a classicist at the University of Toronto, a Victorian liberal turned Fabian by three years of pre-war Oxford and the acquaintance of A. D. Lindsay and G. D. H. Cole, Underhill was caught up during the 1920's in the excitement of prairie politics in the halcyon days of the Progressive movement and of his two Canadian heroes, J. S. Woodsworth and John W. Dafoe. In 1933 he became the author of the founding manifesto of Canada's first social democratic party. By the 1950's, while still a sympathetic if pointed critic of the democratic left in Canada, he was "less interested in the fortunes of political parties as such and more concerned with the climate of opinion . . . which determines to a great extent what parties accomplish or try to accomplish." He became more and more skeptical of doctrinal political solutions. He wished, a little sadly, that he "could be as sure about anything as some people I know are about everything." He compared himself to Huckleberry Finn at the end of his adventures, someone with no political home to go to and needing to light out for the Territory. Certainly much of Underhill's great power as a teacher and a historian came from qualities of candor and humility, gentleness and human sympathy very like those of Huckleberry Finn. But he also had a little of Mark Twain's showman about him. Like George Bernard Shaw he sometimes could be too easily typecast and dismissed as a brilliant clown by the dominions and powers he made fun of. He once compared himself, not altogether inaccurately, to the man who applied to John Morley for a job on the *Pall Mall Gazette* but denied special knowledge of any of a dozen fields Morley named, and when pressed said, "My specialty is general invective."

A good deal of Underhill's important historical writing, along with some samples of his invective, has been collected in *In Search of Canadian Liberalism* (1960).

A useful summary of Underhill's approach to his central theme, the history of party politics, is to be found in his pamphlet *Canadian Political Parties* (1957). Taking the American political tradition for his point of reference as he did so often, Underhill states that the main agent in the making of Confederation and in Canadian political history since has been a kind of Hamiltonian federalist party. This party has been a coalition of diverse sectional, racial, and religious interests whose chief dynamic has been supplied by the transcontinental drive for power and profit of the big business interests of Toronto and Montreal. For thirty years Macdonald's Conservative party played this role, until it was displaced after 1896 by Laurier's Liberals during the great period of western settlement. A third "governmental" party forged by Mackenzie King has held power with only two major interruptions from 1921 down to the present day, although in this period the business interests were more divided and more sophisticated than in the era of the Great Barbecue, and the party leadership was no longer so bold and exciting. Underhill recognized a kind of historical necessity in the existence of the first two parties, if the nation was to be built at all. For the last, however, King's party "of the extreme centre," which effectively dulled the edge of intelligent political debate that made America and British politics so lively, Underhill reserved some of his bitterest attacks. Nevertheless Mackenzie King's very skill in hanging on to power, and his ability to find policies to keep both French and English Canadians together in the same party, in the end won his grudging admiration.

> The essential task of Canadian statesmanship is to discover the terms on which as many as possible of the significant interest-groups of our country can be induced to work together in a common policy. . . . Mr. King has been the only political leader of the last generation who has understood [this]. . . . His statesmanship has been a more subtly accurate, a more flexibly adjustable Gallup poll of Canadian public opinion than statisticians will ever be able to devise. He has been the representative Canadian, the typical Canadian, the essential Canadian, the ideal Canadian, the Canadian as he exists in the mind of God.

> . . . Mr. King . . . was not the traditional kind of parliamentary leader that you read about in the textbooks. . . . He obviously disliked Parliament. The representative side of democracy he did not find congenial, and he worked out a much more direct but also much more indefinable relationship between himself and the Canadian people. . . . And without any of the apparatus of mass hypnosis and police coercion to which vulgar practitioners of the art like Hitler and Mussolini had to have recourse, he succeeded with hardly a mistake for twenty-five years in giving expression, by way of that curious cloudy rhetoric of his, to what lay in the Canadian sub-conscious mind.

The commonest criticism of Mr. King was that he never gave

a definite lead in any direction or committed himself in advance to anything concrete and tangible. . . . But there was one field in which he did . . . —external affairs. And it is in this field that we can now see most clearly that intuitive quality of Mr. King's mind. . . . He grasped what Canadians wanted better than they did themselves, and he was very clear-headed and persistent in moving towards a goal which he saw from the start. . . . He was primarily a North American. He resisted all attempts to make a political or economic or military unit out of the British Commonwealth. . . . Even in the emotional atmosphere of the war he declined all Churchillian invitations into an Imperial War Cabinet. Instead, he was vigorous both in peace and war in strengthening our American ties. . . . He never consulted parliament or people about these steps; he simply kept us informed. [Quotations are from the chapter "W. L. Mackenzie King," in *In Search of Canadian Liberalism*.]

Like King, Underhill was "primarily a North American." Yet to develop and maintain the best of the North American democratic tradition in Canada has not been easy; liberalism and the political left have never flourished here. In Underhill's view the oldest and strongest of Canadian traditions from the "great refusal of 1776" to the Reciprocity issue of 1911 and to the Diefenbaker era, has been "our determination not to become Americans." "We were born saying 'No' " to the Enlightenment and the American Revolution, and for a century and a half we have regularly indulged in outbursts of anti-American feeling and rejected the best that American thought and society has had to offer us. "But if we allow ourselves to be obsessed by the danger of American cultural annexation, so that the thought preys on us day and night, we shall only become a slightly bigger Ulster. The idea that by taking thought, and with the help of some government subventions, we can become another England—which, one suspects, is Mr. [Vincent] Massey's ultimate idea—is purely fantastic."

In his 1946 presidential address to the Canadian Historical Association, Underhill made a plea for two kinds of history little studied in Canada. He asked first for more Canadian intellectual history—political ideas, religion, and education—as a means of correcting and supplementing the Environmentalist emphasis on geographical determinants and abstract forces which often made Canadian history appear to be "a ghostly ballet of bloodless economic categories." Secondly, he noted with regret that Canadian historians concentrated so much on the writing of their own parochial national history and that *Christianity and Classical Culture* (1940) by C. N. Cochrane (1889–1945) was one of the few important books on world history written by a Canadian. He looked forward to the time when "we have asserted our full partnership in the civilization of our day by Canadian writing on the great subjects of permanent and universal interest."

It has been Marshall McLuhan who, by developing an approach to the study of technology and communications first tentatively explored in the later work of Harold Innis, has made the most original Canadian contribution to the interpretation of the history of civilization. When some Canadian historians take McLuhan's *The Gutenberg Galaxy* (1962) seriously enough to try to grapple with its explosive, jargon-proud, joke-filled, non-linear prose, and to let its insights or its errors act as a stimulus to the examination of their own canons of interpretation, their writing might well reach that level of maturity and excitement to which Frank Underhill looked forward a generation ago. As one of the most perceptive contemporary critics, Frank Kermode, has said of *The Gutenberg Galaxy*, "In a truly literate society this book would start a long debate."

The last best word on the subject of the historian and literature (and the sharpest comment on what Canadian historical writing most often neglects) is still that of the young Thomas Macaulay: "Our historians neglect the art of narration, the art of interesting the affections and presenting pictures to the imagination. ... The perfect historian gives to truth those attractions which have been usurped by fiction. In his narrative a due subordination is observed: some transactions are prominent; others retire. But the scale on which he represents them is increased or diminished according to the degree in which they elucidate the condition of society and the nature of man. ... A history which in every particular incident may be true, may, on the whole, be false." William Morton has shrewdly remarked that the first and perhaps the only major choice made by the historian as artist is the choice of his subject-matter, the act of seeing the whole form of his narrative, its beginning, its middle and its end. However, within the strict and difficult limits of what can be known about what actually happened, the historian does have a kind of freedom not easily achieved by the novelist. He need not strain for plausibility or limit his plot to what merely might have been. He need not use elaborate devices to establish the credibility of the narrative voice. He is free, by the very nature of his art, his discipline, and his subject, to explore and show forth in all its variety and complexity and strangeness the incredible truth.

V

F. H. UNDERHILL

French-English Relations in Canada

Wilfrid Laurier was the greatest of all Canadians. Let us remember this today in the midst of all our troubled discussions between English-Canadians and French-Canadians. The name of Laurier and the Laurier tradition are not popular, so I gather, in present-day Quebec. Yet, if we are to solve our difficulties between the two main communal groups today, we need men with Laurier's qualities both in Quebec and in English-speaking Canada.

He was the greatest of all Canadian public men because he devoted his life to this most intractable of all problems, the finding of the terms on which English-speaking and French-speaking Canadians can learn to live together here in Canada more or less amicably. I stress the phrase "more or less" because it is foolish to pretend to believe that we are likely to turn good neighborhood, if we achieve it, into good brotherhood within the lifetime of any individuals now living. There has been too much bitterness in our generation for that. At the end of the 1940s the Frenchman, André Siegfried, who had been studying Canada for fifty years, concluded that all that we had achieved was a *"modus vivendi* without cordiality."[1] We need to aim at something a little better than this. At present, we seem to be moving toward something a good deal worse.

But if we are to achieve this something a little better, it can only be done through leaders from both sides who achieve something a good deal better in their personal relations with each other, who reach a degree of understanding and cordiality that approaches brotherhood. There will always be leaders springing

From F. H. Underhill, *The Image of Confederation*, commissioned and broadcast by the CBC in 1963 as the third series of Massey Lectures and subsequently published by them in paperback under the same title. Copyright © CBC, 1964.
[1] André Siegfried, *Canada, an International Power* (London, 1947), p. 224.

up who make profit for themselves by extremist exploitation of mean tribal suspicions and selfish particularist ambitions. We cannot eliminate these adventurers. We can only hope to counteract their bad influence through the leadership given by another type of statesman who appeals to our better selves, who tries to induce us to stretch our imaginations and sympathies, to display a generosity of spirit toward people who are different from ourselves.

Incidentally this problem of the relations between different groups inside Canada is at bottom the same as the problem of international relations in the world at large. Neither problem will be solved by paper documents, by constitution-making, but only by the emergence in all groups of a general feeling that it is our duty to act as if we were a little better than our normal parochial selves.

Laurier should be our great example because he tried to practice what he preached. Of course, the mouthing of noble *bonne entente* sentiments has become a ritual in our public life. O Canada, O Canada, O can a day go by without some orator orating on this theme of harmony between the two communal groups! Here I am doing it myself at this moment. What distinguished Laurier as a Canadian statesman was, firstly, that he never gave up warning his own French community against the particular form of sin that doth so easily beset it; and, secondly, that he steadily tried to keep in personal touch with the other community. He is unique among Canadian leaders in both respects. Today, more than ever, we need leaders who are capable of both forms of action.

The tendency against which French-Canadians need to be on guard is that toward the particularist, isolationist, Sinn Fein type of tribal nationalism to which they have always been tempted when things have been going wrong—under Mercier, under Bourassa, under Duplessis. This is a tendency natural to all uncomfortable minorities. The tendency against which we English-Canadians need to be on guard is that toward the unconscious or subconscious assumption that, because British sovereignty displaced French sovereignty over Canada in 1763, and because since then the English-speaking population has become an overwhelming majority, therefore Canada is fundamentally an English-speaking community, and our English-Canadian habits, methods, forms of social organization, and way of life generally, must in the end be accepted by the French-Canadians as their way of life also. This is a tendency natural to all comfortable majorities. And we have always lacked English-Canadian Lauriers to warn us against our besetting English-Canadian sins.

Laurier spent a considerable part of his career warning his community against the temptation to form a racial national party for political purposes. He pointed out to them that this would only lead to a combination of the English majority against them, as it did in 1917. He told them the unpleasant truth that as a minority they must from time to time make adjustments to what the majority wanted. He did his best to get minority and majority to divide on political issues as Liberals and Conservatives rather than to confront each other as French-Catholics and English-Protestants.

He did not preach moderation and concession only to his own group. He was always going on political tours into English-speaking Canada, especially into Ontario, speaking to English-Canadians in their own language, which he used with a special gracefulness and polish. More than any other Canadian leader whose speeches I have read, he followed the honest but unpopular practice of saying the same thing on controversial issues to both English and French audiences. He was always preaching the principles of British constitutional liberalism to both. He mixed readily and naturally with members of the other racial group; he had many personal friends among that group. By his generous bearing, his good manners, and his moderation, he built up a personal following in English- as well as in French-Canada. Men who had once worked with him nearly always found it painful to part company with him on political issues. Even Bourassa, who attacked him most bitterly over a long period of years, declared that he loved the man.

This was the happy warrior. This was he that every man in arms should wish to be. Yet Laurier ended his career in defeat.

Laurier's dealings with the intellectuals of the two racial groups are specially noteworthy today. In Quebec he had to fight first the group of fanatical, doctrinaire, ultramontane Catholics,[2] he had to fight them for the right of Catholic voters

---

[2] Laurier's long fight with the ultramontanes, who came to be nicknamed the Castors, is dealt with in the Skelton and Willison biographies. For contemporary comment by English-Canadians on the dangers of ultramontane ambitions, see Goldwin Smith, *Canada and the Canadian Question*, chap. 2, "The French Province"; and Charles Lindsey, *Rome in Canada* (Toronto, 1877).

to vote Liberal freely. And then he had to fight his own Liberal lieutenant Bourassa. Both of these opponents accused him of disloyalty to the French-Catholic group, and of giving in to pressures from the English majority who presented a threat to the French-Catholic way of life. In English-Canada he had Willison of Toronto against him for the opposite reason, for giving in to the sinister ambitions of the French-Catholic hierarchy over Saskatchewan schools and for betraying the principle of provincial rights. And then later he had Dafoe of Winnipeg against him for being so afraid of losing Quebec to Bourassa that he failed to rise to the necessities of the world struggle against German aggression.

Laurier had to steer a difficult middle course between these two opposed sets of intellectual doctrinaires, and to try to make them see that liberal principles as he interpreted them furnished the only guide for peace and freedom within Canada. It is in his discussion of principles, in his frank, face-to-face argument with men of both racial groups who professed to be mainly interested in principle, that Laurier is so superior to both Macdonald and King, who shared his belief that the supreme necessity of statesmanship in Canada is to find a way of conciliation between French and English. One of these two prime ministers disliked talking about principles; and the other, in spite of his Harvard Ph.D., was incapable of handling abstract ideas.

The root of our current difficulties is that French-Canadians and English-Canadians have different pictures in their minds of what the meaning of Confederation was in 1867, of what our national purpose was or should have been in the years since then, and of what Confederation has accomplished so far.

To the French, as they look back on their two centuries of history since 1763, the two centuries have been clearly and unhappily divided. In the first, from being a conquered people they won their way, after long struggles, which included an armed revolt under Papineau, to political liberty, to Responsible Government with full French participation under Lafontaine, Morin, and Cartier. Then came the second century, in which they have had to suffer a series of defeats—over the settlement of the West, over Riel, over schools and language outside Quebec, over our Canadian relations with Britain, over conscription; a century in which they have seen their Quebec economy, as their province entered fully into the second industrial revolution, fall more and more under the control of English-Canadian and American capitalism.

To the English-Canadian, it seems that Quebec is suffering today because she deliberately isolated herself in the nineteenth century under the guidance of a church that was determined to keep its people separated as far as possible from dangerous contacts with Anglo-Saxondom. She accepted the clerical doctrine that in order to preserve her language and religion she should adhere to a static, agrarian, habitant economy. Curiously enough, this agrarian gospel was preached by clerics, journalists, and writers, who themselves lived in cities. Clerically directed education in classical colleges meant that a small élite was turned out who lacked training in science, technology, and business enterprise, and thereby the province cut itself off from the possibilities of economic advance that were so eagerly being seized by the English-Canadians west of the Ottawa River. Quebec lost the competition with Ontario for the West because her teeming surplus population drifted southward to find employment in the American factories, and because she showed no willingness to try to assimilate some of the non-French and non-English population that poured into Canada after the turn of the century. If she fell behind, it was her own doing.

English-speaking Canada has another point to make also. The demands for separate French-Catholic schools outside of Quebec have always been demands for clerically controlled teaching. It is this to which English-Canada generally objects, it seems to me, rather than to the teaching in another language. If Quebec in her present revolution should put her own education under lay control, would English-Canadian distaste for French schools be so marked, so obstinate, so fundamentalist?

I think it might be enlightening at this point to quote some of the criticisms made by André Siegfried of both the French and the English groups as he saw them in Canada in the period just after the Boer War. It was at this time that he published his first book on our country, *The Race Question in Canada*, 1907. Siegfried came from Alsatian-Protestant stock; and he is an interesting commentator because, as a Frenchman, he felt a natural sympathy with the fortunes of the French people in America, while as a Protestant anti-clerical, he had no sympathy with the far-reaching ambitions of the French-Canadian church.

He gives a striking picture of the control that the church exercised over the mind of Quebec through its domination of education and its interference in politics. And he concludes:

> The protection of the church is precious, but the price paid for it is exorbitant. Are not the intellectual bondage in which the church would keep them, the narrow authority she exercises, the antiquated doctrines she persists in inculcating, all calculated to hinder the evolution of the race and to handicap it in its rivalry with the Anglo-Saxons, long since freed from the outworn shackles of the past.[3]

This analysis and conclusion will not surprise us Anglo-Saxons. What may surprise us, however, is what he has to say about the relation of English-Canadian education to politics.

> If Catholicism is one of the essential factors in the development of the French-Canadians, Protestantism does not count for less in that of the English race in the Dominion. . . . To all appearances the independence of these [Protestant] churches in regard to the State has been absolutely established. Perhaps it would not be safe to say quite so positively that the State's independence of them is established in the same degree. . . . They have never been able to imagine a State entirely devoid of religious prepossessions. The Protestant clergy do not aim at controlling the government in the ultramontane Catholic fashion, but they do aim at informing it with their spirit. . . . Canada, never having had its 1789, has no real comprehension of the theory of the neutrality of the State.[4]

As English-speaking Canada intends the State to be Protestant, so also, says Siegfried, it intends it to be Anglo-Saxon:

> Another characteristic of the English school is the very keen national spirit that flourishes in it. Public opinion decides that the boys shall have instilled into them a throughgoing Anglo-Saxon patriotism. . . . This is precisely why the French, who don't wish at any price to be absorbed, have a deep distrust of the distinctively English public school. . . . Both French and English school systems are national in spirit. That is to say, that the one seeks to produce French-Canadians, the other English-Canadians. . . . Both schools are permeated by religion.[5]

[3] André Siegfried, *The Race Question in Canada* (London, 1907), p. 50.
[4] Ibid., p. 52.
[5] Ibid., p. 79.

Siegfried went on to deal with Canadian political parties. He is interesting on this subject, too, because he came from a country in which parties were so much more ideological than with us, and political controversy, especially at this moment of the separation of Church and State, was concerned with the principles on which the good society should be based to a degree that we English-Canadians would find nearly incomprehensible:

> Originally formed to subserve a political idea, these parties are often to be found quite detached from the principles which gave them birth, and with their own self-preservation as their chief care and aim. Even without a programme, they continue to live and thrive, tending to become mere associations for the securing of power. . . . This fact deprives the periodical appeals to the voting public of the importance they should have . . . Whichever side succeeds, the country, it is well known, will be governed in just the same way; the only difference will be in the personnel of the Government . . . Canadian statesmen . . . seem to stand in fear of great movements of public opinion, and seek to lull them rather than to encourage them and bring them to fruition . . . The reason for this attitude is easy to comprehend. Canada, as we have seen, with its rival creeds and races, is a land of fears and jealousies and conflicts. The absence of ideas and programmes and convictions is only apparent. Let a question involving religion or nationality be boldly raised and . . . the elections will be turned into real political fights, passionate and sincere. This is exactly what is dreaded by farsighted and prudent politicians, whose duty it is to preserve the national equilibrium . . . They exert themselves, therefore, to prevent the formation of homogeneous parties, divided according to creed or race or class. The purity of political life suffers from this, but perhaps the very existence of the Federation is the price.[6]

Siegfried was so French in his understanding of how politics should be carried on that he was not quite fair, in this rather cynical account, to our Canadian parties. For the composite bi-racial, bi-cultural party, uniting both French and English voters, had been one of our great political inventions. It has been the only effective instrumentality that we have been able to devise for overcoming the deep cleavages between the two communal groups and for keeping them going along together in some kind of rough jolting co-operation.

[6] Ibid., p. 141.

The experiment began with the Reform party of Lafontaine and Baldwin in the 1840s, which won Responsible Government. When it broke up after ten years, it was succeeded in 1854 by the Liberal-Conservative party of Macdonald and Cartier, which dominated Canadian politics for forty years, taking over the French majority group that had called itself Reform under Lafontaine and Baldwin. Then came the Liberal party of Laurier, which took over most of the Quebec Bleus who had supported Macdonald. With some short breaks, it provided the government from 1896 to 1957. Apparently we are capable of producing only one of these bi-racial parties at a time. The opposition party is never able to function so efficiently as the government party because the French have instinctively given the bulk of their support to the party that sits on the right of Mr. Speaker.

These successful bi-racial governing parties are marked by certain characteristics. Whatever their name, they are really coalitions of the moderate men in each of the French and English communities. Above all, their leaders are moderates. The extremists after 1854, the Grits and Rouges, never quite succeeded for a long time in forming a nation-wide party that was a going concern. The Diefenbaker and the Duplessis groups have been equally unsuccessful in our day. The successful party is based on the men of the center.

This composite party, with membership from the two races, is always in a state of internal tension, and is frequently torn by dissension. Its unity is always somewhat doubtful, for French and English find it difficult to understand each other even when they can speak one another's language. What holds the party together in the end is the quality of its leaders, their determination to stick together personally through thick and thin, their loyalty to one another and fondness for one another—usually, also, their similarity in temperament as well as in political philosophy. The party, in effect, has had a joint leadership when it was most successful—Lafontaine and Baldwin, Macdonald and Cartier, King and Lapointe.

To judge from the fact that this experiment has been going on with more or less success continuously since the 1840s, this kind of a bi-racial party would seem to be essential if political co-operation between French- and English-Canadians is to work in practice. This is our *articulus stantis aut cadentis imperii*. It does not matter what else we may do or try to do in the next few years; if we can not keep in operation a governing party at Ottawa composed in this way, Confederation will fail. If leaders of the requisite quality, who will devote themselves to holding together a party of this kind, do not arise from both communal groups, Confederation will fail.

The most alarming feature of our present situation is that so many of the French leaders no longer seem to be led by ambition or by a wider patriotism to play their part in federal politics. If they are not attracted to our national capital, what hope is there of the ultimate loyalty of the masses of French-Canadians being attached to the larger Canadian experiment? The future of Confederation depends upon the future of this bi-racial, bi-cultural political party.

There is a great tradition in Quebec of service in this larger party; and it is one of Quebec's essential traditions, just as much as is the tradition of the narrow provincial nationalism—though there seems to be a strange reluctance among leading figures in Quebec just now to come out bluntly and say so. Consider the names that are attached to this wider national tradition: Lafontaine, Morin, Cartier, Dorion, Chapleau, Laurier, Lapointe, St. Laurent.

At present the more vocal nationalist thinkers in Quebec tend to sneer at efforts to make the Ottawa government work successfully, on the ground that Ottawa is in reality only the seat of an English-Canadian government, and that the only government that matters to French-Canadians is their own governmen in Quebec. They are forgetting a large part of their Quebec political history.

It is true that we English-Canadians, the overwhelming majority of us anyway, take for granted that our first loyalty is to the federal government in Ottawa rather than to our particular provincial government. Good heavens, how could a citizen of Ontario, since the days of the rise of Mitch Hepburn, possibly feel that he was first an Ontarioite and only secondly a Canadian? French-Canadians have found it more difficult to feel in this way, especially in this last generation when their younger men have been subjected to passionate teaching in the classical colleges, which inculcated narrow, provincialist nationalist doctrines. But Quebec's destiny as part of a larger whole has never quite disappeared from their minds as an ideal.

It was Bourassa who first enlarged the conception that French-Canadians had of themselves as full citizens of the Dominion, and who also unfortunately encouraged them toward a narrow, tribal nationalism. When he started his campaign against Laurier at the time of the Boer War, he was functioning, as he himself emphasized, as a Liberal. He was demanding that Canada's constitutional autonomy should not be infringed by a gradual process of getting entangled in British military imperialism overseas. This was a good Liberal cause; Laurier shared Bourassa's abhorrence of militarism and his constitutional objection to any infringement of Canadian autonomy. This was also a cause on which both French-Canadians and English-Canadians might be hoped to unite. They did rally around it in the next generation, in the King era. It might have been a great unifying cause in these early years of the twentieth century, as Bourassa hoped it would be.

But at the same time he was caught up in a great struggle for French rights within Canada. He put himself at the head of a campaign to protect these rights as he understood them, in the controversies, first, over schools in Saskatchewan and Alberta, and then, over schools in Ontario and Manitoba. He insisted that French-Canadians had the right to be equal citizens with English-Canadians all across Canada, and that they must not allow themselves to be herded into something like an Indian reserve in Quebec. This also was surely a good Liberal cause for which he was fighting. But he became so emotionally wrought up over it, so violent in his attacks on English-Canadians, that he defeated any hopes he might have had earlier of uniting the two races in a common Canadianism. His liberalism gradually transformed itself into a militant, ultramontane Catholicism. The Castor side of his nature overwhelmed the Rouge side. The issue of Regulation xvii overshadowed for him the issue of the war. The real enemy, he told his fellow French-Canadians, was not German militarism in Europe but Anglo-Saxon materialism in North America. Let the French-Canadians collect money, not for the wounded in France and Flanders, but for the French-Catholic sufferers in Ontario, *"les blessés d'Ontario."*

And Laurier became to him more and more a pure villain. Laurier's doctrine of mutual concession became purely evil. "When Sir Wilfrid Laurier arrives at the gates of Paradise, the first thing he will do is to propose a compromise between God and Satan" he declared. This was a brilliant sarcastic sentence, not without considerable point. But it revealed more about

Bourassa than about Laurier. Canadian domestic politics had become for him a struggle between God and the Devil. Peaceful constitutional politics is impossible on that basis.

Bourassa's pilgrimage of passion up and down Quebec inevitably stirred up an extremist form of Quebec provincial nationalism, especially among his excitable younger followers. Yet he himself never gave up his belief in the wider Canadian nation. The charge against him is that you cannot advance this wider nationality by preaching that the differences between the two branches of the nation are part of a great struggle between God and the Devil.

Later, after the war was over, Bourassa became critical of the excesses of this provincial nationalist spirit that he had helped to foster by his impassioned oratorical campaigns. In an audience with the Pope in 1926, he apparently received a long lecture on the evils that excessive nationalism of this kind was producing in the contemporary world and on the incompatibility of this kind of nationalism with the Catholic religion. When he came home, he proclaimed that his Catholicism was more important to him than his politics, and he tried to dampen down some of the racial feeling he had helped to stir up.

It would be difficult to over-emphasize the importance of Bourassa's career. He was one of our greatest Canadians. As an intellectual he insisted on issues always being clearly defined, and was thus a useful trouble-maker, though a confounded nuisance to the practical politicians of both parties who do not like to have party unity upset by too much clarity. He always saw the relation of Canadian issues to wider world affairs, and helped in this way to make his people, English-Canadian as well as French-Canadian, more mature. The process of becoming mature, however, is apt to be a painful one for peoples as well as for individuals. And you cannot unite a people in a common Canadianism by continuously declaiming at the top of your voice on the grievances that separate one group of Canadians from another.

The epigons who followed Bourassa in Quebec narrowed his appeal, and the sad result is our present situation. We need a return to the spirit of Laurier.

Today, it seems to me, many of the claims put forward by the spokesmen of Quebec nationalism must be accepted as valid by reasonable English-Canadians. Equality is always a difficult concept to define in practice; but some of their claims to equality in our common country need wider recognition. However, the exaggerated language in which these claims are phrased, the presentation of claims in the form of ultimata, do not bode well for our future. What we should ask now of the spokesmen of Quebec is not so much a definition of what they claim for their province and for their racial group as of what they consider all of us still to have in common if their claims are granted. Nothing is so alarming in these French-Canadian speeches as the almost complete absence of any consideration of what French and English can still look forward to doing together through their common government in Ottawa, if Confederation is to continue for a second century. A nation is a body of men who have done great things together in the past and who hope to do great things together in the future. Confederation will not be saved by any new constitution-making between now and 1967 if the minds and hearts of men of both groups are not moved by dreams of the great things that we may yet do together in the future.

VI

GEORGE GRANT

The Disappearance of Canada

Perhaps we should rejoice in the disappearance of Canada. We leave the narrow provincialism and our backwoods culture; we enter the excitement of the United States where all the great things are being done. Who would compare the science, the art, the politics, the entertainment of our petty world to the overflowing achievements of New York, Washington, Chicago, and San Francisco? Think of William Faulkner and then think of Morley Callaghan. Think of the Kennedys and the Rockefellers and then think of Pearson and E. P. Taylor. This is the profoundest argument for the Liberals. They governed so as to break down our parochialism and lead us into the future.

Before discussing this position, I must dissociate myself from a common philosophic assumption. I do not identify necessity and goodness. This identification is widely assumed during an age of progress. Those who worship "evolution" or "history" consider that what must come in the future will be "higher," "more developed," "better," "freer" than what has been in the past. This identification is also common among those who worship God according to Moses or the Gospels. They identify necessity and good within the rubric of providence. From the assumption that God's purposes are unfolded in historical events, one may be led to view history as an ever-fuller manifestation of good. Since the tenth century of the Christian era, some Western theologians have tended to interpret the fallen sparrow as if particular events could be apprehended by faith as good. This doctrine of providence was given its best philosophical expression by Hegel: "*Die Weltgeschichte ist das Weltgericht*"— "World history is the world's judgment." Here the doctrines of progress and providence have been brought together. But if

From George Grant, *Lament for a Nation*, 1965, reprinted by permission of the Canadian Publishers, McClelland and Stewart Limited, Toronto.

history is the final court of appeal, force is the final argument. Is it possible to look at history and deny that within its dimensions force is the supreme ruler? To take a progressive view of providence is to come close to worshipping force. Does this not make us cavalier about evil? The screams of the tortured child can be justified by the achievements of history. How pleasant for the achievers, but how meaningless for the child.

As a believer, I must then reject these Western interpretations of providence. Belief is blasphemy if it rests on any easy identification of necessity and good. It is plain that there must be other interpretations of the doctrine. However massive the disaster we might face—for example, the disappearance of constitutional government for several centuries, or the disappearance of our species—belief in providence should be unaffected. It must be possible within the doctrine of providence to distinguish between the necessity of certain happenings and their goodness. A discussion of the goodness of Canada's disappearance must therefore be separated from a discussion of its necessity.

Many levels of argument have been used to say that it is good that Canada should disappear. In its simplest form, continentalism is the view of those who do not see what all the fuss is about. The purpose of life is consumption, and therefore the border is an anachronism. The forty-ninth parallel results in a lower standard of living for the majority to the north of it. Such continentalism has been an important force throughout Canadian history. Until recently it was limited by two factors. Emigration to the United States was not too difficult for Canadians, so that millions were able to seek their fuller future to the south. Moreover, those who believed in the primacy of private prosperity have generally been too concerned with individual pursuits to bother with political advocacy. Nevertheless, this spirit is bound to grow. One has only to live in the Niagara peninsula to understand it. In the mass era, most human beings are defined in terms of their capacity to consume. All other differences between them, like political traditions, begin to appear unreal and unprogressive. As consumption becomes primary, the border appears an anachronism, and a frustrating one at that.

The disadvantages in being a branch-plant satellite rather than in having full membership in the Republic will become obvious. As the facts of our society substantiate continentalism, more people will explicitly espouse it. A way of life shaped by con-

tinental institutions will produce political continentalism.
Young and ambitious politicians will arise to give tongue to it.
The election of 1963 was the first time in our history that a
strongly nationalist campaign did not succeed, and that a government was brought down for standing up to the Americans.
The ambitious young will not be slow to learn the lesson that
Pearson so ably taught them about what pays politically. Some
of the extreme actions of French Canadians in their efforts to
preserve their society will drive other Canadians to identify
themselves more closely with their southern neighbors than with
the strange and alien people of Quebec.

Of course continentalism was more than a consumption-
ideology. In the nineteenth century, the United States appeared
to be the haven of opportunity for those who had found no
proper place in the older societies. Men could throw off the
shackles of inequality and poverty in the new land of opportunity. To many Canadians, the Republic seemed a freer and
more open world than the costive colonial society with its
restraints of tradition and privilege. The United States appeared
to be the best society the world had ever produced for the
ordinary citizen. Whatever the mass society of prosperity has
become, the idea that the United States is the society of freedom,
equality, and opportunity will continue to stir many hearts. The
affection and identification that a vast majority of Canadians
have given to the publicly expressed ideals of such leaders as
Roosevelt and Kennedy is evidence of this.

Continentalism as a philosophy is based on the liberal interpretation of history. Because much of our intellectual life has
been oriented to Great Britain, it is not surprising that our chief
continentalists have been particularly influenced by British liberalism. The writings of Goldwin Smith and F. H. Underhill carry
more the note of Mill and Macaulay than of Jefferson and Jackson. This continentalism has made two main appeals. First, Canadians need the greater democracy of the Republic. To the
continentalists, both the French and British traditions in Canada
were less democratic than the social assumptions of the United
States. In such arguments, democracy has not been interpreted
solely in a political sense, but has been identified with social
equality, contractual human relations, and the society open
to all men, regardless of race or creed or class. American history is seen to be the development of the first mass democ-

GEORGE GRANT

racy on earth.[1] The second appeal of continentalism is that
humanity requires that nationalisms be overcome. In moving
to larger units of government, we are moving in the direction
of world order. If Canadians refuse this, they are standing back
from the vital job of building a peaceful world. After the horrors
that nationalistic wars have inflicted on this century, how can
one have any sympathy for nationalism? Thank God the world
is moving beyond such divisive loyalties.

Both these arguments were used with particular literacy by
F. H. Underhill in his appeals for the Liberal party in the
Toronto Star at the time of the 1963 election.[2] In his use of both
these arguments it was sometimes difficult to know whether
Underhill was appealing to the order of good or to the order of
necessity, or whether in his mind the two were identical. For
example, closeness to the United States was identified in this
writing with true internationalism. The argument from necessity
is that nationalism must disappear and that we are moving inevitably to a world of continental empires. But this inevitable
movement does not in itself mean that we are moving to a better
and more peaceful world order. The era of continental rivalries
may be more ferocious than the era of nationalism. Only when
one adds to this argument the liberal faith in progress does one
believe that continentalism must be a step toward a nobler internationalism. The argument for continentalism is different when
it appeals to inevitability than when it is based on the brotherhood of man. This ambiguity in Underhill was mirrored in the
whole Liberal campaign of 1963, in which Pearson wrapped his
acceptance of continental atomic arms in the language of inter-

[1] In our generation this interpretation is expounded at length in the
sermons of Arthur Schlesinger, Jr.

[2] Professor F. H. Underhill is a key figure in the intellectual history of
Canadian liberalism. See his book *In Search of Canadian Liberalism* (Toronto: Macmillan, 1960). Underhill gave many years to building the CCF.
He found himself on the opposite side from the business community in
Toronto on nearly every public question. Yet in a speech in Toronto in
1964, he could in his seventies announce that the liberal hope lies now
with the great corporations. This conversion surely shows how consistently he continues to work out the consequences of his thought. He
has recognized that the business community in America is no longer the
propertied classes of his youth but managers whose ideology is liberal. He
is right to believe that corporations and not doctrinaire socialism are the
wave of the future.

national obligations and his loyalty to the United Nations.

To those outside the progressive view of history, there was a note of high comedy in the use of the Tennysonian "parliament of man" language to attack Diefenbaker's defense of national sovereignty, when the issue at stake was the acquisition of nuclear arms. The Sifton and Southam papers made any fear of dominance by the American Empire seem a retreat from true internationalism. This note of comedy went further in the summer of 1963, when the CBC made misty-eyed television programs about Pearson's return to the United Nations as the true Canadian internationalist, at a time when he was negotiating with the United States for the spread of nuclear arms to Canada.

However, laughter should not allow us to fail in charity toward liberalism. It was easier to use its language consistently in the era of Goldwin Smith than in the twentieth century. Liberalism was, in origin, criticism of the old established order. Today it is the voice of the establishment. It could sound a purer note when it was the voice of the outsider than today when it is required to legislate freedom. For example, Harvard liberalism was surely nobler when William James opposed the Spanish-American war than when Arthur Schlesinger, Jr., advised Kennedy on Cuban policy.

It has already been argued that, because of our modern assumptions about human good, Canada's disappearance is necessary.[3] In deciding whether continentalism is good, one is making a judgment about progressive political philosophy and its interpretation of history. Those who dislike continentalism are in some sense rejecting that progressive interpretation. It can only be with an enormous sense of hesitation that one dares to question modern political philosophy. If its assumptions are false, the age of progress has been a tragic aberration in the history of the species. To assert such a proposition lightly would be the height of irresponsibility. Has it not been in the age of progress that disease and overwork, hunger and poverty, have been drastically

[3] In our day, necessity is often identified with some fate in the atoms or the "life force." But historical necessity is chiefly concerned with what the most influential souls have thought about human good. Political philosophy is not some pleasant cultural game reserved for those too impotent for practice. It is concerned with judgments about goodness. As these judgments are apprehended and acted upon by practical men, they become the unfolding of fate.

reduced? Those who criticize our age must at the the same time contemplate pain, infant mortality, crop failures in isolated areas, and the sixteen-hour day. As soon as that is said, facts about our age must also be remembered: the increasing outbreaks of impersonal ferocity, the banality of existence in technological societies, the pursuit of expansion as an end in itself. Will it be good for men to control their genes? The possibility of nuclear destruction and mass starvation may be no more terrible than that of man tampering with the roots of his humanity. Interference with human nature seems to the moderns the hope of a higher species in the ascent of life; to others it may seem that man in his pride could corrupt his very being. The powers of manipulation now available may portend the most complete tyranny imaginable. At least, it is feasible to wonder whether modern assumptions may be basically inhuman.

To many modern men, the assumptions of this age appear inevitable, as being the expression of the highest wisdom that the race has distilled. The assumptions appear so inevitable that to entertain the possibility of their falsity may seem the work of a madman. Yet these assumptions were made by particular men in particular settings. Machiavelli and Hobbes, Spinoza and Vico, Rousseau and Hegel, Marx and Darwin originated this account of human nature and destiny. Their view of social excellence was reached in conscious opposition to that of the ancient philosophers. The modern account of human nature and destiny was developed from a profound criticism of what Plato and Aristotle had written. The modern thinkers believed that they had overcome the inadequacies of ancient thought, while maintaining what was true in the ancients.

Yet Plato and Aristotle would not have admitted that their teachings could be used in this way. They believed that their own teaching was the complete teaching for all men everywhere, or else they were not philosophers. They believed that they had considered all the possibilities open to man and had reached the true doctrine concerning human excellence. Only the thinkers of the age of progress considered the classical writers as a preparation for the perfected thought of their own age. The classical philosophers did not so consider themselves. To see the classics as a preparation for later thought is then to think within the assumptions of the age of progress. But this is to beg the question, when the issue at stake is whether these assumptions are true. It is this very issue that is raised by the tragedies and ambiguities of our day.[4]

Ancient philosophy gives alternative answers to modern man concerning the questions of human nature and destiny. It touches all the central questions that man has asked about himself and the world. The classical philosophers asserted that a universal and homogeneous state would be tyranny. To elucidate their argument would require an account of their total teaching concerning human beings. It would take one beyond political philosophy into the metaphysical assertion that changes in the world take place within an eternal order that is not affected by them. This implies a definition of human freedom quite different from the modern view that freedom is man's essence. It implies a science different from that which aims at the conquest of nature.

The discussion of issues such as these is impossible in a short writing about Canada. Also, the discussion would be inconclusive, because I do not know the truth about these ultimate matters. Therefore, the question whether it is good that Canada should disappear must be left unsettled. If the best social order is the universal and homogeneous state, then the disappearance of Canada can be understood as a step toward that order. If the universal and homogeneous state would be a tyranny, then the disappearance of even this indigenous culture can be seen as the removal of a minor barrier on the road to that tyranny. As the central issue is left undecided, the propriety of lamenting must also be left unsettled.

My lament is not based on philosophy but on tradition. If one cannot be sure about the answer to the most important questions, then tradition is the best basis for the practical life. Those who loved the older traditions of Canada may be allowed to lament what has been lost, even though they do not know whether or not that loss will lead to some greater political good. But lamentation falls easily into the vice of self-pity. To live with courage is a virtue, whatever one may think of the dominant assumptions of one's age. Multitudes of human beings through the course of

[4] The previous paragraph is dependent on the writings of Professor Leo Strauss who teaches at the University of Chicago. For Strauss's account of political philosophy, see, for example, *What Is Political Philosophy?* (Glencoe: The Free Press, 1959) and *The City and Man* (Chicago: Rand McNally, 1964). I only hope that nothing in the foregoing misinterprets the teaching of that wise man.

GEORGE GRANT

history have had to live when their only political allegiance was irretrievably lost. What was lost was often something far nobler than what Canadians have lost. Beyond courage, it is also possible to live in the ancient faith, which asserts that changes in the world, even if they be recognized more as a loss than a gain, take place within an eternal order that is not affected by their taking place. Whatever the difficulty of philosophy, the religious man has been told that process is not all. *"Tendebantque manus ripae ulterioris amore."*[5]

[5] Virgil *Aeneid*, bk. 6: "They were holding their arms outstretched in love toward the further shore."

II

THE THEORETICAL CONTEXT

I

NORTHROP FRYE

The Road of Excess

It will be easiest for me to begin with a personal reference. My first sustained effort in scholarship was an attempt to work out a unified commentary on the prophetic books of Blake. These poems are mythical in shape: I had to learn something about myth to write about them, and so I discovered, after the book was published, that I was a member of a school of "myth criticism" of which I had not previously heard. My second effort, completed ten years later, was an attempt to work out a unified commentary on the theory of literary criticism, in which again myth had a prominent place. To me, the progress from one interest to the other was inevitable, and it was obvious to anyone who read both books that my critical ideas had been derived from Blake. How completely the second book was contained in embryo in the first, however, was something I did not realize myself until I recently read through *Fearful Symmetry*, for the first time in fifteen years, in order to write a preface to a new paperback edition. It seems perhaps worth while to examine what has been so far a mere assumption, the actual connecting links between my study of Blake and my study of the theory of criticism. At least the question is interesting to me, and so provides the only genuine motive yet discovered for undertaking any research.

Blake is one of the poets who believe that, as Wallace Stevens says, the only subject of poetry is poetry itself, and that the writing of a poem is itself a theory of poetry. He interests a critic because he removes the barriers between poetry and criticism. He defines the greatest poetry as "allegory addressed to the intellectual powers," and defends the practice of not being too explicit on the ground that it "rouzes the faculties to act." His language in his later prophecies is almost deliberately collo-

Reprinted from *Myth and Symbol*, ed. Bernice Slote, by permission of University of Nebraska Press. Copyright 1963 by University of Nebraska Press.

quial and "unpoetic," as though he intended his poetry to be also a work of criticism, just as he expected the critic's response to be also a creative one. He understood, in his own way, the principle later stated by Arnold that poetry is a criticism of life, and it was an uncompromising way. For him, the artist demonstrates a certain way of life: his aim is not to be appreciated or admired, but to transfer to others the imaginative habit and energy of his mind. The main work of criticism is teaching, and teaching for Blake cannot be separated from creation.

Blake's statements about art are extreme enough to make it clear that he is demanding some kind of mental adjustment to take them in. One of the Laocoon Aphorisms reads: "A Poet, a Painter, a Musician, an Architect: the Man Or Woman who is not one of these is not a Christian." If we respond to this in terms of what we ordinarily associate with the words used, the aphorism will sound, as Blake intended it to sound, like someone in the last stages of paranoia. Blake has an unusual faculty for putting his central beliefs in this mock-paranoid form, and in consequence has deliberately misled all readers who would rather believe that he was mad than that their own use of language could be inadequate. Thus when a Devil says in *The Marriage of Heaven and Hell*: "those who envy or calumniate great men hate God; for there is no other God," our habitual understanding of the phrase "great men" turns the remark into something that makes Carlyle at his worst sound by comparison like a wise and prudent thinker. When we read in the *Descriptive Catalogue*, however, that Chaucer's Parson is "according to Christ's definition, the greatest of his age," we begin to wonder if this paradoxical Devil has really so sulphurous a smell. Similarly, Blake's equating of the arts with Christianity implies, first, that his conception of art includes much more than we usually associate with it, and, second, that it excludes most of what we do associate with it. Blake is calling a work of art what a more conventional terminology would call a charitable act, while at the same time the painting of, say, Reynolds is for him not bad painting but anti-painting. Whether we agree or sympathize with Blake's attitude, what he says does involve a whole theory of criticism, and this theory we should examine.

One feature of Blake's prophecies which strikes every reader is the gradual elimination, especially in the two later poems *Milton* and *Jerusalem* that form the climax of this part of his work, of anything resembling narrative movement. The following passage occurs in Plate 71 of *Jerusalem*:

What is Above is Within, for every-thing in Eternity is translucent:
The Circumference is Within, Without is formed the Selfish Center,
And the Circumference still expands going forward to Eternity,
And the Center has Eternal States; these States we now explore.

I still have the copy of Blake that I used as an undergraduate, and I see that in the margin beside this passage I have written the words "Something moves, anyhow." But even that was more of an expression of hope than of considered critical judgment. This plotless type of writing has been discussed a good deal by other critics, notably Hugh Kenner and Marshall McLuhan, who call it "mental landscape," and ascribe its invention to the French *symbolistes*. But in Blake we not only have the technique already complete, but an even more thoroughgoing way of presenting it.

If we read *Milton* and *Jerusalem* as Blake intended them to be read, we are not reading them in any conventional sense at all: we are staring at a sequence of plates, most of them with designs. We can see, of course, that a sequence of illustrated plates would be an intolerably cumbersome and inappropriate method of presenting a long poem in which narrative was the main interest. The long poems of other poets that Blake illustrated, such as Young's *Night Thoughts* and Blair's *Grave*, are meditative poems where, even without Blake's assistance, the reader's attention is expected to drop out of the text every so often and soar, or plunge, whichever metaphor is appropriate, although perhaps wander is even more accurate. No doubt the development of Blake's engraving technique had much to do with the plotlessness of the engraved poems. We notice that the three poems of Blake in which the sense of narrative movement is strongest—*Tiriel*, *The French Revolution*, *The Four Zoas*— were never engraved. We notice too that the illustration on a plate often does not illustrate the text on the same plate, and that in one copy of *Jerusalem* the sequence of plates in Part Two is slightly different. The elimination of narrative movement is clearly central to the structure of these poems, and the device of a sequence of plates is consistent with the whole scheme, not a mere accident.

The theme of *Milton* is an instant of illumination in the mind of the poet, an instant which, like the moments of recognition in Proust, links him with a series of previous moments stretching back to the creation of the world. Proust was led to see men as giants in time, but for Blake there is only one giant, Albion, whose dream is time. For Blake in *Milton,* as for Eliot in *Little Gidding*, history is a pattern of timeless moments. What is said, so to speak, in the text of *Milton* is designed to present the context of the illuminated moment as a single simultaneous pattern of apprehension. Hence it does not form a narrative, but recedes spatially, as it were, from that moment. *Jerusalem* is conceived like a painting of the Last Judgment, stretching from heaven to hell and crowded with figures and allusions. Again, everything said in the text is intended to fit somewhere into this simultaneous conceptual pattern, not to form a linear narrative. If I ever get a big enough office, I shall have the hundred plates of my *Jerusalem* reproduction framed and hung around the walls, so that the frontispiece will have the second plate on one side and the last plate on the other. This will be *Jerusalem* presented as Blake thought of it, symbolizing the state of mind in which the poet himself could say: "I see the Past, Present & Future existing all at once Before me." In the still later Job engravings the technique of placing the words within a pictorial unit is of course much more obvious.

Many forms of literature, including the drama, fiction, and epic and narrative poetry, depend on narrative movement in a specific way. That is, they depend for their appeal on the participation of the reader or listener in the narrative as it moves along in time. It is continuity that keeps us turning the pages of a novel, or sitting in a theater. But there is always something of a summoned-up illusion about such continuity. We may keep reading a novel or attending to a play "to see how it turns out." But once we know how it turns out, and the spell ceases to bind us, we tend to forget the continuity, the very element in the play or novel that enabled us to participate in it. Remembering the plot of anything seems to be unusually difficult. Every member of this audience is familiar with many literary narratives, could even lecture on them with very little notice, and yet could not give a consecutive account of what happened in them, just as all the evangelical zeal of the hero of *The Way of All Flesh* was not equal to remembering the story of the resurrection of Christ in the Gospel of John. Nor does this seem particularly regrettable.

Just as the pun is the lowest form of wit, so it is generally agreed, among knowledgeable people like ourselves, that summarizing a plot is the lowest form of criticism.

I have dealt with this question elsewhere, and can only give the main point here. Narrative in literature may also be seen as theme, and theme *is* narrative, but narrative seen as a simultaneous unity. At a certain point in the narrative, the point which Aristotle calls *anagnorisis* or recognition, the sense of linear continuity or participation in the action changes perspective, and what we now see is a total design or unifying structure in the narrative. In detective stories, when we find out who done it, or in certain types of comedy or romance that depend on what are now called "gimmicks," such as Jonson's *Epicoene*, the point of *anagnorisis* is the revelation of something which has previously been a mystery. In such works Aristotle's word *anagnorisis* is best translated "discovery." But in most serious works of literature, and more particularly in epics and tragedies, the better translation is "recognition." The reader already knows what is going to happen, but wishes to see, or rather to participate in, the completion of the design.

Thus the end of reading or listening is the beginning of critical understanding, and nothing that we call criticism can begin until the whole of what it is striving to comprehend has been presented to it. Participation in the continuity of narrative leads to the discovery or recognition of the theme, which *is* the narrative seen as total design. This theme is what, as we say, the story has been all about, the point of telling it. What we reach at the end of participation becomes the center of our critical attention. The elements in the narrative thereupon regroup themselves in a new way. Certain unusually vivid bits of characterization or scenes of exceptional intensity move up near the center of our memory. This reconstructing and regrouping of elements in our critical response to a narrative goes on more or less unconsciously, but the fact that it goes on is what makes remembering plot so difficult.

Thus there are two kinds of response to a work of literature, especially one that tells a story. The first kind is a participating response in time, moving in measure like a dancer with the rhythm of continuity. It is typically an uncritical, or more accurately a pre-critical response. We cannot begin criticism, strictly speaking, until we have heard the author out, unless he is a bore, when the critical response starts prematurely and, as we say, we can't get into the book. The second kind of response is thematic, detached, fully conscious, and one which sees and is capable of examining the work as a simultaneous whole. It may be an act of understanding, or it may be a value-judgment, or it may be both. Naturally these two types of response overlap more in practice than I suggest here, but the distinction between them is clear enough, and fundamental in the theory of criticism. Some critics, including Professors Wimsatt and Beardsley in *The Verbal Icon*, stress the deficiencies of "holism" as a critical theory; but we should distinguish between "holism" as a critical theory and as a heuristic principle.

There are of course great differences of emphasis within literature itself, according to which kind of response the author is more interested in. At one pole of fiction we have the pure storyteller, whose sole interest is in suspense and the pacing of narrative, and who could not care less what the larger meaning of his story was, or what a critic would find in it afterward. The attitude of such a storyteller is expressed in the well-known preface to *Huckleberry Finn*: "Persons attempting to find a motive in this narrative will be prosecuted; persons attempting to find a moral in it will be banished; persons attempting to find a plot in it will be shot." Motive and moral and plot certainly are in *Huckleberry Finn*, but the author, or so he says, doesn't want to hear about them. All the storyteller wants to do is keep the attention of his audience to the end: once the end is reached, he has no further interest in his audience. He may even be hostile to criticism or anti-intellectual in his attitude to literature, afraid that criticism will spoil the simple entertainment that he designed. The lyrical poet concerned with expressing certain feelings or emotions in the lyrical conventions of his day often takes a similar attitude, because it is natural for him to identify his conventional literary emotions with his "real" personal emotions. He therefore feels that if the critic finds any meaning or significance in his work beyond the intensity of those emotions, it must be only what the critic wants to say instead. Anti-critical statements are usually designed only to keep the critic in his place, but the attitude they represent, when genuine, is objective, thrown outward into the designing of the continuity. It is the attitude that Schiller, in his essay on *Naive and Sentimental Poetry*, means by naive, and which includes what we mean in English by naive. Naive writers'

The Road of Excess

obiter dicta are often repeated, for consolation, by the kind of critic who is beginning to suspect that literary criticism is a more difficult discipline than he realized when he entered into it. But it is not possible for any reader today to respond to a work of literature with complete or genuine naivete. Response is what Schiller calls sentimental by its very nature, and is hence to some degree involved with criticism.

If we compare, let us say, Malory with Spenser, we can see that Malory's chief interest is in telling the stories in the "French book" he is using. He seems to know that some of them, especially the Grail stories, have overtones in them that the reader will linger with long after he has finished reading. But Malory makes no explicit reference to this, nor does one feel that Malory himself, preoccupied as he was with a nervous habit of robbing churches, would have been much interested in a purely critical reaction to his book. But for Spenser it is clear that the romance form, the quest of the knight journeying into a dark forest in search of some sinister villain who can be forced to release some suppliant female, is merely a projection of what Spenser really wants to say. When he says at the end of Book II of *The Faerie Queene*:

> Now gins this goodly frame of Temperaunce
> Fayrely to rise

it is clear that his interest is thematic, in the emergence of a fully articulated view of the virtue of Temperance which the reader can contemplate, as it were, like a statue, seeing all of its parts at once. This simultaneous vision extends over the entire poem, for Temperance is only one of the virtues surrounding the ideal Prince, and the emergence of the total form of that Prince is the thematic mold into which the enormous narrative is finally poured. The stanza in Spenser, especially the final alexandrine, has a role rather similar to the engraved design in Blake: it deliberately arrests the narrative and forces the reader to concentrate on something else.

In our day the prevailing attitude to fiction is overwhelmingly thematic. Even as early as Dickens we often feel that the plot, when it is a matter of implausible mysteries unconvincingly revealed, is something superimposed on the real narrative, which is more like a procession of characters. In our day the born storyteller is even rather peripheral to fiction, at best a border-

131

line case like Somerset Maugham, and the serious novelist is as a rule the novelist who writes not because he has a story to tell but because he has a theme to illustrate. One reason for this present preference of the thematic is that the ironic tone is central to modern literature. It is the function of irony, typically in Greek tragedy, to give the audience a clearer view of the total design than the actors themselves are aware of. Irony thus sets up a thematic detachment as soon as possible in the work, and provides an additional clue to the total meaning.

There may be, then, and there usually is, a kind of empathic communion set up in the reader or audience of a work of literature, which follows the work continuously to the end. The sense of empathy may be established by a story, where we read on to see what happens. Or by a pulsating rhythm, such as the dactylic hexameter in Homer, which has a surge and sweep that can carry us through even the longueurs referred to by Horace. We notice the effectiveness of rhythm in continuity more clearly in music, and most clearly in fast movements. I recall a cartoon of a tired man at a concert consulting his program and saying: "Well, the next movement is *prestissimo molto ed appassionato*, thank God." Or by the fluctuating intensity of a mood or emotion, again most clearly in music and in lyrical poetry. Or by a continuous sense of lifelikeness in realistic fiction, a sense which can extend itself even to realistic painting, as the eye darts from one detail to another. All these empathic responses are "naive," or essentially pre-critical.

Certain forms of art are also designed to give us the strongest possible emphasis on the continuous process of creation. The sketch, for example, is often more prized than the finished painting because of the greater sense of process in it. *Tachisme* and action-painting, spontaneous improvisation in swing, jazz, or more recently electronic music, and the kind of action-poetry, often read to jazz, which evokes the ghosts of those primeval jam-sessions postulated by early critics of the ballad, are more complete examples. All forms of art which lay great stress on continuous spontaneity seem to have a good deal of resistance to criticism, even to the education which is the natural context of criticism. We are told in Professor Lord's *Singer of Tales* that the most continuous form of poetry ever devised, the formulaic epic, demands illiteracy for success on the part of the poet, and there seems to be an inevitable affinity between the continuous and the unreflecting.

It is this continuity which is particularly Aristotle's imitation of an action. One's attention is completely absorbed in it: no other work of art is demanding attention at the same time, hence one has the sense of a unique and novel experience, at least as an ideal (for of course one may be rereading a book or seeing a familiar play). But, as in the world of action itself, one cannot participate and be a spectator at the same time. At best one is what Wyndham Lewis calls a "dithyrambic spectator." Lewis's disapproval of the dithyrambic spectator indicates an opposed emphasis on the detached contemplation of the entire work of art, and one so extreme that it talks of eliminating the sense of linear participating movement in the arts altogether. It would not clarify our argument to examine Lewis's very muddled polemics at this point, but they have some interest as documents in a tradition which strongly emphasized a visual and contemplative approach to art. Blake's plotless prophecies are, somewhat unexpectedly, in a similar (though by no means identical) tradition.

Just as the sense of participation in the movement of literature is absorbed, unique and novel, isolated from everything else, so the contemplative sense of its simultaneous wholeness tends to put the work of literature in some kind of framework or context. There are several such contexts, some of them indicated already. One of them is the allegorical context, where the total meaning or significance of the literary work is seen in relation to other forms of significance, such as moral ideas or historical events. A few works of literature, such as *The Pilgrim's Progress*, are technically allegories, which means that this explicit relation to external meaning is also a part of its continuity. Most literary works are not allegorical in this technical sense, but they bear a relation to historical events and moral ideas which is brought out in the kind of criticism usually called commentary. As I have explained elsewhere, commentary allegorizes the works it comments on.

We notice that Blake is somewhat ambiguous in his use of the term "allegory." He says in a letter to Butts, "Allegory addressed to the Intellectual powers . . . is My Definition of the Most Sublime Poetry." But in commenting on one of his paintings of the Last Judgment, he says: "The Last Judgment is not

Fable or Allegory, but Vision. Fable or Allegory are a totally distinct & inferior kind of Poetry." The first use of the term recognizes the fact that "the most sublime poetry," including his own prophecies, will demand commentary. The second use indicates that his own poems and pictures are not allegorical in the Spenserian or continuous sense, nor are they allegorical in a much more obvious and central way. They do not subordinate their literary qualities to the ideas they convey, on the assumption that the latter are more important. In the second passage quoted above Blake goes on to say with great precision: "Fable is allegory, but what Critics call The Fable, is Vision itself." Fable is here taken in its eighteenth-century critical sense of fiction or literary structure. Aristotle's word for intellectual content, *dianoia*, "thought," can be understood in two ways, as a moral attachment to a fable, or as the structure of the fable itself. The latter, according to Blake, contains its own moral significances by implication, and it destroys its imaginative quality to assume that some external moral attached to it can be a definitive translation of its "thought."

We touch here on a central dilemma of literature. If literature is didactic, it tends to injure its own integrity; if it ceases wholly to be didactic, it tends to injure is own seriousness. "Didactic poetry is my abhorrence," said Shelley, but it is clear that if the main body of Shelley's work had not been directly concerned with social, moral, religious, philosophical, political issues he would have lost most of his self-respect as a poet. Nobody wants to be an ineffectual angel, and Bernard Shaw, one of Shelley's most direct descendants in English literature, insisted that art should never be anything but didactic. This dilemma is partly solved by giving an ironic resolution to a work of fiction. The ironic resolution is the negative pole of the allegorical one. Irony presents a human conflict which, unlike a comedy, a romance, or even a tragedy, is unsatisfactory and incomplete unless we see it in a significance beyond itself, something typical of the human situation as a whole. What that significance is, irony does not say: it leaves that question up to the reader or audience. Irony preserves the seriousness of literature by demanding an expanded perspective on the action it presents, but it preserves the integrity of literature by not limiting or prescribing for that perspective.

Blake is clearly not an ironic writer, however, any more than he is an allegorist, and we must look for some other element in his thematic emphasis. A third context to which the theme of a literary work may be attached is its context in literature itself, or what we may call its archetypal framework. Just as continuous empathy is naive and absorbed in a unique and novel experience, so the contemplation of a unified work is self-conscious, educated, and one which tends to classify its object. We cannot in practice study a literary work without remembering that we have encountered many similar ones previously. Hence after following a narrative through to the end, our critical response includes the establishing of its categories, which are chiefly its convention and its genre. In this perspective the particular story is seen as a *projection* of the theme, as one of an infinite number of possible ways of getting to the theme. What we have just experienced we now see to be a comedy, a tragedy, a courtly love lyrical complaint, or one of innumerable treatments of the Tristan or Endymion or Faust story.

Further, just as some works of literature are explicitly or continuously allegorical, so some works are continuously, or at least explicitly, allusive, calling the reader's attention to their relation to previous works. If we try to consider *Lycidas* in isolation from the tradition of the pastoral elegy established by Theocritus and Virgil, or *Ash Wednesday* in isolation from its relation to Dante's *Purgatorio*, we are simply reading these works out of context, which is as bad a critical procedure as quoting a passage out of context. If we read an Elizabethan sonnet sequence without taking account of the conventional nature of every feature in it, including the poet's protests that he is not following convention and is really in love with a real person, we shall merely substitute the wrong context for the right one. That is, the sonnet sequence will become a biographical allegory, as the sonnets of Shakespeare do when, with Oscar Wilde, we reach the conclusion that the profoundest understanding of these sonnets, the deepest appreciation of all their eloquence and passion and power, comes when we identify the "man in hue" of Sonnet 20 with an unknown Elizabethan pansy named Willie Hughes.

Blake's prophecies are intensely allusive, though nine-tenths of the allusions are to the Bible. "The Old & New Testaments are the Great Code of Art," Blake says, and he thinks of the framework of the Bible, stretching from Creation to Last Judgment and surveying the whole of human history in between, as indicating the framework of the whole of literary experience, and establishing the ultimate context for all works of literature whatever. If the Bible did not exist, at least as a form, it would be necessary for literary critics to invent the same kind of total and definitive verbal structure out of the fragmentary myths and legends and folk tales we have outside it. Such a structure is the first and most indispensable of critical conceptions, the embodiment of the whole of literature as an order of words, as a potentially unified imaginative experience. But although its relation to the Bible takes us well on toward a solution of the thematic emphasis in Blake's illuminated poetry, it does not in itself fully explain that emphasis. If it did, the prophecies would simply be, in the last analysis, Biblical commentaries, and this they are far from being.

Blake's uniqueness as a poet has much to do with his ability to sense the historical significance of his own time. Up to that time, literature and the arts had much the same educational and cultural value that they have now, but they competed with religion, philosophy, and law on what were at best equal and more usually subordinate terms. Consequently when, for example, Renaissance critics spoke of the profundity of poetry, they tended to locate that profundity in its allegorical meaning, the relations that could be established between poetry and ideas, more particularly moral and religious ideas. In the Romantic period, on the other hand, many poets and critics were ready to claim an authority and importance for poetry and the imaginative arts prior to that of other disciplines. When Shelley quotes Tasso on the similarity of the creative work of the poet to the creative work of God, he carries the idea a great deal further than Tasso did. The fact of this change in the Romantic period is familiar, but the trends that made it possible are still not identified with assurance.

My own guess is that the change had something to do with a growing feeling that the origin of human civilization was human too. In traditional Christianity it was not: God planted the garden of Eden and suggested the models for the law, rituals, even the architecture of human civilization. Hence a rational understanding of "nature," which included the understanding of the divine as well as the physical origin of human nature, took precedence over the poetic imagination and supplied a criterion for it. The essential moral ideas fitted into a divine scheme for the redemption of man; we understand the revelation of this scheme rationally; literature forms a series of more indirect parables or emblems of it. Thus poetry could be the companion of camps, as Sidney says: it could kindle an enthusiasm for virtue by providing examples for precepts. The sense of excitement in participating in the action of the heroic narrative of, say, the Iliad was heightened by thinking of the theme or total meaning of the Iliad as an allegory of heroism. Thus, paradoxically, the Renaissance insistence on the allegorical nature of major poetry preserved the naivete of the participating response. We see this principle at work wherever poet and audience are completely in agreement about the moral implications of a poetic theme, as they are, at least theoretically, in a hiss-the-villain melodrama.

Blake was the first and the most radical of the Romantics who identified the creative imagination of the poet with the creative power of God. For Blake God was not a superhuman lawgiver or the mathematical architect of the stars; God was the inspired suffering humanity of Jesus. Everything we call "nature," the physical world around us, is sub-moral, subhuman, sub-imaginative; every act worth performing has as its object the redeeming of this nature into something with a genuinely human, and therefore divine, shape. Hence Blake's poetry is not allegorical but mythopoeic, not obliquely related to a rational understanding of the human situation, the resolution of which is out of human hands, but a product of the creative energy that alone can redeem that situation. Blake forces the reader to concentrate on the meaning of his work, but not didactically in the ordinary sense, because his meaning is his theme, the total simultaneous shape of his poem. The context into which the theme or meaning of the individual poem fits is not the received ideas of our cultural tradition, of which it is or should be an allegory. It is not, or not only, the entire structure of literature as an order of words, as represented by the Bible. It is rather the expanded vision that he calls apocalypse or Last Judgment: the vision of the end and goal of human civilization as the entire universe in the form that human desire wants to see it, as a heaven eternally separated from a hell. What Blake did was closely related to the Romantic movement, and Shelley and Keats at least are mythopoetic poets for reasons not far removed from Blake's.

Since the Romantic movement, there has been a more conservative tendency to deprecate the central place it gave to the creative imagination and to return, or attempt to return, to the older hierarchy. T. S. Eliot is both a familiar and a coherent exponent of this tendency, and he has been followed by Auden, with his Kierkegaardian reinforcements. According to Eliot, it is the function of art, by imposing an order on life, to give us the sense of an order in life, and so to lead us into a state of serenity and reconciliation preparatory to another and superior kind of experience, where "that guide" can lead us no further. The implication is that there is a spiritually existential world above that of art, a world of action and behavior, of which the most direct imitation in this world is not art but the sacramental act. This latter is a form of uncritical or pre-critical religious participation that leads to a genuinely religious contemplation, which for Eliot is a state of heightened consciousness with strong affinities to mysticism. Mysticism is a word which has been applied both to Blake and to Saint John of the Cross: in other words it has been rather loosely applied, because these two poets have little in common. It is clear that Eliot's mystical affinities are of the Saint John of the Cross type. The function of art, for Eliot, is again of the subordinated or allegorical kind. Its order represents a higher existential order, hence its greatest ambition should be to get beyond itself, pointing to its superior reality with such urgency and clarity that it disappears in that reality. This, however, only happens either in the greatest or the most explicitly religious art: nine-tenths of our literary experience is on the subordinate plane where we are seeing an order in life without worrying too much about the significance of that order. On this plane the naive pre-critical direct experience of participation can still be maintained, as it is in Renaissance critical theory. The Romantics, according to this view, spoil both the form and the fun of poetry by insisting so much on the profundity of the imaginative experience as to make it a kind of portentous *ersatz* religion.

This leads us back to the aphorism of Blake with which we began, where the artist is identified with the Christian. Elsewhere he speaks of "Religion, or Civilized Life such as it is in the Christian Church," and says that poetry, painting and music are "the three Powers in Man of conversing with Paradise, which the flood did not Sweep away." For Blake art is not a substitute for religion, though a great deal of religion as ordinarily conceived is a substitute for art, in that it abuses the mythopoeic faculty by creating fantasies about another world or rationalizing the evils of this one instead of working toward genuine human life. If we describe Blake's conception of art independently of the traditional myth of fall and apocalypse that embodies it, we may say that the poetic activity is fundamentally one of identifying the human with the nonhuman world. This identity is what the poetic metaphor expresses, and the end of the poetic vision is the humanization of reality, "All Human Forms identified," as Blake says at the end of *Jerusalem*. Here we have the basis for a critical theory which puts such central conceptions as myth and metaphor into their proper central place. So far from usurping the function of religion, it keeps literature in the context of human civilization, yet without limiting the infinite variety and range of the poetic imagination. The criteria it suggests are not moral ones, nor are they collections of imposing abstractions like Unity, but the interests, in the widest sense, of mankind itself, or himself, as Blake would prefer to say.

In this conception of art the productive or creative effort is inseparable from the awareness of what it is doing. It is this unity of energy and consciousness that Blake attempts to express by the word "vision." In Blake there is no either-or dialectic where one must be either a detached spectator or a preoccupied actor. Hence there is no division, though there may be a distinction, between the creative power of shaping the form and the critical power of seeing the world it belongs to. Any division instantly makes art barbaric and the knowledge of it pedantic—a bound Orc and a bewildered Urizen, to use Blake's symbols. The vision inspires the act, and the act realizes the vision. This is the most thoroughgoing view of the partnership of creation and criticism in literature I know, but for me, though other views may seem more reasonable and more plausible for a time, it is in the long run the only one that will hold.

II

MARSHALL McLUHAN

The Medium Is the Message

In a culture like ours, long accustomed to splitting and dividing all things as a means of control, it is sometimes a bit of a shock to be reminded that, in operational and practical fact, the medium is the message. This is merely to say that the personal and social consequences of any medium—that is, of any extension of ourselves—result from the new scale that is introduced into our affiairs by each exension of ourselves, or by any new technology. Thus, with automation, for example, the new patterns of human association tend to eliminate jobs, it is true. That is the negative result. Positively, automation creates roles for people, which is to say depth of involvement in their work and human association that our preceding mechanical technology had destroyed. Many people would be disposed to say that it was not the machine, but what one did with the machine, that was its meaning or message. In terms of the ways in which the machine altered out relations to one another and to ourselves, it mattered not in the least whether it turned out cornflakes or Cadillacs. The restructuring of human work and association was shaped by the technique of fragmentation that is the essence of machine technology. The essence of automation technology is the opposite. It is integral and decentralist in depth, just as the machine was fragmentary, centralist, and superficial in its patterning of human relationships.

The instance of the electric light may prove illuminating in this connection. The electric light is pure information. It is a medium without a message, as it were, unless it is used to spell out some verbal ad or name. This fact, characteristic of all media, means that the "content" of any medium is always another medium. The content of writing is speech, just as the written word is the content of print, and print is the content of the telegraph. If it is asked, "What is the content of speech?," it is necessary to say, "It is an actual process of thought, which is in itself nonverbal." An abstract painting represents direct manifestation of creative thought processes as they might appear in computer designs. What we are considering here, however, are the psychic and social consequences of the designs or patterns as they amplify or accelerate existing processes. For the "message" of any medium or technology is the change of scale or pace or pattern that it introduces into human affairs. The railway did not introduce movement or transportation or wheel or road into human society, but it accelerated and enlarged the scale of previous human functions, creating totally new kinds of cities and new kinds of work and leisure. This happened whether the railway functioned in a tropical or a northern environment, and is quite independent of the freight or content of the railway medium. The airplane, on the other hand, by accelerating the rate of transportation, tends to dissolve the railway form of city, politics, and association, quite independently of what the airplane is used for.

Let us return to the electric light. Whether the light is being used for brain surgery or night baseball is a matter of indifference. It could be argued that these activities are in some way the "content" of the electric light, since they could not exist without the electric light. This fact merely underlines the point that "the medium is the message" because it is the medium that shapes and controls the scale and form of human association and action. The content or uses of such media are as diverse as they are ineffectual in shaping the form of human association. Indeed, it is only too typical that the "content" of any medium blinds us to the character of the medium. It is only today that industries have become aware of the various kinds of business in which they are engaged. When IBM discovered that it was not in the business of making office equipment or business machines, but that it was in the business of processing information, then it began to navigate with clear vision. The General Electric Company makes a considerable portion of its profits from electric light bulbs and lighting systems. It has not yet discovered that, quite as much as A.T.&T., it is in the business of moving information.

The electric light escapes attention as a communication

medium just because it has no "content." And this makes it an invaluable instance of how people fail to study media at all. For it is not till the electric light is used to spell out some brand name that it is noticed as a medium. Then it is not the light but the "content" (or what is really another medium) that is noticed. The message of the electric light is like the message of electric power in industry, totally radical, pervasive, and decentralized. For electric light and power are separate from their uses, yet they eliminate time and space factors in human association exactly as do radio, telegraph, telephone, and TV, creating involvement in depth.

A fairly complete handbook for studying the extensions of man could be made up from selections from Shakespeare. Some might quibble about whether or not he was referring to TV in these familiar lines from *Romeo and Juliet:*

> But soft! what light through yonder window breaks?
> It speaks and yet says nothing.

In *Othello*, which, as much as *King Lear*, is concerned with the torment of people transformed by illusions, there are these lines that bespeak Shakespeare's intuition of the transforming powers of new media:

> Is there not charms
> By which the property of youth and maidhood
> May be abus'd? Have you not read Roderigo,
> Of some such thing?

In Shakespeare's *Troilus and Cressida*, which is almost completely devoted to both a psychic and social study of communication, Shakespeare states his awareness that true social and political navigation depend upon anticipating the consequences of innovation:

> The providence that's in a watchful state
> Knows almost every grain of Plutus' gold
> Finds bottom in the uncomprehensive deeps,
> Keeps place with thought, and almost like the gods
> Does thoughts unveil in their dumb cradles.

The increasing awareness of the action of media, quite independently of their "content" or programming, was indicated in the annoyed and anonymous stanza:

> In modern thought, (if not in fact)
> Nothing is that doesn't act,
> So that is reckoned wisdom which
> Describes the scratch but not the itch.

The same kind of total, configurational awareness that reveals why the medium is socially the message has occurred in the most recent and radical medical theories. In his *Stress of Life*, Hans Selye tells of the dismay of a research colleague on hearing of Selye's theory:

> When he saw me thus launched on yet another enraptured description of what I had observed in animals treated with this or that impure, toxic material, he looked at me with desperately sad eyes and said in obvious despair: "But Selye, try to realize what you are doing before it is too late! You have now decided to spend your entire life studying the pharmacology of dirt!"
>
> (Hans Selye, *The Stress of Life*)

As Selye deals with the total environmental situation in his "stress" theory of disease, so the latest approach to media study considers not only the "content" but the medium and the cultural matrix within which the particular medium operates. The older unawareness of the psychic and social effects of media can be illustrated from almost any of the conventional pronouncements.

In accepting an honorary degree from the University of Notre Dame a few years ago, General David Sarnoff made this statement: "We are too prone to make technological instruments the scapegoats for the sins of those who wield them. The products of modern science are not in themselves good or bad; it is the way they are used that determines their value." That is the voice of the current somnambulism. Suppose we were to say, "Apple pie is in itself neither good nor bad; it is the way it is used that determines its value." Or, "The smallpox virus is in itself neither good nor bad; it is the way it is used that determines its value." Again, "Firearms are in themselves neither good nor bad; it is the way they are used that determines their value." That is, if the slugs reach the right people firearms are good. If the TV tube fires the right ammunition at the right people it is good. I am not being perverse. There is simply nothing in the Sarnoff statement that will bear scrutiny, for it ignores the nature of the medium, of any and all media, in the true Narcissus style of one hypnotized by the amputation and extension of his own being in a new technical form. General Sarnoff went on to explain his attitude to the technology of print, saying that it was true that print caused much trash to circulate, but it had also disseminated the Bible and the thoughts of seers and philosophers. It has never occurred to General Sarnoff that any technology could do anything but *add* itself on to what we already are.

Such economists as Robert Theobald, W. W. Rostow, and John Kenneth Galbraith have been explaining for years how it is that "classical economics" cannot explain change or growth. And the paradox of mechanization is that although it is itself the cause of maximal growth and change, the principle of mechanization excludes the very possibility of growth or the understanding of change. For mechanization is achieved by fragmentation of any process and by putting the fragmented parts in a series. Yet, as David Hume showed in the eighteenth century, there is no principle of causality in a mere sequence. That one thing follows another accounts for nothing. Nothing follows from following, except change. So the greatest of all reversals occurred with electricity, that ended sequence by making things instant. With instant speed the causes of things began to emerge to awareness again, as they had not done with things in sequence and in concatenation accordingly. Instead of asking which came first, the chicken or the egg, it suddenly seemed that a chicken was an egg's idea for getting more eggs.

Just before an airplane breaks the sound barrier, sound waves become visible on the wings of the plane. The sudden visibility of sound just as sound ends is an apt instance of that great pattern of being that reveals new and opposite forms just as the earlier forms reach their peak performance. Mechanization was never so vividly fragmented or sequential as in the birth of the movies, the moment that translated us beyond mechanism into the world of growth and organic interrelation. The movie, by sheer speeding up the mechanical, carried us from the world of sequence and connections into the world of creative configuration and structure. The message of the movie medium is that of transition from lineal connections to configurations. It is the transition that produced the now quite correct observation: "If it works, it's obsolete." When electric speed further takes over from the mechanical movie sequences, then the lines of force in structures and in media become loud and clear. We return to the inclusive form of the icon.

To a highly literate and mechanized culture the movie appeared as a world of triumphant illusions and dreams that money could buy. It was at this moment of the movie that cubism occurred, and it has been described by E. H. Gombrich (*Art and Illusion*) as "the most radical attempt to stamp out ambiguity and to enforce one reading of the picture—that of a man-made construction, a colored canvas." For cubism substitutes all facets of an object simultaneously for the "point of view" or facet of perspective illusion. Instead of the specialized illusion of the third dimension on canvas, cubism sets up an interplay of planes and contradiction or dramatic conflict of patterns, lights, textures that "drives home the message" by involvement. This is held by many to be an exercise in painting, not in illusion.

In other words, cubism, by giving the inside and outside, the top, bottom, back, and front and the rest, in two dimensions, drops the illusion of perspective in favor of instant sensory awareness of the whole. Cubism, by seizing on instant total awareness, suddenly announced that *the medium is the message*. Is it not evident that the moment that sequence yields to the simultaneous, one is in the world of the structure and of configuration? Is that not what has happened in physics as in painting, poetry, and in communication? Specialized segments of attention have shifted to total field, and we can now say, "The medium is the message" quite naturally. Before the electric speed and total field, it was not obvious that the medium is the message. The message, it seems, was the "content," as people used to ask what a painting was *about*. Yet they never thought to ask what a melody was about, nor what a house or a dress was about. In such matters, people retained some sense of the whole pattern, of form and function as a unity. But in the electric age this integral idea of structure and configuration has become so prevalent that educational theory has taken up the matter. Instead of working with specialized "problems" in arithmetic, the structural approach now follows the lines of force in the field of number and has small children meditating about number theory and "sets."

Cardinal Newman said of Napoleon, "He understood the grammar of gunpowder." Napoleon had paid some attention to other media as well, especially the semaphore telegraph that gave him a great advantage over his enemies. He is on record for saying that "Three hostile newspapers are more to be feared than a thousand bayonets."

Alexis de Tocqueville was the first to master the grammar of print and typography. He was thus able to read off the message of coming change in France and America as if he were reading aloud from a text that had been handed to him. In fact, the nineteenth century in France and in America was just such an open book to de Tocqueville because he had learned the grammar of print. So he, also, knew when that grammar did not apply. He was asked why he did not write a book on England, since he knew and admired England. He replied:

> One would have to have an unusual degree of philosophical folly to believe oneself able to judge England in six months. A year always seemed to me too short a time in which to appreciate the United States properly, and it is much easier to acquire clear and precise notions about the American Union than about Great Britain. In America all laws derive in a sense from the same line of thought. The whole of society, so to speak, is founded upon a single fact; everything springs from a simple principle. One could compare America to a forest pierced by a multitude of straight roads all converging on the same point. One has only to find the center and everything is revealed at a glance. But in England the paths run criss-cross, and it is only by travelling down each one of them that one can build up a picture of the whole.

De Tocqueville, in earlier work on the French Revolution, had explained how it was the printed word that, achieving cultural saturation in the eighteenth century, had homogenized the French nation. Frenchmen were the same kind of people from north to south. The typographic principles of uniformity, continuity, and lineality had overlaid the complexities of ancient feudal and oral society. The Revolution was carried out by the new literati and lawyers.

In England, however, such was the power of the ancient oral traditions of common law, backed by the medieval institution of Parliament, that no uniformity or continuity of the new visual print culture could take complete hold. The result was that the most important event in English history has never taken place; namely, the English Revolution on the lines of the French Revolution. The American Revolution had no medieval legal institutions to discard or to root out, apart from monarchy. And many have held that the American Presidency has become very much more personal and monarchical than any European monarch ever could be.

De Tocqueville's contrast between England and America is clearly based on the fact of typography and of print culture creating uniformity and continuity. England, he says, has rejected this principle and clung to the dynamic or oral common-law tradition. Hence the discontinuity and unpredictable quality of English culture. The grammar of print cannot help to construe the message of oral and nonwritten culture and institutions. The English aristocracy was properly classified as barbarian by Matthew Arnold because its power and status had nothing to do with literacy or with the cultural forms of typography. Said the Duke of Gloucester to Edward Gibbon upon the publication of his *Decline and Fall:* "Another damned fat book, eh, Mr. Gibbon? Scribble, scribble, scribble, eh, Mr. Gibbon?" De Tocqueville was a highly literate aristocrat who was quite able to be detached from the values and assumptions of typography. That is why he alone understood the grammar of typography. And it is only on those terms, standing aside from any structure or medium, that its principles and lines of force can be discerned. For any medium has the power of imposing its own assumption on the unwary. Prediction and control consist in avoiding this subliminal state of Narcissus trance. But the greatest aid to this end is simply in knowing that the spell can occur immediately upon contact, as in the first bars of a melody.

A Passage to India by E. M. Forster is a dramatic study of the inability of oral and intuitive oriental culture to meet with the rational, visual European patterns of experience. "Rational," of course, has for the West long meant "uniform and continuous and sequential." In other words, we have confused reason with literacy, and rationalism with a single technology. Thus in the electric age man seems to the conventional West to become irrational. In Forster's novel the moment of truth and dislocation from the typographic trance of the West comes in the Marabar Caves. Adela Quested's reasoning powers cannot cope with the total inclusive field of resonance that is India. After the Caves: "Life went on as usual, but had no consequences, that is to say, sounds did not echo nor thought develop. Everything seemed cut off at its root and therefore infected with illusion."

A Passage to India (the phrase is from Whitman, who saw America headed Eastward) is a parable of Western man in the electric age, and is only incidentally related to Europe or the Orient. The ultimate conflict between sight and sound, between written and oral kinds of perception and organization of existence is upon us. Since understanding stops action, as Nietzsche observed, we can moderate the fierceness of this conflict by understanding the media that extend us and raise these wars within and without us.

Detribalization by literacy and its traumatic effects on tribal man is the theme of a book by the psychiatrist J. C. Carothers, *The African Mind in Health and Disease* (World Health Organization, Geneva, 1953). Much of his material appeared in an article in *Psychiatry* magazine, November, 1959: "The Culture, Psychiatry, and the Written Word." Again, it is electric speed that has revealed the lines of force operating from Western technology in the remotest areas of bush, savannah, and desert. One example is the Bedouin with his battery radio on board the camel. Submerging natives with floods of concepts for which nothing has prepared them is the normal action of all of our technology. But with electric media Western man himself experiences exactly the same inundation as the remote native. We are no more prepared to encounter radio and TV in our literate milieu than the native of Ghana is able to cope with the literacy that takes him out of his collective tribal world and beaches him in individual isolation. We are as numb in our new electric world as the native involved in our literate and mechanical culture.

Electric speed mingles the cultures of prehistory with the dregs of industrial marketeers, the nonliterate with the semi-literate and the postliterate. Mental breakdown of varying degrees is the very common result of uprooting and inundation with new information and endless new patterns of information. Wyndham Lewis made this a theme of his group of novels called *The Human Age*. The first of these, *The Childermass*, is concerned precisely with accelerated media change as a kind of massacre of the innocents. In our own world as we become more aware of the effects of technology on psychic formation and manifestation, we are losing all confidence in our rights to assign guilt. Ancient prehistoric societies regard violent crime as pathetic. The killer is regarded as we do a cancer victim. "How terrible it must be to feel like that," they say. J. M. Synge took up this idea very effectively in his *Playboy of the Western World*.

If the criminal appears as a nonconformist who is unable to meet the demand of technology that we behave in uniform and continuous patterns, literate man is quite inclined to see others who cannot conform as somewhat pathetic. Especially the child, the cripple, the woman, and the colored person appear in a world of visual and typographic technology as victims of injustice. On the other hand, in a culture that assigns roles instead of jobs to people—the dwarf, the skew, the child create their own spaces. They are not expected to fit into some uniform and repeatable niche that is not their size anyway. Consider the phrase "It's a man's world." As a quantitative observation endlessly repeated from within a homogenized culture, this phrase refers to the men in such a culture who have to be homogenized Dagwoods in order to belong at all. It is in our I.Q. testing that we have produced the greatest flood of misbegotten standards. Unaware of our tpyographical cultural bias, our testers assume that uniform and continuous habits are a sign of intelligence, thus eliminating the ear man and the tactile man.

C. P. Snow, reviewing a book of A. L. Rowse *(The New York Times Book Review,* December 24, 1961) on *Appeasement* and the road to Munich, describes the top level of British brains and experience in the 1930s. "Their I.Q.'s were much higher than usual among political bosses. Why were they such a disaster?" The view of Rowse, Snow approves: "They would not listen to warnings because they did not wish to hear." Being anti-Red made it impossible for them to read the message of Hitler. But their failure was as nothing compared to our present one. The American stake in literacy as a technology or uniformity applied to every level of education, government, industry, and social life is totally threatened by the electric technology. The threat of Stalin or Hitler was external. The electric technology is within the gates, and we are numb, deaf, blind, and mute about its encounter with the Gutenberg technology, on and through which the American way of life was formed. It is, however, no time to suggest strategies when the threat has not even been acknowledged to exist. I am in the position of Louis Pasteur telling doctors that their greatest enemy was quite invisible, and quite unrecognized by them. Our conventional response to all media, namely that it is how they are used that counts, is the numb stance of the technological idiot. For the "content" of a medium is like the juicy piece of meat carried by the burglar to distract the watchdog of the mind. The effect of the medium is made strong and intense just because it is given another medium as "content." The content of a movie is a novel or a play or an opera. The effect of the movie form is not related to its program content. The "content" of writing or print is speech, but the reader is almost entirely unaware either of print or of speech.

Arnold Toynbee is innocent of any understanding of media as they have shaped history, but he is full of examples that the student of media can use. At one moment he can seriously suggest that adult education, such as the Workers Educational Association in Britain, is a useful counterforce to the popular press. Toynbee considers that although all of the oriental societies have in our time accepted the industrial technology and its political consequences: "On the cultural plane, however, there is no uniform corresponding tendency." (Somervell, I. 267) This is like the voice of the literate man, floundering in a milieu of ads, who boasts, "Personally, I pay no attention to ads." The spiritual and cultural reservations that the oriental peoples may have toward our technology will avail them not at all. The effects of technology do not occur at the level of opinions or concepts, but alter sense ratios or patterns of perception steadily and without any resistance. The serious artist is the only person able to encounter technology with impunity, just because he is an expert aware of the changes in sense perception.

The operation of the money medium in seventeenth-century Japan had effects not unlike the operation of typography in the West. The penetration of the money economy, wrote G. B. Sansom (in *Japan*, Cresset Press, London, 1931) "caused a slow but irresistible revolution, culminating in the breakdown of feudal government and the resumption of intercourse with foreign countries after more than two hundred years of seclusion." Money has reorganized the sense life of peoples just because it is an *extension* of our sense lives. This change does not depend upon approval or disapproval of those living in the society.

Arnold Toynbee made one approach to the transforming power of media in his concept of "etherialization," which he holds to be the principle of progressive simplification and efficiency in any organization or technology. Typically, he is ignoring the *effect* of the challenge of these forms upon the response of our senses. He imagines that it is the response of our opinions that is relevant to the effect of media and technology in society, a "point of view" that is plainly the result of the typographic spell. For the man in a literate and homogenized society ceases to be sensitive to the diverse and discontinuous life of forms. He acquires the illusion of the third dimension and the "private point of view" as part of his Narcissus fixation, and is quite shut off from Blake's awareness or that of the Psalmist, that we become what we behold.

Today when we want to get our bearings in our own culture, and have need to stand aside from bias and pressure exerted by any technical form of human expression, we have only to visit a society where that particular form has not been felt, or a historical period in which it was unknown. Professor Wilber Schramm made such a tactical move in studying *Television in the Lives of Our Children*. He found areas where TV had not penetrated at all and ran some tests. Since he had made no study of the peculiar nature of the TV image, his tests were of "content" preferences, viewing time, and vocabulary counts. In a word, his approach to the problem was a literary one, albeit unconsciously so. Consequently, he had nothing to report. Had his methods been employed in 1500 A.D. to discover the effects of the printed book in the lives of children or adults, he could have found out nothing of the changes in human and social psychology resulting from typography. Print created individualism and nationalism in the sixteenth century. Program and "content" analysis offer no clues to the magic of these media or to their subliminal charge.

Leonard Doob, in his report *Communication in Africa*, tells of one African who took great pains to listen each evening to the BBC news, even though he could understand nothing of it. Just to be in the presence of those sounds at 7 P.M. each day was important for him. His attitude to speech was like ours to melody—the resonant intonation was meaning enough. In the seventeenth century our ancestors still shared this native's attitude to the forms of media, as is plain in the following sentiment of the Frenchman Bernard Lam expressed in *The Art of Speaking* (London, 1696):

> 'Tis an effect of the Wisdom of God, who created Man to
> be happy, that whatever is useful to his conversation (way of
> life) is agreeable to him . . . because all victual that con-
> duces to nourishment is relishable, whereas other things that
> cannot be assimulated and be turned into our substance are
> insipid. A Discourse cannot be pleasant to the Hearer that is not
> easie to the Speaker; nor can it be easily pronounced unless it be
> heard with delight.

Here is an equilibrium theory of human diet and expression such
as even now we are only striving to work out again for media
after centuries of fragmentation and specialism.

Pope Pius XII was deeply concerned that there be serious
study of the media today. On February 17, 1950, he said:

> It is not an exaggeration to say that the future of modern
> society and the stability of its inner life depend in large part
> on the maintenance of an equilibrium between the strength
> of the techniques of communication and the capacity of the
> individual's own reaction.

Failure in this respect has for centuries been typical and total
for mankind. Subliminal and docile acceptance of media impact
has made them prisons without walls for their human users. As
A. J. Liebling remarked in his book *The Press*, a man is not free
if he cannot see where he is going, even if he has a gun to help
him get there. For each of the media is also a powerful weapon
with which to clobber other media and other groups. The result
is that the present age has been one of multiple civil wars that
are not limited to the world of art and entertainment. In *War and
Human Progress*, Professor J. U. Nef declared: "The total wars
of our time have been the result of a series of intellectual mistakes."

If the formative power in the media are the media themselves,
that raises a host of large matters that can only be mentioned
here, although they deserve volumes. Namely, that technological
media are staples or natural resources, exactly as are coal and
cotton and oil. Anybody will concede that society whose economy is dependent upon one or two major staples like cotton,
or grain, or lumber, or fish, or cattle is going to have some obvious social patterns of organization as a result. Stress on a few
major staples creates extreme instability in the economy but great
endurance in the population. The pathos and humor of the

American South are embedded in such an economy of limited staples. For a society configured by reliance on a few commodities accepts them as a social bond quite as much as the metropolis does the press. Cotton and oil, like radio and TV, become "fixed charges" on the entire psychic life of the community. And this pervasive fact creates the unique cultural flavor of any society. It pays through the nose and all its other senses for each staple that shapes its life.

That our human senses, of which all media are extensions, are also fixed charges on our personal energies, and that they also configure the awareness and experience of each one of us, may be perceived in another connection mentioned by the psychologist C. G. Jung:

> Every Roman was surrounded by slaves. The slave and his psychology flooded ancient Italy, and every Roman became inwardly, and of course unwittingly, a slave. Because living constantly in the atmosphere of slaves, he became infected through the unconscious with their psychology. No one can shield himself from such an influence [*Contributions to Analytical Psychology*, London, 1928].

III

FRANCIS SPARSHOTT

Art and Criticism

PERFORMANCE AND THE ARTS

In discussing what determines the nature of a performance and
the way in which it is classified we have come increasingly to
cast our discussion in terms of the fine arts. This requires no
apology, since no considerations were introduced that did not
hold for performances generally, and our ultimate interest is
after all in the criticism of the arts. Besides, problems of the
identification and classification of performances are characteristic of the arts, if not entirely restricted to them. We might ask,
however, whether this is merely an institutional accident; and
we might further ask whether the close association between
criticism and the arts is also a mere matter of habitual practice,
or whether the arts are by their nature peculiarly adapted to
critical activity.

Anything whatever, we have repeatedly insisted, may be regarded as a performance and so criticized, and indeed may be
regarded as a performance of almost any kind; but to do so may
be more or less appropriate. What will most suitably be regarded
as a performance will be something that is, on the one hand, an
unmistakable manifestation of human agency and, on the other
hand, self-contained to the point of practical isolation. But this
is precisely the condition ascribed to works of art by the esthetic
theories most widely current nowadays. Consequently, prevailing theory makes works of art performances *par excellence*, and
hence objects of criticism *par excellence*. Since the concept of
performance was introduced with just this in mind, we can
hardly affect to be surprised at this result. None the less, we
could not have reached it had current ideas about the arts been
other than what they are. Many writers on esthetics have re-

From F. E. Sparshott, *The Concept of Criticism*, 1967. By permission of
the author and Oxford University Press.

marked on the significance of frames, physical or conceptual devices that mark a work of art off from its surroundings and isolate it for attention: the stage of the drama, the wood or straight boundary of the picture frame, the pedestal of the statue (cf. my *The Structure of Aesthetics*, pp. 92–93 and 218–20). And the concept of performance is, precisely, a framing concept.

It may be argued that current esthetic theory is not securely enough based to justify anything. But it should be enough to consider the immediate function of works of fine art themselves. If one asks oneself, without theorizing about ulterior uses, what paintings are for, the obvious answer is that they are for looking at; and music is for listening to. Directly and immediately, then, they are designed for contemplation; and to consider as a work of art anything that is not so designed is to consider it as an object for contemplation. But to consider it so is, simply, to isolate it for attention and disregard its human setting and its natural functions, if any, and that falls short of regarding it as a performance only in its making no reference to intelligent agency.

If works of art exist to be objects of contemplation, to be looked at or listened to, that means that looking at or listening to them must be inherently desirable; otherwise we could not specify the contemplation as the end, but would have to go on and say what end the contemplation served. But that entails that the value in some measure determines the fact: works of art may not exist to be valued, but certainly must exist to be enjoyed and appreciated. Thus the criticism of art cannot be merely and independently descriptive. Even if it were not true that every description must be made from the point of view of some interest or set of interests, it would remain true that the description of an object of appreciation as such must describe what there is about it to be appreciated. Thus the idea of a value-free discussion of works of art as such is chimerical. It may thus appear that criticism as we have described it is simply the form of discourse appropriate to works of art as such.

Criticism is not only peculiarly appropriate to the fine arts; a continuation of the same line of argument shows that it is usually necessary. To be a proper object of contemplation a thing must be such as to make contemplation rewarding. That is to say, it must not yield to a casual glance all that it has to give. But if that is the case it cannot be immediately obvious which

works of arts are successful and will ultimately reward contemplation and which will not; and presumably some people will
be better and quicker than others at differentiating them.
Thus an overtly evaluative criticism is both possible and desirable: possible, because the complexity in the work's structure
that requires close attention will mean that there is enough to say;
desirable, because without it one might waste a lot of time dis-
covering that time had been wasted. But perhaps the same facts
show an even greater need for the interpretative side of the critical appraisal. Those with the best vision must help those with
dimmer sight to see.

The foregoing argument assumes that some potential con-
sumers of the arts are more adept than others, and also that works
of art receive concentrated attention; it does not therefore hold
for societies of which those assumptions are not true. But in a
society of which the latter was not true there would be no concept of art: the concept is peculiar to highly developed civilizations and reflects precisely the custom of esthetic scrutiny. As
for the assumption of differential expertness, that too would not
hold for a society all of whose arts were folk-arts with the
products of which all members of the society were, so to speak,
attuned. In such a society one cannot think that there would be
critics, or any criticism beyond such a straightforward evaluation as anyone might make. Such criticism there would indeed
be, since even there artists would have to learn their arts, but
where every man is an artist every man may be a critic. But in
societies where labor is divided and where there is a leisure class
the fine arts are, for better or worse, an acquired taste, and
wherever there are acquired tastes some will have acquired
more than others, and among those who have acquired most
some will be more articulate than the rest. These are the critics.
The more describably complex the structure of an object of an
acquired taste is, the more articulate connoisseurs can be about
it. The more complex the work, the more elaborate the criticism.

The possibility of critical performance depends not only on
the existence of arts that need interpretation but on their allocation to a separate and important compartment of human life.
Without that allocation one might indeed have occasional
criticism, but no regular art or industry of criticism in which
critiques that are themselves performances could figure.

The uses of the term "performance" in everyday life, which

we have not yet exploited or even disentangled, correspond neatly enough to modes of criticism of the arts. The term is used in several differentiable ways. When we speak of a man's performance of a task we do not mean quite the same as when we speak of a machine's performance or simply of a performance, and criticism of the three will have different emphases. In assessing a man's performance of his task one considers how well he has carried out a definite prescribed assignment. The criteria of success are fixed beforehand. We have insisted that the criticism of the arts wields no such criteria, that artistic performance generally reveals its problems by their solution. But from the artist's point of view this is less than the whole truth: his work is dominated by the idea of a task to be fulfilled. And however unfashionable it may be to say so, even in the fine arts one must acknowledge that things may be done right or wrong, that the importance of spontaneity and invention does not make technical skill and competence unnecessary.

A machine's "performance" is not its carrying out of any task or action, but the quality of its "activity," how well it does in general the sort of things the machine is designed to do. The criteria are fixed, but the question is not whether something has been done properly but whether something is done well. That criticism of this kind has a place in the arts we have seen: it is especially characteristic of performances in the "performing arts," where the styles and techniques of actors and musicians are discussed, but such "textural" criticism is applicable to all arts.

Next, there is a sense of "performance," as in "putting on a performance," in which the word means something like a show or display, something done with spectators in mind. And it is important to remember that the fine arts are performances in this sense and are criticized as such, as matters in which there is a legitimate public interest because a public is invoked. It is this public interest that gives the critic his privilege of speaking his mind both as and when he pleases. Some high-minded theorists would indeed deny that the arts are thus essentially public, just as they deny that questions of competence enter; but these are mere forms of piety, or cant. The activities of the fine arts make sense only as displays, only as implying a public of potential audiences. Of course one can do these things for oneself alone, just as one can talk to oneself, or shadow-box, but these solitary exercises are derivative activities only intelligible in the light of the social ones.

By "a performance" one may also mean something like what is often meant by "a production," not merely something done for an audience but an elaborate affair on which much trouble has been expended. And we have already observed that art-criticism presupposes elaboration. Artifacts have always been prized at least in part for the work that has gone into them; and this philistinism, if that is what it is, is understandable. We like to feel that someone has taken trouble for us, and at least a part of the satisfaction we find in works of art is in the triumph of human agency.

The idea of the performance of a task and that of a performance as a display meet in the sense of "performance" peculiar to the arts in which performance amounts to publication: the sense in which we speak of the performance of a symphony. Of the criticism of such performances at least the point we wished to make generally is unmistakably true, that the standards by which an appraisal is made are partly derived from the performance itself and partly predetermined by known standards of competence and fidelity. Such a performance may be marred by mistakes, fluffs, wrong notes, misreadings, etc., but to avoid such errors is not enough to ensure a fine performance. Conversely, a performance may be full of life and fire, but if it is full of mistakes too it will be defective. The area where interpretations become controversial is the most interesting to the critic, but he can only avail himself of it once competence can be taken for granted.

To conclude our discussion of the relation between performance and art: the existence of criticism, and of the habit of thinking in terms of isolable performance, reveals an important and pervasive aspect of human valuation. People tend to get interested in what they are doing for its own sake, whatever it may be, just as they tend to sympathize most with the people in whose company they are. Thus whatever might have been a means becomes an end in itself, and thus we load our lives with all the value they will bear. In the arts this intensification of the value of the present moment reaches its steepest pitch. It was because he realized this, and not because he was a sadist, that Nietzsche spoke of the cruelty of art and of cruelty as the condition of all positive worth.

CRITICISM AND THE INSTITUTIONS OF ART

Now that we have drained the concept of performance of its last dregs of significance and related it to the fine arts, we are free to turn to the efficient cause of criticism: the institution of criticism itself, the organization of the production of critiques. But this organization is fused with that of its object, with the institutional aspects of the arts; and, since we have just been discussing the arts, it will be logical to approach our new topic from this angle.

We have seen that the actual close connection between criticism and the fine arts reflects the outstandingly performance-like characteristics of the latter. Thus the unity of criticism mirrors the functional unity of the arts. No doubt it is impossible to criticize art with constant reference to its functions, for any assigned function will be simple and criticism is endlessly complex. Even so, it seems plain that both the call for criticism and general ideas of what will pass muster as criticism will be controlled, if only loosely, by ideas about what sort of activity art is, or what sort of activities the arts embody, and what in general the arts are good for and meant for. One would expect changing ideas about the arts and changing ideas about criticism to go together. But ideas about criticism and its unity may well reflect, not merely the functional unity of the fine arts in their character of performance, but all the unity they have. And the unity of the arts, whatever its historical origins and theoretical justification, is in current practice largely institutional. Painting is a unity, largely because it is accepted as one sort of thing to do, and because there are channels for the exhibition and sale of paintings, schools and academies for providing and regularizing instruction in painting, and counter-academies and anti-salons wherein protests against the over-institutionalization of painting find institutional expression. What passes as painting is whatever is produced in the appropriate fashion in this nexus of institutions: as Dadaist and post-dadaist practices show, almost any object presented in this framework is in some sense a "painting." The same is true, *mutatis mutandis*, for each of the fine arts. Moreover, most of such unity as the fine arts have among themselves is institutional, being constituted by the custom of grouping these activities together for purposes of teaching, journalism, and historiography. The very fact that many attempts have been made to demonstrate the unity of the fine arts shows that that unity is not basically functional, but is primarily an accepted social fact whose non-conventional ground needs to be shown.

Granted that the institutional unity of the arts supports the functional unity of criticism, the reverse may be equally true. By treating the various arts in the same way criticism inevitably suggests that they are similar activities, and may encourage and reinforce or even create their institutional unity. Whether the influence was originally reciprocal, or which of the two fields established its unity first, is a question of historical fact that lies beyond our competence. At present, the two unities reinforce each other.

The unifying effect of criticism on the arts is suggested by one of our pervasive lines of argument. To be a performance is to be treated as a performance, and that is to be regarded as a potential object of criticism; to be a certain kind of performance is to be regarded as a potential object of a certain kind of criticism. Thus to be a work of art is to be regarded as a potential object of art criticism, and the idea of "art" is a product of the idea and practice of art criticism. It used indeed to be maintained, in effect if not in set terms, that the unity of the fine arts *(arts du beau)* lay in their susceptibility to criticism in terms of beauty and kindred concepts, in the fact that a common critical terminology suited them. It was thought, of course, that what united them was their shared function of being beautiful or giving esthetic delight; but the actual evidence of this unity was nothing but the use of a standard critical vocabulary in discussing them. The artist's intention was postulated to fit this vocabulary—he must have meant to do what everyone says he has done—and the "esthetic experience" of the beholder was merely the ghost in the critical machinery. Alternatively, one can say (as we said ourselves) in scholastic-Aristotelian terms that the peculiarity of the fine arts is that they are endotelic, that they seek no end beyond themselves; but again, the real evidence for this is neither the purity of the artist's art nor the disinterestedness of the beholder's attitude but the viability of a criticism that ignores ulterior ends. Or again, we have noted that some theorists identify excellence in all the arts with a kind of coherent complexity; but we also noted that the evidence for this complexity is just that critics can find a lot to say and contrive to say it all in a single critique.

Art and Criticism

If critical theory is closely related to the institutional as well as the functional unity of the arts, critical practice is no less obviously and notoriously related to the commercial aspects of that institution. Free copies of books and free tickets for shows are passed out to critics. No hand-out, no critique. Even if their critiques make no reference to commercial viability, what they say affects the economic destinies of artistic products. Paradoxically, the more strongly commercial considerations prevail over artistic ones the more important the critical appraisal may be. Personal taste can get by without criticism, but valuations not based on personal taste are based on repute, and repute follows appraisal, so that wherever patrons have more money than taste the critic's word is supreme. This partly explains the career of the late Bernard Berenson, and the crucial importance of good notices for Broadway shows. Wealthy collectors pay for authenticated pictures rather than good ones, and a visiting fireman must be taken to a well-reviewed show rather than one worth seeing—when he gets back home, his family and colleagues must be able to recognize the name of what he has seen.

THE EFFICIENT CAUSE: CRITICISM AS INSTITUTION

It is not surprising that criticism, functioning as part of the great complex of artistic institutions, should itself have an institutional aspect. The critic appears as a special type of person producing a standard kind of commodity to meet a regular demand, and the idea of "criticism" itself figures among the concepts by which we get our bearings. Fundamentally, criticism as an institution lies in what critics do to supply their markets. What we have to ask, then, is who the critic is and what his markets are. In so far as markets differ in scope or interests, the demands on critics will differ. Some critics may then be torn between conflicting demands, forced either to compromise or to please some by displeasing others. Other critics will specialize in satisfying one market; criticism for scholarly journals will then be in other hands than those which supply the daily press. To list and classify all the markets for criticism would be a task for the sociologist. We shall content ourselves here with naming four main types of market that professional critics supply: the mass-medium market for spoken or written ephemera; the academic-scholarly market; the academic instructional market; and the market for quasi-permanent literature. Of course, given these markets, it is not only professional critics who supply them: anyone who gets caught up in the machinery is a critic for the nonce, as is anyone who is called on to criticize in any context. But although a wide variety of people are called to supply critiques from time to time (to review work in their line of expertise, to judge beauty contests, to report on how their underlings do their jobs, to give an "average housewife's" opinion on sample products), we do not say that such people are critics if we are asked what they are or what they do. We classify people as critics only if they criticize regularly and habitually and as part of a policy or a way of life.

Critics of the first kind fill slots on a radio or TV timetable or in the critical columns of the press. Their functions seem to be three. They may carry on the evaluative and interpretative debates about performances whose place in the accepted corpus of the cultural tradition is prima facie secure. Or they may introduce, or decline to introduce, new performances or new kinds of performance into that mainstream. Or finally their activity may be merely vestigial, space-filling or traditional: it is accepted that certain media should devote so much space or time to "criticism" and the ritual of filling it up must be followed. In such cases, common among newspapers of the English-speaking world, it becomes quite fortuitous what is discussed, what is said about it and who says it. But the prayer-wheel turns.

The second kind of critic is the scholastic or academic teacher of literature. Since all these people may be called critics, it may be said (Mr. Righter has in fact said) that most criticism nowadays is done in the classroom. Hence the worries of teachers, who ask themselves, "Can this be criticism? Can I be a critic? How, and why?" For such a person may feel that neither taste nor training nor talent has endowed him with the critical authority that he must professionally assume. However, only academics suppose that teaching literature is criticism. The source of the supposition seems to be the academic continuity of teaching and scholarship. A university teacher is supposed to be an authority on his subject, which means that his teaching should reflect his research and his research should be into what he teaches. Now, the teaching of literature used to consist of systematic endeavors to make sure that young people got to know the standard literary works of the society into which they were being initiated. That was a major part of their indoctrination into the received values or "cultural heritage" of their people. It was a study without scholarly pretensions, preintellectual and propaedeutic. Nowadays, when intellectual infancy has been prolonged and the teaching of literature has been pushed up into the universities, the basic function of that teaching is still the same, as the enormous reading-lists of college English courses show; but it has to be pretended that the study of literature is a serious and systematic academic discipline. The simple and unpretentious task of getting young people to read standard literature appreciatively has to be presented as something like a science. In the classroom, understanding must be made out to go by rules; and the teacher's "research" must provide a theoretical underpinning for these pretensions and exemplify them on a more formal and formidable scale. Literary research thus goes beyond establishing texts and historical connections to embrace critical studies differing from those of public critics only in that the performances that embody them differ in style and intended audience: footnotes replace style, circumlocution wit. And so academic criticism is born.

Sneering is always fun, but we cannot leave that as our last word on academic criticism. Even if our account of its origins and foibles is correct, origins do not compromise success and weaknesses do not nullify achievements. Academic critics include some of the best critics there are, and the rise of academic criticism has raised the tone of criticism generally: that literature can be systematically studied as literature is not a pretense but a real discovery. And the alternative to a serious academic criticism is that historical and philological criticism should take over the classroom teaching of literature, a horrifying prospect.

The problem of classroom critical pretensions arises only with literature. No one claims that the teaching of the history and appreciation of music or the visual arts should be called "criticism"or that the teachers are critics. A possible explanation of the discrepancy is that one can acquaint young people with art by teaching them its history far more readily than one can acquaint them with literature by teaching literary history. In either field, historical teaching demands that many representative works be cited and compared; but in art history slides of these works can be shown, whereas in literary history only descriptions and summaries can be given. Admittedly, any reproduction of a work of visual art is very far from being the work itself, but it is much closer to it than any précis or description can be to a literary work. On the other hand, though acquaintance with the visual arts through reproductions is vicarious, it is the only sort of acquaintance that most of the students can ever have; but the teacher of literary history, though he cannot embed his examples in his discourse, can rely on the original works being available to his students. Thus a course in the history of art can be self-contained, needing to be reinforced rather than supplemented; but a course in literary history is about something that it does not contain. It must therefore take on the elaboration of critical discourse, whereas the lecturer on the visual arts need say little more than "Next, please."

Besides journalists and the janus-faced scholar-teachers of the universities there is a third kind of professional critic, the critic *pur sang*, a literary man whose literary productions take the form of critiques. Like other literary men, he must either have independent means or a second job, or else must have worked his way up to independence from journalistic slot-filling. The market that he supplies is the world of art-fanciers, and more especially that of book-fanciers: a book about books is as booksy a thing as you can have, not even excelled by books about books about books (histories or theories of literary criticism) and books about books about books about books (discussions and comparisons of such histories and theories), which provide not distillation but specialization.

Such an interest-group market as we have just mentioned, being defined solely by its shared interest, may be defined by a more specialized taste. This taste may be for criticism, as such. And so we arrive at a purely autonomous criticism, whose standards are not determined by the needs of the consumer but rather determine what the consumer will get and will have to like. The situation here is the same as that in the fine arts. As painters paint to satisfy themselves and (perhaps) other painters, and survive either because other people take the trouble to acquire their tastes (or pretend to do so) or by earning their living by other means or because (as often happens) the standards they have introjected are those actually already current around them, so a critic may say just what he feels like saying about whatever he feels like saying it about, and survive either because he does not have to sell his criticism or because he bends others to his taste or because he is the unconscious spokesman of a popular point of view. This is indeed, as we remarked before, the ultimate ground and pure spring of criticism, that people have things to say and want to say them. The arts after all exist to arouse interest, and nothing could be more natural than that people should wish to share their excitements, enjoyments, resentments, disappointments, and insights. The procedure becomes institutionalized because it is equally natural to take an interest in what other people have to say about what interests them. The complexities of the arts and the diffusion through space and time of those who share interests in them combine to make improvisation and casual social contact inadequate to this interchange of views, and thus systematic criticism is born. But now, we may ask, what comes of criticism as a craft? The critic as such is surely the recognized exponent of a recognized skill; and how is this compatible with the critical autonomy and spontaneity that we have just vindicated? Once again the analogy of the fine arts lies to hand. It is possible that painting should be autonomous not in the sense that each painter paints as he personally thinks proper, but that the community of painters should share criteria and practices that they develop communally. (A situation is certainly conceivable, and may actually be developing, in which all professionally respectable composers of music would employ a methodology and associated canons of success that no one who was not a composer shared.) Alternatively, it is possible that it should be accepted that serious artists please none but themselves, and that the criterion of serious painterhood should simply be that one painted seriously, the mark of seriousness being either simple devotion to one's painting or acceptance as a compeer by other painters. Thus by analogy one might be accepted as a serious critic simply because one set out seriously to criticize, or because one was accepted as a critic by other serious critics, or because one's critical canons were those adopted by other serious critics no matter how crackbrained they might seem to the educated public at large. Nor, in fact, are these theoretical possibilities very far from what seems to be the way things actually are.

There now seem to be three ways of looking at the institutional side of critics and their criticism. To be a critic may be to have a socially recognized position as such, or it may be to be regularly and systematically active in accordance with certain recognized standards, or it may be to be regularly productive of what is institutionally recognized as criticism. Criticism may be material produced to meet certain recognized requirements, or it may be institutionally identified either as the work of a recognized critic or by the circumstances of its marketing. And this may be simplified into saying that criticism may be identified either as a technique, a type of skilled activity with its own canons, or as an institution defined by its social relations.

The institutionalization of the critic and that of his product do not quite coincide. The institution of criticism is basically that of a market, and whoever supplies the market is criticizing though he be no critic. Conversely, critics are critics even when they are not criticizing, and it is at least theoretically possible that one should be a recognized critic without ever criticizing, just as it is alleged that certain bars in New York are full of painters who never paint. But I do not know of any cases where this has actually happened yet. The two institutionalizations, however, do exercise a pull on each other. From the idea of critic as recognized purveyor of critiques derives the notion of criticism as whatever the recognized critic purveys. Thus if a critic is someone whose byline appears on a page headed "criticism" or some such word or phrase, "criticism" may be whatever appears under that byline. This is, as it were, criticism by association. We need say no more about it than that, in general, institutions have their own dynamic and whatever forms part of the set of practices that define an institution bears the name of the institution whether it contributes to its supposed funcions or not.

CRITICISM AS ART

The fact that criticism is essentially discourse about performances but is also itself performance may, as we have seen, be used to support the more general thesis that criticism is homogenous with its object. But the typical objects of criticism are works of literature and the fine arts. The general thesis then suggests that criticism is itself a fine art, and that critiques are works of art. Of course nothing that has been said has proved this, nor would the analogy itself suggest more than that the typical critique was a work of art. Rather, the analogy would suggest that a classification of types of objects of criticism, of which works of art are only one, would also serve to classify types of critique. None the less, it has often been held that the critic is a type of literary artist, and it seems plain from our last section that the critic *pur sang* actually is. And why not? Why should not critical writings be works of coherent complexity designed to reward contemplation—or whatever other formula we may use to characterize works of art?

The main objection to making criticism a fine art is that one cannot suppose criticism to be endotelic. A critique is essentially a critique of something, not merely in the sense that it has a content but in the sense that it has a really existing external referent. Criticism differs from portraiture, with which we compared it before, in the manner in which its interpretative and appraising function is primary. The quality of a portrait as such may indeed depend on its merits as likeness and interpretation of character, but it may fail in these respects and still be a fine painting. But if a critique sheds no light on the work criticized one is puzzled to say what excellence it has. There are many portraitists to whom their subjects are just opportunities for painting, but there are no critics to whom their subjects are just opportunities for writing; or, if there are, they will not admit it.

The contrast between criticism and portraiture is not limited to supposed function and intention. It is important that the original to which a critique refers is normally accessible to his public, while the original stimulus, if any, to which a painting refers is accessible only in special cases and usually by accident. The evidence on which a critic relies for his interpretations is accessible to his readers, and the critic relies not only on their being able to get it but often on their actually having it. Curiously, although this puts the critic on the spot, it also sets him free. Unless he is reviewing new work, he is not so much informing the ignorant as guiding or persuading the informed; and because no one has to take his word for anything he can exaggerate or play.

It is the very freedom that the accessibility of the referent gives him that raises for the critic the problem of the status of his work. The artistic freedom that he would like to claim and the apparent overriding demand that he should be faithful to his original pull in opposite directions. Surely his creative freedom is not confined to tarting up with fine writing a lump of technical prose, but extends to his interpretation itself. But he differs from other artists in that his subject as such is already ordered and has its own artistic integrity. Surely he can only respect this integrity by suppressing his own personal view-point; but, equally surely, it is only his own personal viewpoint that gives him anything to say. If he merely uses the criticized performance as a stimulus, he is not a critic at all; if he exploits it, he is a bad critic; but if he merely reports it his genius is rebuked.

The critical dilemma just outlined is theoretically somewhat factitious. If he is worried about his precious autonomy and integrity, let him write and speak as he pleases, and let others decide whether what he has done is "criticism" or not. Of all writers, the critic or near-critic or paracritic should be sophisti-cated enough not to worry about what generic pigeon-hole he will be filed in. What gives his dilemma its sharp horns is that criticism has the formidable institutional aspect that we have discussed. The critic appears to be publicly committed to meet-ing incompatible requirements.

Besides being theoretically factitious, the critic's problem is practically nugatory. Criticism is very difficult to do well, but not because it is practically hard to determine what sort of thing one should do. Critical practice varies, but not so much as critical theory might lead one to think: critics are all going to heaven, and A. C. Bradley is of the company. The problem is of a more baffling though very familiar kind, that of giving a con-sistent and colorable account of what one is doing. Particular answers to the question of what the art of criticism is constitute theories about criticism, and therefore lie beyond the scope of this essay; but we may mention some of the ways in which one might seek to reconcile the artistic integrity of the critic with his critical responsibility to that of his subject.

One possible solution is to produce a theory of the fine arts (if you prefer, the *other* fine arts) which demands of them a fidelity comparable with the most that can be asked of a critic. This means constructing a sort of shadow-referent for every poem or painting, an original "moment" or "experience" for which the artist has to find an equivalent in words or paint (cf. *The Structure of Aesthetics*, ch. xvi). The critic's task can then be made out to be just the same, that of reconstructing the esthetic moment or whatever else the corresponding original may turn out to be. The trouble with this *tu quoque* solution is that it relies on an account of artistic creation that is highly controversial, and may also suggest that critics have to deal with something more vaporous than the criticized work itself, a suggestion that we have seen many critics resist and resent.

The opposite solution to that just considered is to deny that the work criticized has any, or much, or enough structure before it is criticized. Nature without art, we may be told, has no order or dignity; and the art that orders and dignifies nature has itself no dignity or order of its own until the critic bestows them by his interpretation. Less ambitiously and more plausibly, one may say that the world is indeed in part and in some ways orderly, but that its order is too complex to be grasped in its wholeness, or that the different kinds of order that it partly shows get in each other's way. The artist substitutes for this ungraspable patterning a simpler order of his own, that the mind can grapple with: an order partly selected from, partly educed from, and partly imposed on nature. Similarly it may be argued that any work complex enough to deserve and demand criticism will have an order too complex and perhaps too ramshackle to be grasped as a whole; the critic substitutes for this a simpler pattern that he partly selects, partly educes, partly supplies. Alternatively, one may say that the world's order is not too complex to be taken in but is really only partial; the artist takes up the suggestions of orderliness and develops them into a single complete form. So too the novelist or the painter merely adumbrates a world for his public to complete for themselves; the critic offers satisfactory completions on the basis of the hints supplied. On this interpretation, the critic really does the organizing work traditionally assigned to the artist, and the artist himself merely supplies the opportunities. Whether one says that the artist provides too much pattern or too little, on either interpretation the order he imparts is indeterminate; it is the critic who gives it a single pattern. And because of that we may take the metaphor of "giving" order so fas as to say that the gift once bestowed is a permanent possession. Once a viable interpretation has been put forward, that becomes what the work means; or, if there are rival interpretations, each of them will be one of the definite things the work means.

The idea that the critic's interpretative art is the sole source of determinate order is supported by the thesis previously put forward, that the ideas of total meaning and full understanding have no content, that one can never say that explanation is complete. There is an obvious sense in which an uninterpreted work has no determinate meaning: no one has determined it.

It is, after all, not true that a partial view is an imperfect view. Superimposition of views taken from many viewpoints yields, not one complete view, but a blur. To have a viewpoint of one's own is not a drawback but a necessity of vision, and a succession of views retain their value only while they remain distinct. But, if this is accepted, it has one important consequence. It entails that there can be no such thing as evaluation or appraisal of the work, insofar as both those terms refer to overall summative judgments that purport to be definitive. One could only say how good a work was, or in what ways it was good, insofar as one supposed oneself to have understood it completely. One's personal interpretation would indeed have important evaluative consequences, it would bring out part of the worth of the work, but it could have no claim to the status of verdict. This consideration would not in itself tell against the thesis, except for people who like to have things definitive; what does tell against it is the plain fact that one-sidedness is a defect in an interpretation. The possibility of achieving total understanding represents a theoretical limit rather than a serious practical problem, and the analogy from vision and viewpoint was only an analogy. Interpretations and appraisals do indeed differ from one another in comprehensiveness as well as in the angle of approach. But these considerations do not undermine the main point of the thesis, that interpretations serve as necessary simplifications or supplements.

If one maintains that the order of a work of art, even if undetected, must be determinately what the artist imparted to it, and the critic's formal task can only be to recover this order, two ways of saving the critic's artistic autonomy remain open. One is to say that his task is to divine and make plain a latent order, for example a pattern of myth and imagery, that is implicit in the original work. The artist-critic produces a work of a different logical level in which these hidden implications are made plain. This, however, is a view with little actual appeal, for the justification of such systematic exegesis must usually be some theory of symbolic or mythological significances, and critics who embark on such projects are therefore likely to regard themselves as scientists rather than as artists. The onlooker, however, may take their products as a sort of poetic rhapsodizing rather than in the way it was intended. In either case, the analogy with the fine arts is easy. Nature, one says, is indeed orderly, with just the nature that it has; what the artist does is to ignore the obvious order and bring out the hidden correspondences, the signatures in all things. One is inclined to say that it is rather a special way of looking at art, or a way of looking at a special sort of art; but then, its analogue is perhaps a rather special sort of criticism.

Finally, one may say that nature has the order that it has, but it is dead. The artist filters this order through his consciousness and brings it to life by imparting his own vital power to it. So too we may say that a critic takes a dead work and breathes life into it, lending it his own vitality. But this again is a highly specialized interpretation of the critic's task. It supposes that the critic's work is somehow more vital than the work he is writing about. I am not sure what that means if taken literally, and I am sure that the situations about which one would feel impelled to say it are few. It applies to a critic expounding authors of a distant age to his contemporaries, and may apply to a first-rate critic expounding second-rate work. But most obviously it applies to the man in the classroom trying to make the classics "come alive." He is then a real person really present to his students, but the works he expounds are merely words on paper. But surely in this aspect of his work he is not critic but prophet or necromancer, making (as Wilamowitz said) the ghosts speak by feeding them on blood.

My own preferences among the views put forward in this section will be evident here, but it is not my present task to promote any of them. Indeed, it is not even my concern to defend the basic thesis that gives rise to the problem, that the function of criticism is in important ways like that of the fine arts.

CONCLUSION

The discussion of the production of criticism in its institutional aspects, both organizational and methodological, concludes the account of what criticism is and brings us to the end of our task. To go beyond this would lead into territory whose marches we already tread, that of positive critical theory itself. We cap off our remarks about the intension of the concept of criticism with a few words about its extension: about what is

criticism and what is not. Most of what is said here will merely
resume points made before; even so, we shall find that the dis-
criminations we are called upon to make commit us to sides in
controversies belonging to critical theory proper. Our treatment will accordingly be cursory, not to say perfunctory.

The ultimate basis of criticism in literature and the arts is
that some people have things they want to say, and others have
things they want to know, about performances of these kinds.
No doubt the degree and manner of their success and failure is
the most obvious and important of these things: direction and
warning are more urgent than information, and it is the best
and the worst that one feels most strongly impelled to bring to
the attention of others. But, given any interest in performances
of a certain kind, anything whatever that pertains to those performances will come to share that interest, because of the
cumulative and contagious nature of curiosity to which Aristotle
already drew attention as the mainspring of the sciences. And
this interest in performances will extend to the unperformance-
like aspects of whatever actions and artifacts constitute and
cause them. Just as a specialist purveyor of merchandise to a
restricted market may slip into the habit of supplying, as a side-
line, the less specialized wants of his clientèle, without thereby
feeling that he has stepped beyond the limits of his calling, so a
critic may come to write in a quite general way about matters
that pertain to art and artists without necessarily being conscious
of straying beyond the bounds of criticism, or caring whether
he has strayed or not. Since, as we have seen, there is also an
institutional basis for accepting as criticism whatever critics
write on company time, we should not be surprised to find this
peripheral writing classified as criticism, nor should we think
that this classification tells in any way against either the validity
or the utility of the more restricted account of what the concept
of criticism involves that this essay has excogitated. Let us then
list a few varieties of what we might pejoratively call pseudo-
criticism: kinds of utterance that are excluded from criticism
by our definitions, but might be included in it by a more
generous account, or that are associated with criticism in the
way sketched in this paragraph.

One kind of near-criticism puts forward a general thesis about
art or literature, or about the state of society or the world, and
merely uses discussions of particular performances as pegs to

hang the discussion on. Since the merits and actual nature of those works are not the main concern, and sometimes not even a subsidiary concern, of such discussions, they do not really earn the title of "criticism" that is in practice often conferred on them.

Next comes the very large class of biographical writings that do not come closer to dealing with their subjects' performances than saying how they came to perform and how they acted in performing. The traditional "Life and Works" is often like that, the "works" part being limited to summary and to remarks on circumstances of production and reception. But it is of course perfectly possible for genuinely critical discussions to be conjoined to biographies. There really should be no danger of confusing biography with criticism, except in those cases where the performer makes or purports to make his life his subject. In practice, however, the colors often run: what the biographer knows of the life affects his reading of the work, or he infers the life (as biographers in classical antiquity regularly did) from what he finds in the work.

Histories often come closer to real criticism than biographies do. Although the life of an artist is interesting only because of his art, his biography will deal with his whole lifetime; but a history of art has nothing but performances for its subject. However, its concern as history is not with the performances as such but with their origins and effects. Like a biography, a history can embody critical judgments and, if there is room, critical discussions; indeed, it usually does; but they form no necessary part of its historical content. But histories do, at least indirectly, perform a critical service, since knowledge of the contemporary setting of a work may so modify one's understanding of it as altogether to change one's appreciation. If one way of evaluating is to show that a performance conforms to given requirements, another way may be to show that there are requirements to which it does after all conform or by which it falls unexpectedly short, and any evaluation that one can understand can be made one's own and may also come to serve as the basis of one's own appreciation.

Philological writing comes closer to criticism than biography and history do: it does at least devote itself to what a particular work contains rather than to its relations with other things. The same is true of technical or archeological studies in the plastic arts. But none of these are generally classed as criticism, nor do they qualify under our definitions. The descriptions to which they devote themselves are of a kind that cannot ground evaluations, since what they describe is not so much the performance itself as its material basis. Again, however, like historical studies, they may bring information that changes a perspective and sways a judgment. Besides, the material cause of a performance is among its causes and is a necessary aspect of it. It may be said that it is a necessary part of it as act or object rather than as performance, since "performance" itself is as we have seen a strictly aspect-denoting word; but it may reasonably be replied that to perform is always to do something *with* something, and ignorance of what it was done with must maim understanding of what was done.

Still on the margin of criticism, in that it charts reactions to performances rather than the performances themselves, is that well-known form of writing that records the adventures of the soul among masterpieces. We have remarked before that there are good reasons for thinking of some good criticism in this way; much depends on how it is done. The adroit account of a response gives a good idea of what is responded to, and of course there is a sense in which one knows nothing except through one's responses to it. But discussing one's reactions may not be the same as talking about one's feelings, and it is very easy for those adventures among masterpieces to degenerate into funny things that happened on the way to the theater. It is true, of course, that any evaluation can be made out to be autobiographical, and so may any interpretation or description: any utterance only tells us what its author thinks. It is also true that every critique reveals as much about the critic as about what he is criticizing. But too much should not be made of these subversive truths. One has to differentiate between three questions, all of which usually admit of definitive answers. One is: Is the ostensible subject of this utterance the performance or its critic? The second is: Is the actual subject of this utterance the performance or its critic? And the third: Does this utterance shed more light on the performance or on its critic? A critique that fails to illuminate its subject but illuminates its critic's prejudices with startling clarity may nonetheless be unmistakably about the work that it purports to criticize; for the logical relation of being about something, taking a thing as subject, is not the same as the pragmatic relation of revealing something about something. And this distinction is not to be classified with the rhetorical device of saying something about one thing while purporting to say something about another thing, as in the celebrated review of a children's book by Dorothy Parker (under the pen-name of "Constant Reader"): "Tonstant Weader fwowed up."

Last among these utterances on the periphery of criticism we may mention the purported criticisms of a performance that are irrelevant to it as performance, or as performance of the kind supposedly being criticized. To use our earlier example: if a reviewer complains that a book is too thin to prop a broken chair, he is not criticizing the literary performance at all, but facetiously criticizing the printer and binder in the capacity, which they never professed, of wedge-suppliers. Such a remark is "criticism" in the vulgar sense, but no one supposes that it is literary criticism except insofar as by making it the critic would be suggesting that the book had no literary significance at all.

Thus far we have mentioned types of discourse that fail to be criticism, if they fail, by being directed on something other than the relevant aspects of the performance itself. Those to which we now turn fail, when they fail, by being directed at the right thing in the wrong way. If they are criticism at all, they are very bad criticism; whereas most of those previously discussed, if they are allowed to be criticism at all, may be quite unobjectionable. The case of the chair-propping book stands on the borderline between the two kinds.

First among these doubtful utterances comes a group very close to that last mentioned, criticisms of a performance in terms of irrelevant standards: criticism, that is, for the performance of tasks not undertaken or otherwise irrelevant. To criticize a playwright for not writing a classical tragedy, unless he had specifically contracted to do so, would be such an irrelevance. It differs from the case of the chair-propping book in that it does point to an alleged defect in the performance itself. One might even here feel inclined to say, and some do say, that the critique is not really concerned with the work as it is, but with something else: an idea of the critic's, perhaps. But with the same justification one could say that any purported critique with which one disagreed was no critique at all, on the grounds that to misinterpret the work is to mistake the kind of performance that it is. Such exclusions would in fact be mere polemical ploys. An irrelevant criticism is nonetheless a criticism of the performance in question, so long as the features upon which it fastens are features of the performance itself.

A special kind of irrelevant criticism is that which treats works of art not as things made but as action or theorem. Since this fails to treat the performance as a performance of the kind recognized by the institution of art and its criticism, it might seem to belong with the chair-prop rather than with the classical tragedy; however, like the latter, it does fasten on at least some of those aspects of the criticized thing that constitute it a performance of the relevant kind. Such criticism would be regarded as inappropriate rather than irrelevant, since although it pertains to the work and may within its limits be well taken, it is not the kind of criticism that the critical situation calls for.

On the border between non-criticism and bad criticism is the comment by illuminating falsehood, the misdescription that yet implies an evaluation. Many criticisms are simply wrong in that the performances they refer to do not have the characters assigned to them. But our previous discussion of such cases left them within the critical pale, and it is plain that a misdescription may be as indirectly illuminating as a caricature or a parody. (Caricatures and parodies themselves, we recall, were excluded from criticism because they do not have the essential character of discourse or discussion about what they take off; and caricatures also because they are not verbal. Nonetheless, they do have an obvious critical use, and may form parts of or adjuncts to criticism proper.)

Mere polemics for or against performances do not constitute criticism at all, we have said, so long as they bear their polemical character on their face. But if they masquerade as judicial in character one must say that they are criticism indeed, but bad criticism. The difference is not one of degree: it is not that some polemics are so blatant as not to be criticisms, but that a critique is not the same sort of thing as a puff or a blast. A puff in the guise of a critique is a critique. Literary genres, of which criticism is one, are altogether a matter of guise.

Finally, we have excluded from criticism the merely extemporaneous and marginal comment, which does not qualify as a performance; the sense in which casual dicta are criticism is one in which we have little interest, and one that our formal word "critique" excludes. The proper province of criticism remains that marked out by the terminology appropriated to complex structures of formal speech: evaluation, appraisal, explanation, interpretation.

Beyond this point our prolegomena cannot go. Already we are more and more dividing our time between repeating ourselves and trespassing on others' land. More and more we are faced with decisions that we cannot take without committing ourselves to a substantive theory of criticism.

Looking back, we are surprised to see how much could be done merely by unpacking the main concepts that we used in defining criticism, and unfolding their implications. An explicative study such as this can hardly be said to reach a conclusion, but we may end by drawing attention to one rather surprising result that has come out. Socrates said that the unexamined life was not fit for men. In the same vein we may say that a life with no place for criticism is not worth living. This is not because of the value inherent in the activity of criticism itself, but because criticism is possible and suitable wherever the complex values of human experience are found. Critical activity seeks and finds, if it does not create, experience that is worth dwelling on. The old fear that criticism might dissolve enjoyment has no ground. Only a mindless enjoyment could be thus melted, and a mindless enjoyment is never enough for people with minds.

III

PATTERNS OF CRITICISM

I

NORTHROP FRYE

Preface to an Uncollected Anthology

The author imagines that he has collected his ideal anthology of English Canadian poetry, with no difficulties about permission, publishers, or expense, and is writing his preface.

Certain critical principles are essential for dealing with Canadian poetry which in the study of English literature as such are seldom raised. Unless the critic is aware of the importance of these principles, he may, in turning to Canadian poets, find himself unexpectedly incompetent, like a giraffe trying to eat off the ground. The first of these principles is the fact that the cultivated Canadian has the same kind of interest in Canadian poetry that he has in Canadian history or politics. Whatever its merits, it is the poetry of his own country, and it gives him an understanding of that country which nothing else can give him. The critic of Canadian literature has to settle uneasily somewhere between the Canadian historian or social scientist, who has no comparative value-judgments to worry about, and the ordinary literary critic, who has nothing else. The qualities in Canadian poetry which help to make Canada more imaginatively articulate for the Canadian reader are genuine literary values, whether they coincide with other literary values or not. And while the reason for collecting an anthology can only be the merit of the individual poems, still, having made such a collection, one may legitimately look at the proportioning of interests, at the pattern of the themes that seem to make Canadian poets eloquent.

It is not a nation but an environment that makes an impact on poets, and poetry can deal only with the imaginative aspect of that environment. A country with almost no Atlantic seaboard,

Originally presented to section 2 of the Royal Society of Canada, June 1956, in a session on Canadian literature. Reprinted from Northrop Frye, "Preface to an Uncollected Anthology," in *Studia Varia*, ed. E. G. Murray, 1957, by permission of the University of Toronto Press.

which for most of its history has existed in practically one dimension; a country divided by two languages and great stretches of wilderness, so that its frontier is a circumference rather than a boundary; a country with huge rivers and islands that most of its natives have never seen; a country that has made a nation out of the stops on two of the world's longest railway lines: this is the environment that Canadian poets have to grapple with, and many of the imaginative problems it presents have no counterpart in the United States, or anywhere else.

In older countries the works of man and of nature, the city and the garden of civilization, have usually reached some kind of imaginative harmony. But the land of the Rockies and the Precambrian Shield impresses painter and poet alike by its raw colors and angular rhythms, its profoundly unhumanized isolation. It is still "The Lonely Land" to A. J. M. Smith, still "A Country without a Mythology" to Douglas LePan. The works of man are even more imaginatively undigested. A Canadian village, unlike an English one, does not "nestle": it sprawls awkwardly along a highway or railway line, less an inhabited center than an episode of communication. Its buildings express an arrogant defiance of the landscape; its roads and telephone wires and machinery twist and strangle and loop. Irving Layton says, looking at an abstract picture,

> When I got the hang of it
> I saw a continent of railway tracks
> coiling about the sad Modigliani necks
> like disused tickertape, the streets
> exploding in the air
> with disaffected subway cars.

The Wordsworth who saw nature as exquisitely fitted to the human mind would be lost in Canada, where what the poets see is a violent collision of two forces, both monstrous. Earle Birney describes the bulldozers of a logging camp as "iron brontosaurs"; Klein compares grain elevators to leviathans.

Poets are a fastidious race, and in Canadian poetry we have to give some place, at least at the beginning, to the anti-Canadian, the poet who has taken one horrified look at the country and fled. Thus Standish O'Grady, writing of *The Emigrant:*

> Here forests crowd, unprofitable lumber,
> O'er fruitless lands indefinite as number;

> Where birds scarce light, and with the north winds veer
> On wings of wind, and quickly disappear,
> Here the rough Bear subsists his winter year,
> And licks his paw and finds no better fare. . . .
> The lank Canadian eager trims his fire,
> And all around their simpering stoves retire;
> With fur clad friends their progenies abound,
> And thus regale their buffaloes around;
> Unlettered race, how few the number tells,
> Their only pride a cariole and bells. . . .
> Perchance they revel; still around they creep,
> And talk, and smoke, and spit, and drink, and sleep!

There is a great deal of polished wit in these couplets of the modern ambiguous kind: the word "lumber," for example, has both its Canadian meaning of wood and its English meaning of junk. We notice that "Canadian" in this poem means French Canadian habitant: O'Grady no more thinks of himself as Canadian than an Anglo-Indian colonel would think of himself as Hindu. Here is an American opinion, the close of a folk song about a construction gang that spent a winter in Three Rivers:

> And now the winter's over, it's homeward we are bound,
> And in this cursed country we'll never more be found.
> Go back to your wives and sweethearts, tell others not to go
> To that God-forsaken country called Canaday-I-O.

Thanks to the efforts of those who remained, this particular theme is now obsolete, although Norman Levine in 1950 spoke of leaving the land of "parchment summers and merchant eyes" for "the loveliest of fogs," meaning England. Still, it will serve as an introduction to two central themes in Canadian poetry: one a primarily comic theme of satire and exuberance, the other a primarily tragic theme of loneliness and terror.

It is often said that a pioneering country is interested in material rather than spiritual or cultural values. This is a cliché, and it has become a cliché because it is not really true, as seventeenth-century Massachusetts indicates. What is true is that the imaginative energy of an expanding economy is likely to be mainly technological. As a rule it is the oppressed or beleaguered peoples, like the Celts and the Hebrews, whose culture makes the greatest imaginative efforts: successful nations usually express a restraint or a matter-of-fact realism in their culture and keep their exuberance for their engineering. If we are looking for imaginative exuberance in American life, we shall find it not in its fiction but in its advertising; not in Broadway drama but in Broadway skyscrapers; not in the good movies but in the vista-visioned and technicolored silly ones. The extension of this life into Canada is described by Frank Scott in *Saturday Sundae*, by James Reaney in *Klaxon*, a fantasy of automobiles wandering over the highways without drivers, "Limousines covered with pink slime / Of Children's blood," and by many other poets.

The poet dealing with the strident shallowness of much Canadian life is naturally aware that there is no imaginative change when we cross the American border in either direction. Yet there is, I think, a more distinctive attitude in Canadian poetry than in Canadian life, a more withdrawn and detached view of life which may go back to the central fact of Canadian history: the rejection of the American Revolution. What won the American Revolution was the spirit of entrepreneur capitalism, an enthusiastic plundering of the natural resources of a continent and an unrestricted energy of manufacturing and exchanging them. In *A Search for America*, which is quite a profound book if we take the precaution of reading it as a work of fiction, Grove speaks of there being two Americas, an ideal one that has something to do with the philosophy of Thoreau and the personality of Lincoln, and an actual one that made the narrator a parasitic salesman of superfluous goods and finally a hobo. At the end of the book he remarks in a footnote that his ideal America has been preserved better in Canada than in the United States. The truth of this statement is not my concern, but some features of my anthology seem to reflect similar attitudes.

In the United States, with its more intensively indoctrinated educational system, there has been much rugged prophecy in praise of the common man, a tradition that runs from Whitman through Sandburg and peters out in the lugubrious inspiration-alism of the Norman Corwin school. Its chief characteristics are the praise of the uncritical life and a manly contempt of prosody. One might call it the Whitmanic-depressive tradition, in view of the fact that it contains Robinson Jeffers. It seems to me signifi-cant that this tradition has had so little influence in Canada. I find in my anthology a much higher proportion of humor than I expected when I began: a humor of a quiet, reflective, observant type, usually in fairly strict meter, and clearly coming from a country with a ringside seat on the revolutionary sidelines.

Preface to an Uncollected Anthology

A song from a poem by Alexander McLachlan called, like
O'Grady's *The Emigrant*, will illustrate what I mean:

> I love my own country and race,
> Nor lightly I fled from them both,
> Yet who would remain in a place
> Where there's too many spoons for the broth.
>
> The squire's preserving his game.
> He says that God gave it to him,
> And he'll banish the poor without shame,
> For touching a feather or limb. . . .
>
> The Bishop he preaches and prays,
> And talks of a heavenly birth,
> But somehow, for all that he says,
> He grabs a good share of the earth.

In this poem there is nothing of the typically American identification of freedom with national independence: the poet is still
preoccupied with the old land and thinks of himself as still within
its tradition. There is even less of the American sense of economic
competition as the antidote to social inequality. The spirit in
McLachlan's poem is that of a tough British radicalism, the radicalism of the Glasgow dock worker or the Lancashire coal
miner, the background of the Tom Paine who has never quite
fitted the American way of life.

We may find something similar in a totally different context:
an episode in the *Malcolm's Katie* of that very shrewd woman
Isabella Crawford. The hero is engaged in cutting down a tree
and singing the praises of the ax as the agent of progress. He is
interrupted by the villian, who is something of a Spenglerian
and who speaks of the eventual downfall of all cycles of civilization. The hero turns indignantly to refute this unhealthy
pessimism, whereupon the tree, which he has forgotten about,
falls over and flattens him. The irony of the scene is all the more
striking for being somewhat out of key with the general romantic tone, as of course the hero gets up again, and his simple-minded
view of life eventually baffles the villain and annexes the heroine.
If we are to read Canadian poetry sympathetically we must often
keep an eye out for such disturbers of poetic convention.

It is not surprising to find a good deal of satiric light verse in
this imaginative resistance to industrial expansion and the gum-
chewing way of life. Frank Scott we have mentioned: his

Canadian Social Register is a ferocious paraphrase of an advertising prospectus, and his *Social Notes* are also something un-American, social poems with an unmistakably socialist moral. The observations of Toronto by Raymond Souster and of Montreal by Louis Dudek, Miriam Waddington, and Irving Layton have much to the same effect: of golfers Layton remarks "that no theory of pessimism is complete/Which altogether ignores them." But of course it is easy for the same satiric tone to turn bitter and nightmarish. Lampman's terrible poem, *The City of the End of Things*, is not only social but psychological, and warns of the dangers not simply of exploiting labor but of washing our own brains. There are other sinister visions in A. J. M. Smith's *The Bridegroom*, in Dudek's *East of the City*, in Dorothy Livesay's *Day and Night*, in P. K. Page's *The Stenographers*, and elsewhere. Canadian poems of depression and drought, like Dorothy Livesay's *Outrider* or Anne Marriott's *The Wind Our Enemy*, often have in them the protest of a food-producing community cheated out of its labor not simply by hail and grasshoppers but by some mysterious financial finagling at the other end of the country, reminding us of the man in Balzac's parable who could make his fortune by killing somebody in China. The same feeling comes out in a poignant folk song that could have come from only one part of the world, southeastern Newfoundland:

> "Oh, mother dear, I wants a sack
> With beads and buttons down the back. . . .
> Me boot is broke, me frock is tore,
> But Georgie Snooks I do adore. . . .
> Oh, fish is low and flour is high,
> So Georgie Snooks he can't have I."

There are of course more positive aspects of industrial expansion. In Canada the enormous difficulties and the central importance of communication and transport, the tremendous energy that developed the fur trade routes, the empire of the St. Lawrence, the transcontinental railways, and the northwest police patrols have given it the dominating role in the Canadian imagination. E. J. Pratt is the poet who has best grasped this fact, and his *Towards the Last Spike* expresses the central comic theme of Canadian life, using the term "comic" in its literary sense as concerned with the successful accomplishing of a human act.

The imagery of technology and primary communication is usually either avoided by poets or employed out of a sense of duty: its easy and unforced appearance in Pratt is part of the reason why Pratt is one of the few good popular poets of our time. Technology appears all through his work, not only in the poems whose subjects demand it, but in other and more unexpected contexts. Thus in *Come Away, Death*:

> We heard the tick-tock on the shelf,
> And the leak of valves in our hearts.

In *The Prize Cat*, where a cat pounces on a bird and reminds the poet of the deliberately summoned-up brutality of the Fascist conquest of Ethiopia, the two themes are brought together by the inspired flash of a technical word:

> Behind the leap so furtive-wild
> Was such ignition in the gleam
> I thought an Abyssinian child
> Had cried out in the whitethroat's scream.

As a student of psychology, before he wrote poetry at all, he was preoccupied with the problems of sensory response to signals, and the interest still lingers in the wireless messages of *The Titanic*, the radar and asdic of *Behind the Log*, and the amiable joggle of *No. 6000*, one of the liveliest of all railways poems:

> A lantern flashed out a command,
> A bell was ringing as a hand
> Clutched at a throttle, and the bull,
> At once obedient to the pull,
> Began with bellowing throat to lead
> By slow accelerating speed
> Six thousand tons of caravan
> Out to the spaces—there to toss
> The blizzard from his path across
> The prairies of Saskatchewan.

In *Behind the Log*, Canadians undertake a mission of war in much the spirit of an exploration: there is a long journey full of perils, many members of the expedition drop off, and those that reach the goal feel nothing but a numb relief. Nothing could be less like the charge of the Light Brigade. Yet perhaps in this poem we may find a clue to the fact that Canada, a country that has never found much virtue in war and has certainly never started one, has in its military history a long list of ferocious conflicts against desperate odds. The Canadian poem best known outside Canada, MacCrae's *In Flanders Fields*, breathes a spirit like that of the Viking warrior whose head continued to gnaw the dust after it had been cut from his body; and it comes from the country of the Long Sault, Chrysler's Farm, St. Julien, and Dieppe. Douglas LePan's *The Net and the Sword*, the title poem of a book dealing with the Italian campaign of the Second World War, mentions something similar:

> In this sandy arena, littered
> And looped with telephone wires, tank-traps, mine-fields,
> Twined about the embittered
> Debris of history, the people whom he shields
> Would quail before a stranger if they could see
> His smooth as silk ferocity.

LePan finds the source of the ferocity in the simplicity of the Canadian soldier's vision: "Skating at Scarborough, summers at the Island," but perhaps it is also a by-product of engineering exuberance. We notice that the looped litter of telephone wires and the like belongs here to Europe, not to Canada, and the same kind of energy is employed to deal with it.

The tragic themes of Canadian poetry have much the same origin as the comic ones. The cold winter may suggest tragedy, but it may equally well suggest other moods, and does so in Lampman's sonnet *Winter Evening*, in Patrick Anderson's *Song of Intense Cold*, in Roberts's *The Brook in February*, in Klein's *Winter Night: Mount Royal*, and elsewhere. Other seasons too have their sinister aspects: none of Lampman's landscape poems is finer than his wonderful Hallowe'en vision of *In November*, where a harmless pasture full of dead mullein stalks rises and seizes the poet with the spirit of an eerie witches' sabbath:

> And I, too, standing idly there,
> With muffled hands in the chill air
> Felt the warm glow about my feet,
> And shuddering betwixt cold and heat,
> Drew my thoughts closer, like a cloak,
> While something in my blood awoke,
> A nameless and unnatural cheer,
> A pleasure secret and austere.

Still the winter, with its long shadows and its abstract black and white pattern, does reinforce themes of desolation and loneliness, and, more particularly, of the indifference of nature to human values, which I should say was the central Canadian tragic theme. The first poet who really came to grips with this theme was, as we should expect, Charles Heavysege. Heavysege's first two long poems, *Saul* and *Count Filippo*, are Victorian dinosaurs in the usual idiom: *Count Filippo*, in particular, like the Albert Memorial achieves a curious perverted beauty by the integrity of its ugliness. His third poem, *Jephthah's Daughter*, seems to me to reflects more directly the influence of his Canadian environment.

He tells us in the introduction that he decided on Jephthah's daughter rather than Iphigeneia because Iphigeneia was, as Samuel Johnson said of the victum of a public hanging, sustained by her audience; the Biblical theme had a solitary bleakness about it that was nearer to what he wanted. During the action Jephthah goes out in the darkness to pray for release from his vow, asking for some sign of that release. He listens a moment and then hears:

> The hill wolf howling on the neighbouring height,
> And bittern booming in the pool below.

He gets of course no other answer, and it is clear that what Jephthah is really sacrificing his daughter to is nature, nature as a mystery of mindless power, with endless resources for killing man but with nothing to respond to his moral or intellectual feelings. The evolutionary pessimism of the nineteenth century awoke an unusual number of echoes in Canada, many of them of course incidental. In a well-known passage from Charles Mair's *Tecumseh*, Lefroy is describing the West to Brock, and Brock comments: "What charming solitudes! And life was there!" and Lefroy answers: "Yes, life was there! inexplicable life,/Still wasted by inexorable death"; and the somber Tennysonian vision of nature red in tooth and claw blots out the sentimental Rousseauist fantasy of the charming solitudes.

In the next generation the tragic theme has all the more eloquence for being somewhat unwanted, interfering with the resolutely cheerful praise of the newborn giant of the north. Roberts, Wilfred Campbell, Wilson Macdonald, and Bliss Carman are all romantics whose ordinary tone is nostalgic, but who seem most deeply convincing when they are darkest in tone, most preoccupied with pain, loss, loneliness, or waste. We notice this in the poems which would go immediately into anyone's anthology, such as Campbell's *The Winter Lakes*, Wilson Macdonald's *Exit*, Carman's *Low Tide on Grand Pré*. It is even more striking when Carman or Roberts writes a long metrical gabble that occasionally drops into poetry, like Silas Wegg, as it is almost invariably this mood that it drops into. Thus in Roberts's *The Great and the Little Weavers:*

> The cloud-rose dies into shadow,
> The earth-rose dies into dust.

The "great gray shape with the paleolithic face" of Pratt's *Titanic* and the glacier of Birney's *David* are in much the same tradition as the gloomy and unresponsive nature of *Jephthah's Daughter*. In fact the tragic features in Pratt mainly derive from his more complex view of the situation of Heavysege's poem. Man is also a child of nature, in whom the mindlessness of the animal has developed into cruelty and malice. He sees two men glare in hatred at one another on the street, and his mind goes

> Away back before the emergence of fur or feather, back to the unvocal sea and down deep where the darkness spills its wash on the threshold of light, where the lids never close upon the eyes, where the inhabitants slay in silence and are as silently slain.

From the very beginning, in *Newfoundland Verse*, Pratt was fascinated by the relentless pounding of waves on the rocks, a movement which strangely seems to combine a purpose with a lack of it. This rhythm recurs several times in Pratt's work: in the charge of the swordfish in *The Witches' Brew;* in the "queries rained upon the iron plate" of *The Iron Door;* in the torpedo launched from *The Submarine;* in the sinking of the *Titanic* itself, this disaster being caused by a vainglorious hubris which in a sense deliberately aimed at the iceberg. In *Brébeuf* the same theme comes into focus as the half-mindless, half-demonic curiosity which drives the Iroquois on through torture after torture to find the secret of a spiritual reality that keeps eluding them.

It is Pratt who has expressed in *Towards the Last Spike* the central comic theme, and in *Brébeuf* the central tragic theme, of the Canadian imagination, and it is Pratt who combines the two in *The Truant*, which is in my anthology because it is the greatest poem in Canadian literature. In it the representative of mankind confronts a "great Panjandrum," a demon of the mathe-

matical order of nature of a type often confused with God. In
the dialectic of their conflict it becomes clear that the great
Panjandrum of nature is fundamentally death, and that the
intelligence that fights him, comprehends him, harnesses him,
and yet finally yields to his power is the ultimate principle of life,
and capable of the comedy of achievement only because capable
also of the tragedy of enduring him:

> We who have learned to clench
> Our fists and raise our lightless sockets
> To morning skies after the midnight raids,
> Yet cocked our ears to bugles on the barricades,
> And in cathedral rubble found a way to quench
> A dying thirst within a Galilean valley—
> No! by the Rood, we will not join your ballet.

We spoke at the beginning of certain principles that become
important in the study of Canadian poetry. One of these is the
fact that while literature may have 'ife, reality, experience, nature
or what you will for its content, the forms of literature cannot
exist outside literature, just as the forms of sonata and fugue
cannot exist outside music. When a poet is confronted by a new
life or environment, the new life may suggest a new content,
but obviously cannot provide him with a new form. The forms
of poetry can be derived only from other poems, the forms of
novels from other novels. The imaginative content of Canadian
poetry, which is often primitive, frequently makes extraordinary
demands on forms derived rrom romantic or later traditions.
Duncan Campbell Scott, for instance, lived in Ottawa as a civil
servant in the Department of Indian Affairs, between a modern
city and the Ungava wilderness. He has a poem on the music
of Debussy, and he has a poem on a starving squaw trying to
catch fish for her child and having nothing but her own flesh
to bait the hook with. To find anything like such incongruity
in English life we have to go clear back to Anglo-Saxon times.
If we think of an Old English poet, with his head full of ancient
battles and myths of dragon-fights, in the position of having to
write for the sophisticated audience of Rome and Byzantium,
we shall have some parallel to the technical problems faced by
a Lampman or a Scott who had only the elaborate conventions of
Tennysonian romanticism to contain his imaginative experience.
Pratt's attempt to introduce the imagery of dragon-killing into a

poem about the Canadian Pacific Railway is another good example; and I have much sympathy for the student who informed me in the examinations last May that Pratt had written a poem called Beowulf and his Brothers.

I think it is partly an obscure feeling for more primitive forms that accounts for the large number of narratives in Canadian poetry. I am aware, of course, that the narrative was a favorite romantic form, but the themes of Canadian narrative, the sacrifice of Jephthah's daughter, the catching of Isabella Crawford's Max in a log jam, Dominique de Gourges's quest for vengeance in D. C. Scott, the death of Birney's David on the glacier, have a primeval grimness about them that is not romantic or even modern fashion. Pratt has also turned to older and more primitive types of narrative: Chaucerian beast-fable in the *Pliocene Armageddon* and *The Fable of the Goats*, saint's legend in *Brébeuf*, heroic rescue in *The Roosevelt and the Antinoe*.

It is more common for a Canadian poet to solve his problem of form by some kind of erudite parody, using that term as many critics now do, to mean adaptation in general rather than simply a lampoon, although adaptation usually has humorous overtones. In Charles Mair's *Winter* some wisps of Shakespearean song are delicately echoed in a new context, and Drummond's best poem, *The Wreck of the Julie Plante*, is an admirable parody of the ballad, with its tough oblique narration, its moralizing conclusion, and its use of what is called incremental repetition:

> For de win' she blow lak' hurricane,
> Bimeby she blow some more.

According to his own account, Pratt, after his college studies in theology, psychology, literature, and the natural sciences, put everything he knew into his first major poetic effort, an epic named *Clay*, which he promptly burnt. Soon afterward all this erudition went into reverse and came out as the fantasy of *The Witches' Brew*, in which parody has a central place. Since then, we have parody in Anne Wilkinson and Wilfred Watson, who use nursery rhymes and ballads as a basis; Birney's *Trial of a City* is among other things a fine collection of parodied styles; and Klein's devotion to one of the world's greatest parodists, James Joyce, has produced his brilliant bilingual panegyric on Montreal:

> Grand port of navigations, multiple
> The lexicons uncargo'd at your quays,
> Sonnant though strange to me; but chiefest, I,
> Auditor of your music, cherish the
> Joined double-melodied vocabulaire
> Where English vocable and roll Ecossic,
> Mollified by the parle of French
> Bilinguefact your air!

Much of Canada's best poetry is now written by professors or others in close contact with universities. There are disadvantages in this, but one of the advantages is the diversifying of the literary tradition by a number of scholarly interests. Earle Birney's *Anglo-Saxon Street* reminds us that its author is a professor of Anglo-Saxon. Louis Mackay, professor of Classics, confronts an unmistakably Canadian landscape with a myth of Eros derived from Catullus:

> The hard rock was his mother; he retains
> Only her kind, nor answers any sire.
> His hand is the black basalt, and his veins
> Are rocky veins, ablaze with gold and fire.

Robert Finch, professor of French, carries on the tradition of Mallarmé and other *symbolistes;* one of his most successful poems, *The Peacock and the Nightingale*, goes back to the older tradition of the medieval *débat.* Klein, of course, has brought echoes from the Talmud, the Old Testament, and the whole range of Jewish thought and history; and the erudition necessary to read Roy Daniells and Alfred Bailey with full appreciation is little short of formidable. It may be said, however, that echoes and influences are not a virtue in Canadian poetry, but one of its major weaknesses. Canadian poetry may echo Hopkins or Auden today as it echoed Tom Moore a century ago, but in every age Echo is merely the discarded mistress of Narcissus. This question brings up the most hackneyed subject in Canadian literature, which I have left for that reason to the end.

Political and economic units tend to expand as history goes on; cultural units tend to remain decentralized. Culture, like wine, seems to need a specific locality, and no major poet has been inspired by an empire, Virgil being, as the *Georgics* show, an exception that proves the rule. In this age of world-states we have two extreme forms of the relationship between culture and politics. When cultural developments follow political ones, we get an anonymous international art, such as we have in many aspects of modern architecture, abstract painting, and twelve-tone music. When a cultural development acquires a political aspect, we frequently get that curious modern phenomenon of the political language, where a minor language normally headed for extinction is deliberately revived for political purposes. Examples are Irish, Norwegian, Hebrew, and Afrikaans, and there are parallel tendencies elsewhere. I understand that there is a school of Australian poets dedicated to putting as many aboriginal words into their poems as possible. As the emotional attachments to political languages are very violent, I shall say here only that this problem has affected the French but not the English part of Canadian culture. As we all know, however, English Canada has escaped the political language only to become involved in a unique problem of self-identification, vis-à-vis the British and American poets writing in the same tongue. Hence in every generation there has been the feeling that whether poetry itself needs any defense or manifesto, Canadian poetry certainly does.

The main result of this has been that Canadian poets have been urged in every generation to search for appropriate themes, in other words to look for content. The themes have been characterized as national, international, traditional, experimental, iconic, iconoclastic: in short, as whatever the propounder of them would like to write if he were a poet, or to read if he were a critic. But the poet's quest is for form, not content. The poet who tries to make content the informing principle of his poetry can write only versified rhetoric, and versified rhetoric has a moral but not an imaginative significance: its place is on the social periphery of poetry, not in its articulate center. The rhetorician, Quintilian tells us, ought to be a learned and good man, but the critic is concerned only with poets.

By form I do not of course mean external form, such as the use of a standard meter or convention. A sonnet has form only if it really is fourteen lines long: a ten-line sonnet padded out to fourteen is still a part of chaos, waiting for the creative word. I mean by form the shaping principle of the individual poem, which is derived from the shaping principles of poetry itself.

Preface to an Uncollected Anthology

Of these latter the most important is metaphor, and metaphor, in its radical form, is a statement of identity: this is that, A is B. Metaphor is at its purest and most primitive in myth, where we have immediate and total identifications. Primitive poetry, being mythical, tends to be erudite and allusive, and to the extent that modern poetry takes on the same qualities it becomes primitive too. Here is a poem by Lampman, written in 1894:

> So it is with us all; we have our friends
>   Who keep the outer chambers, and guard well
> Our common path; but there their service ends,
>   For far within us lies an iron cell
> Soundless and secret, where we laugh or moan
>   Beyond all succour, terribly alone.

And here is a poem by E. W. Mandel, published in 1954:

> It has been hours in these rooms,
> the opening to which, door or sash,
> I have lost. I have gone from room to room
> asking the janitors who were sweeping up
> the brains that lay on the floors,
> the bones shining in the wastebaskets,
> and once I asked a suit of clothes
> that collapsed at my breath and bundled
> and crawled on the floor like a coward.
> Finally, after several stories,
> in the staired and eyed hall,
> I came upon a man with the face of a bull.

Lampman's poem is certainly simpler, closer to prose and to the direct statement of emotion. All these are characteristics of a highly developed and sophisticated literary tradition. If we ask which is the more primitive, the answer is certainly the second poem, as we can see by turning to the opening pages of the anthology to see what primitive poetry is really like. Here is a Haida song translated by Hermia Fraser:

> I cannot stay, I cannot stay!
> I must take my canoe and fight the waves,
> For the Wanderer spirit is seeking me.
>
> The beating of great, black wings on the sun,
> The Raven has stolen the ball of the sun,
> From the Kingdom of Light he has stolen the sun. . . .

> The Slave Wife born from the first clam shell
> Is in love with the boy who was stolen away,
> The lovers have taken the Raven's fire.

When we look for the qualities in Canadian poetry that illustrate the poet's response to the specific environment that we call approximately Canada, we are really looking for the mythopoeic qualities in that poetry. This is easiest to see, of course, when the poetry is mythical in content as well as form. In the long mythopoeic passage from Isabella Crawford's *Malcolm's Katie*, beginning "The South Wind laid his moccasins aside," we see how the poet is, first, taming the landcsape imaginatively, as settlement tames it physically, by animating the lifeless scene with humanized figures, and, second, integrating the literary tradition of the country by deliberately re-establishing the broken cultural link with Indian civilization:

>   for a man
> To stand amid the cloudy roll and moil,
> The phantom waters breaking overhead,
> Shades of vex'd billows bursting on his breast,
> Torn caves of mist wall'd with a sudden gold,
> Reseal'd as swift as seen—broad, shaggy fronts,
> Fire-ey'd and tossing on impatient horns
> The wave impalpable—was but to think
> A dream of phantoms held him as he stood.

And in the mythical figures of Pratt, the snorting iron horses of the railways, the lumbering dinosaurs of *The Great Feud*, the dragon of *Towards the Last Spike*, and above all Tom the Cat from Zanzibar, the Canadian cousin of Roy Campbell's flaming terrapin, we clearly have other denizens of the monstrous zoo that produced Paul Bunyan's ox Babe, Paul Bunyan himself being perhaps a descendant of the giants who roamed the French countryside and were recorded by the great comtemporary of Jacques Cartier, Rabelais.

We are concerned here, however, not so much with myth-opoeic poetry as with myth as a shaping principle of poetry. Every good lyrical poet has a certain structure of imagery as typical of him as his handwriting, held together by certain recurring metaphors, and sooner or later he will produce one or more poems that seem to be at the center of that structure. These poems are in the formal sense his mythical poems, and they are for the critic the imaginative keys to his work. The poet himself often recognizes such a poem by making it the title poem of a collection. They are not necessarily his best poems, but they often are, and in a Canadian poet they display those distinctive themes we have been looking for which reveal his reaction to his natural and social environment. Nobody but a genuine poet ever produces such a poem, and they cannot be faked or imitated or voluntarily constructed. My anthology is largely held together by such poems: they start approximately with D. C. Scott's *Piper of Arll,* and continue in increasing numbers to our own day. I note among others Leo Kennedy's *Words for a Resurrection,* Margaret Avison's *Neverness,* Irving Layton's *Cold Green Element,* Douglas LePan's *Idyll,* Wilfred Watson's *Canticle of Darkness,* P. K. Page's *Metal and the Flower,* and similar poems forming among a younger group that includes James Reaney, Jay Macpherson, and Daryl Hine. Such poems enrich not only our poetic experience but our cultural knowledge as well, and as time goes on they become increasingly the only form of knowledge that does not date and continues to hold its interest for future generations.

II

MILTON WILSON

Recent Canadian Verse

Some critic of critics ought to write an essay on "The Geographical Fallacy." When Sir Donald Tovey discovered from an atlas that Finland was "mainly flat and water-logged with lakes," he decided not to say of the music of Sibelius that "his forms are hewn out of the rocks of his native and Nordic mountains." Very few critics would give up so easily. More certain of his facts, although no doubt equally questionable in his assumptions, Ralph Gustafson has recently called the conditions of Canadian climate and terrain "good for spare lyricism and metaphysical wit"—qualities suspiciously like those of his own best poetry. Perhaps we are wise to suspect such analogies, geographical or otherwise. If the supreme fiction of Canadian history is Confederation, we need not draw any conclusions about the mode of organization of our large-scale poems; if the most conventional subjects of controversy in our newspapers are the national anthem, the Canadian flag and the designs on our postage stamps, this alone may not convince us that Canadian poetry will be self-conscious and exploratory in its symbolism; just because our native poets speak uncertain English in an uncertainly bilingual country, they aren't necessarily driven to inventing their own eclectic idiom in an unstable world of words. But we can be too suspicious of the many plausible determinisms which we inherit from the eighteenth century. The problems of organization, symbolism and diction are real and distinctive in English-Canadian poetry, attribute them to whatever cause you will.

According to James Reaney, "the moment you start thinking about the history of the land's shape you start to think of a poem." His own recent poetry is certainly shaped by history and loaded with fossils. From a higher (and less geological) level of abstrac-

Reprinted from *Queen's Quarterly* 66 (Summer 1959):268–74, by permission of the author.

tion, we can imagine Canada spread out before us in space and time, like the very model of a major poem. In the background lie

> those northern boundaries
> Where in the winter the white pines could brush
> The Pleiades, and at the equinoxes
> Under the gold and green of the Auroras
> Wild geese drove wedges through the zodiac.

Underground lie lost, unassimilated, alien but native cultures, nightmares fading into nuisances. In the middle-ground, out of a funnel of water, shoot tentative lines of cross-country movement; scattered pockets of society emerge *en route* and find unexpected relationships; communications break and join and break again. But the longer the lines, the less linear they become. The panorama starts to close in, the sea approaches as it recedes, the background becomes the foreground. It's all one.

Models aside, any reader of recent English-Canadian poetry is likely to be struck by the way the short poems congregate and the long ones split up. But if same reader also remembers such earlier landmarks as *Malcolm's Katie, Ave, Sappho, The Piper of Arll* and some of the sonnet sequences, he may suspect that the discontinuous long poem, the cyclical short poem and the cycle of lyrics have always been the most fruitful cluster of genres in our poetic history, although (outside of Pratt) the tradition never really found its second wind until Klein and Birney. Northrop Frye, who has written more "portraits of the Canadian poem as landscape" than anybody else, has remarked of Pratt's last long poem: "I have the notion that the technical problems involved in *Towards the Last Spike* are going to be central problems in the poetry of the future." But such problems are not restricted to ostensibly narrative poems on specifically Canadian subjects. We can see them not only in Earle Birney's *Trial of a City* or *North Star West*, Philip Child's *The Victorian House* and James Reaney's *A Suit of Nettles*, but also in E. W. Mandel's *Minotaur Poems*, Jay Macpherson's *The Boatman*, Margaret Avison's *The Agnes Cleves Papers*, Daryl Hine's *The Carnal and the Crane* and even in Louis Dudek's *Europe* or *En México*—to name some obvious examples from the past decade. I can hardly claim that such formal problems are new; just that they are currently central to Canadian and not to British or even American poetry. Perhaps we ought to take more seriously the contention that E. J. Pratt is not merely our greatest but also our most fundamental poet. He writes narratives no doubt, but discontinuous narratives which are always turning, on the one side, into documents, letters and jokes, and on the other, into pure lyrics. When the latter break off completely, we get such epic and historical lyrics as *Myth and Fact*, *Cycles*, *Silences* and *From Stone to Steel*. The point at which Pratt's genres meet is worth calling the center of Canadian poetry. Dead center may not be a very comfortable or lively place to live in, but if James Reaney decides to write an epic after his pastorals, I don't see any other place for him to go.

By beginning with questions of Canadian structure rather than texture, I am going against the natural bias of our culture. We expect the products of our factories to be designed abroad, even if the materials are dug up locally and our own workmen assemble the parts. In practice, this often means that the measure of Canadianism in poetry is the image: tamaracks and totem-poles instead of dryads and nightingales. It might be more fruitful to concentrate less on the merely different images than on the transplanted and transformed ones: romantic blue flowers turning into local corn-flowers, as in a famous sonnet by Roberts. When a Canadian poet writes a melodrama, an idyll, a birthday ode, an elegy, what happens to the traditional settings and images? If they survive what adjustment (if any) has preserved them? If they change, what has changed into what?

By appropriate comparisons we may even observe Canadian poets in the very act of transformation and discovery. Take, for example, Roberts's best-known poem, *The Tantramar Revisited*, in which he tries to make the wind-swept, sun-drenched, net-laden shore (half-present and half-past) a symbol of permanence in the midst of flux. The obvious comparison is with Wordsworth's *Tintern Abbey*. But for Wordsworth the abbey on the Wye becomes a stable, recurrent image built into the poet's identity by both memory and repetition. Roberts, on the contrary, finds his image slipping out of his grasp and joining the flux. Only if it stays on the horizon can it retain the illusion of permanence. Roberts, like some of his successors, maintained his Canadianism by emigrating and taking the long view. Part of the trouble in *The Tantramar Revisited* may even lie in the image itself, which stretches back beyond New Brunswick into the

Mediterranean world of Roberts's classical studies. In *Ave* Roberts tries to use the drowned Shelley as an intermediary between shore and shore.

But the classical heritage of our early scholar-poets is an unexplored field and resists dogmatism. A more obvious and more insistent source of images waiting to be transformed is the Bible. Not the least unlikely thing about the literature of the Jews is the way its beasts, birds and plants, as well as its natural conditions, have made their way north and west, surviving in new guises, acquiring new relations, and acting as though there were no such thing as natural selection in iconography. The process is already well under way in the Bible itself, in both the Old Testament and the New. Understandably enough, the farther north and west they go, the stronger the challenge to survival. Even Milton had some doubts about telling the story of *Paradise Lost* in a cold climate. From a Canadian point of vantage, we can watch crocodiles turning into dragons, whales and sea serpents, and ending up as the Rockies in *Towards the Last Spike*. We can watch the flood becoming a glacier in Raymond's spring song from *A Suit of Nettles*. "It's possible to read the Bible with North American eyes," James Reaney has remarked, but he himself likes to complicate the matter by crossing it with Indian legends. We can watch the Biblical green pastures in Miriam Waddington's green world, or the Song of Solomon in her Montreal; or, moving farther west and north, watch the old problem of northern canticles or cold pastorals in the recent poetry of E. W. Mandel, although the pipe-line is no substitute for the olive, and Northern Alberta may be an uncooperative bride.

In this Biblical movement from south to north an appropriate guardian angel would be the William Blake,[1] who once thought he saw "a Serpent in Canada who courts me to his love." For some Canadian poets the snows of Urizen may provide an appropriate station on the way from the deserts of Isaiah or Ezekiel; for others Blake may seem an inevitable guide for peopling what Douglas LePan has called "a country without a mythology"; still others may feel a special affinity between their Canadian poetic world and the period of Ossian, Chatterton, Smart, Blake

[1] The emphasis on Blake arises from the fact that a surprising number of poems in the collection to which this article serves as an introduction happen to refer to him (author's note, 1969).

and Fuseli; some, of course, may prefer more recent poets (Yeats, Thomas, Stevens) as convenient intermediaries. But it is important to distinguish such conscious and thoroughgoing mythologists as James Reaney, Jay Macpherson, Wilfred Watson and Anne Wilkinson from those whose myth-making seems less a matter of direct endeavor than a part of their everyday cultural inheritance, some of it being merely a by-product of very different poetic concerns. As we start to move from the first group to the second, we meet Douglas LePan, then E. W. Mandel, then Miriam Waddington; finally, Leonard Cohen and Irving Layton. For Irving Layton William Blake isn't a guide to the underworld but just one of the friends he has picked up on the way, like Lawrence, Nietzsche and many others. The natural temptation is to call my two groups "School of Pratt" and "School of Klein" (with "School of Frye," a possible alternative to the first). But maybe a more obvious, three-part division is better: from its Classical and Christian strands Canadian poetry gets most of its brilliance and organization; from the Hebraic strand most of its vitality.

Irving Layton is the owner of the largest and least exotic zoo in Canadian poetry. The domestic animals outnumber the wild beasts; the insects overshadow the birds; the fish are surpassed by the frogs. These creatures are always getting killed, or, rather, sacrificed. A crushed fly is "a smudge of blood smoking/On my fingers"; a bull-calf about to be slaughtered makes the poet think of Richard the Second. The whole natural world (including the poet himself) is one gigantic scapegoat. The spring leaves which uncurl at the end of that gay and grim Nativity Ode *The Birth of Tragedy*, curl again in *Chokecherries*. "Still, the leaves' sacrifice/is acrid on the tongue." Death is the tragic fact, murder the one perverse act, envy the one deadly sin. Layton's Adam is Cain. But if death is a curse it is also a consolation, as the grass goes to the annual bonfire; and what if Cain is the natural poet and Abel his unnatural enemy, beloved of the gods that be? Layton's poetry exemplifies this unresolved contradiction, this mixture of cruelty and compassion at the heart of things. His poet-heroes find joy in the sacrificial fire of nature but they do not wish to transcend it, even when he calls them resurrected Christs. Leonard Cohen also specializes in sacrifices, but his richly ornamented ritualistic love poems are equally memorable. If Layton's affinities are with late Klein, Cohen's are with early. But what gives his poetry its unique and exciting flavor is the way he merges the Biblical with the medieval, the canticle with the ballad or chanson, like a French *trouvère* at the court of Solomon. Maybe it could only ' happen in Montreal.

This last fancy is the point where many of our cultural historians would like to begin. Regional criticism would observe in the poetry of John Glassco a kind of lyrical cross between the English nineteenth-century tradition of realistic pastoral and the French provincial tradition (most familiar in the novel). If to this evidence we add the fact that Glassco is one of the most accomplished translators of French-Canadian poetry, it is something of an anticlimax to point out that he lives in the Eastern Townships of rural Quebec. But a regional method of criticism has its obvious limitations. Perhaps the most promising of our younger regional poets is Alden A. Nowlan, born in Nova Scotia and now living in New Brunswick. His best poetry is vigorous, but also remarkably disquieting. In his scenes and portraits we watch the thin, strenuous line of pastoral routine and sanity constantly being threatened by fear, hysteria and egotism. Obviously even a Maritime critic is going to be cautious about drawing regional conclusions here. Moreover, the nomadic culture of contemporary North America makes the wandering poet the norm, and in as varied a country as Canada he is always having to set his digestion on fresh images: from dawn on *Anglo-Saxon Street* to *Dusk on English Bay*, from the ambiguous Avon flowing through Stratford, Ontario, to an equally ambiguous streetcar running down Main Street in Winnipeg, from "the blue men of Saskatchewan" to "the blue women of Quebec" and more than back again, from Newfoundland to the Last Spike. Indeed the poet who moves west (or returns west) already has a niche in our gallery of poet-archetypes right opposite the poet who can never get out of Montreal.

The diction of English-Canadian poetry has the same scope and stretch as its imagery but few of the important problems are simply a matter of regional dialect. I remember arguing on one occasion that Jay Macpherson's mixed idiom was Canadian in the sense that the mixed, unstable diction of Burns, Whitman and Joyce was Scotch, American or Irish; as if it were her melting-pot rhetoric, her juxtaposition of disparate idioms and her use of puns as cement that identify her as a colonial poet. Perhaps a better parallel would be Wordsworth, struggling to move from Northern dialect to *lingua communis,* or even T. S. Eliot, struggling to "purify the language of the tribe" three thousand miles from Missouri. However that may be, a few Canadian Jonsons have already suggested that in at least one section of *The Boatman* Miss Macpherson "writ no language." They could say the same of James Reaney's neo-Spenserian set of eclogues, *A Suit of Nettles,* and with more obvious relevance. Reaney puts in perspective the problems of a Canadian poetic idiom by forcing the reader to recall Spenser's similar yet very different ones. His recreated idiom, like Spenser's, must be synthetic; but the perspective has expanded. He can mix not merely the archaic with the up-to-date, but the cleft palate of the colony with the whole stretch of the mother tongue. Maybe it could only have begun in Stratford, Ontario. However, our idiomatic self-consciousness has other guises. Ralph Gustafson's search for a style has led him into many of the back-waters of contemporary taste; to read his work chronologically from beginning to end would be quite an historical experience; but his recent free-wheeling, disjunctive, epigrammatic verse (the new Senecanism) would certainly make the journey worthwhile. In the recent poems of A. W. Purdy, the idiomatic center only just holds, and we expect an explosion of words any minute. Purdy's recurrent theme has been the relation between identity and history, or (in his love poems) between the held image and the moving object, but the theme keeps turning into the problem of language.

In all these poets (and the same might be said of that very striking poet, Phyllis Gotlieb) the handling of diction is something of a *tour-de-force;* even when it comes off, the reader has a sense of strain. No such strain is apparent in the *tours-de-force* of Raymond Souster and George Johnston. Souster's language has immediate conviction and authenticity; the reader can imagine a voice speaking and shifting its idiom, but never losing its chosen tone or hitting a false note. His best poems have the fresh and varied inflections of a perfectly improvised solo: they would go well on a saxophone. The instrument for playing George Johnston's poems would have to be invented for the purpose, and it could have no other use. When he makes a misstep, he does it just right, like a clown on a tight-rope. Before such a combination of ease and awkwardness idiomatic difficulties exist only as advantages. The wings of the dilemma are there to fly on.

Merely to observe how certain problems of diction, imagery and form recur in recent Canadian poetry is a more modest and defensible task than to define our national identity or (even worse) to chart an English-Canadian poetic tradition. You can hardly expect any real continuity from a poetic history which consists of one half-baked phoenix after another. Nor do the materials available to our sensibility suggest the leisurely conception of tradition as organic growth. In our world the skyscraper and the totem-pole, the ghost town and the museum are brothers under the skin; one step takes us from the forest primeval to reforestation. If we use the dubious word tradition at all, it will have to be redefined. Among our older living poets, Pratt and Klein are the only ones with any appreciable influence on their young successors. No dead Canadian poet has any influence at all. James Reaney likes to recall the "dear bad Poets/ Who wrote/Early in Canada/And never were of note," but any line of influence will go from him to them. For Reaney the peculiar opportunity of the modern Canadian poet is that he can make up for the failures of his predecessors, he can rewrite and complete the fragmentary gestures of our literary history, he can redeem our wasted poetic time. But, as Raymond Souster puts it, in *The Need for Roots,*

> If all of us
> Who need roots
> Start digging
> At the same time
> There just aren't
> Going to be enough spades
> To go around.

III

PAUL WEST

Ethos and Epic: Aspects of Contemporary Canadian Poetry

An outsider who has read no Canadian poets might justifiably expect them to supply something rather American: the frontier rather than the sophisticated, the blunt rather than the subtle, the heroic rather than the maisonette, the didactic rather than the oblique. He might add something about the unlikeliness, for a long time, of estheticism and preciosity; and there he stops. Not all that is distinctly Canadian bears upon poetry written by Canadians. Much that is American does. The outsider deserves some sympathy, as well as license to get as personal as he likes. For (and here I must judge by my own experience) there are many subtle differences from the European and American traditions. With those I cannot be concerned here. But I do want to examine three aspects which seem reasonably obvious: the first two go together—the sharply visual quality of much Canadian poetry, and the unpoeticised bluntness of tone; the third is a potentiality which I hope will come to something like an epic of heterogeneous daily life.

Canadian poets writing now seem to have at their disposal most of the European modes. The Parnassian keeps pace with the Whitmanish when one might have expected the latter to dominate the scene with barbaric yawp, rambling exposition and asymmetrical shape. There is a strong tradition of it in the United States, sustained in varying ways by William Carlos Williams, Robinson Jeffers, E. E. Cummings, and such poems as Allan Ginsberg's *Howl*. It is the sort of thing produced when the picaresque sensibility tries to write poems; it is far from the lapidary, but it does not seem to predominate in Canada any

Reprinted from *Canadian Literature* 4 (Spring 1960):7–17, by permission of the author.

more than it does in America. At one extreme we have something like Louis Dudek's *Europe*; at the other, the Parnassian (Robert Graves-like) poems of Jay Macpherson. It would be idle to propose a dichotomy: obviously, at times, the two modes mingle; obviously most poets attempt both modes of expression, although they usually manage one end of the formal spectrum better than the other—Dudek and Raymond Souster the Whitmanish, Miss Macpherson and R. A. D. Ford the Parnassian.

But having proposed the extremes as points of reference at least, let me allude to them at once by saying that I think the Whitmanish mode more suited to what I find the essentially Canadian manner of utterance. There is a brusqueness, a visual punchiness about this utterance which might seem to evoke, say, Carl Sandburg or Carlos Williams, but which is in fact less literary and less overlaid with allusions. Take Irving Layton's magnificent poem, *The Bull Calf*, for instance:

> Struck,
> the bull calf drew in his thin forelegs
> as if gathering strength for a mad rush . . .
> tottered . . . raised his darkening eyes to us,
> and I saw we were at the far end
> of his frightened look, growing smaller and smaller
> till we were only the ponderous mallet
> that flicked his bleeding ear
> and pushed him over on his side, stiffly,
> like a block of wood.

This is the mallet rather than the lyre—for good reasons: the poem has to suggest the brutality of a necessary indifference. But, just as in this instance it is particularly true, so it is true generally that the thumping, emphatic and non-iambic quality of Canadian poetry lingers in the ear and prodigiously enriches its moments of tenderness. (Norman Levine's reading of this poem on the BBC Third Programme made this even more evident: Mr. Levine's deadpan voice, which Canada made, seemed to fit the poem extremely well. An Englishman reading the same poem would sound stagey and would probably force upon the lines rhythms of the wrong kind.) The curt context has no sound of the literarized, and that explains why an etiolated and almost hackneyed word like "beautiful" is restored to an astonishing, pre-Tennysonian power:

PAUL WEST

> Settled, the bull calf lay as if asleep,
> one foreleg over the other,
> bereft of pride and so beautiful now,
> without movement, perfectly still in the cool pit,
> I turned away and wept.

In that, the poem's conclusion, "bereft" comes to us from an archaic world of "poesy"; but instead of sticking out like a sore muse, it is subsumed by the regenerated word "beautiful." Regeneration in poetry is always an art of context. That is why the sudden self-exposure of the last line escapes the trite; we can think of other lines which might have preceded it and would have degraded it into a conventional trope. For example:

> I strayed through the midst of the city
> On, through the lovely Archipelago;
> That night I felt the winter in my veins;
> Was it a year or lives ago
> I turned away and wept?

That doesn't quite make sense: the first line is Lampman, the second Charles Sangster, the third Wilfred Campbell and the fourth Bliss Carman. But the lines' connotations might evoke, say, James Thomson's *The City of Dreadful Night* or certain parts of *In Memoriam*. The traditionally poetic voice, with its usual images, terms of grief and approbation, rhymes and calls to attention, renders certain words impotent and creates a monotony of tone. It is the singular asset of the Canadian voice that it can manage potent contrasts by giving its utterances a disheveled, unsystematic look: there is little concern with attracting the reader's eye to the maintenance of form. Life and meditation are presented in a manner no more symmetrical or homogeneous than that of a newspaper page. But this manner can make the trivial arresting, make us look thoroughly at things over-familiar. Here is an example of this typically haphazard, disjointed way of writing; the excerpt is from Jean Arsenault's *Canada Canto*, published in *Delta* Number Eight:

> And poor suckers bring
> their pennies to upstairs
> office, "bring coppers on time",
> shouts Joe
> As Riel wrote to Grant, but
> that's all past & everything

                              west of Ontario went
                              Canadian, with its black oil,
                              & rushing gas
              So, it's penny interest now,
                              each copper counted,
                              added, subtracted,
                              multiplied, divided to make
              principle, all added to Joe's acct.

The Poundian gimmicks and money-mania apart, not to mention
the signs of a faltering parody, this passage does bring into relief
some of the dull data of living. An old decorum is being broken:
there is nothing that cannot turn up in such a medium. And in
this respect the poetry of indiscriminate cataloging fulfills
Santayana's demand for attention to the world about us—as well
as Berenson's fastidious plea for sheer physical impact.

    Of course, it also opens the gate to all kinds of charlatanry,
messy musing and feeble posturing. But, for all its incoherence,
it makes easier a poetry that seems to *enact* the very muddle it
describes. This is the poetic method of a booming, over-busy
world; it is omnivorous rather than exiguous, a satchel rather
than a form. It appears to be what Louis Dudek has in mind in
his *Functional Poetry: A Proposal*, which appears in the same
issue of *Delta:*

              Williams of course
              did the right thing, so far as rhythm and language
                              go
              He simply did not have a lot (enough) to say.
                              Williams is a joy
              to read—the senses live
                              in his lines—the senses
              are a good beginning
                      with which to breach the wall
                                              of prose.

Such a scattered presentation may well be an excuse for not
trying to write either prose or verse; but it may equally well
be an attempt to replace a useless dichotomy with a rich and
flexible medium. True, it has so far (in Pound himself, as well
as in its Canadian practitioners) released a torrent of self-
conscious flippancy. But perhaps this only indicates that such a
method, so close to rubbish, so apparently undisciplined, must
operate by means of irony—its principal device being that of

ironic juxtaposition in order to convey the exact impact of a kaleidoscopic world. Only time will show; and we should not expect from this method an absolute of any kind, whether of lyricism or starkness, whether of reportage or fantasy. The synoptic, which is its aim, is a genre apart. And there are not likely to be any rules.

The prerequisites for such a method are principally two: a robust, matter-of-fact tone (which I think many modern Canadian poets already have) and a complete view—of worlds pastoral, industrial, urban and commercial—which most of them seem to lack. What of the tone? It appears in the following, from Raymond Knister's *The Plowman*, as a rural factualness:

> For Danny whistling slowly
> "Down in Tennessee"
> A fat white shoat by the trough
> Lifts his snout a moment to hear,
> Among the guzzling and slavering comrades,
> Squeezing and forcing . . . .

It turns up in this: *Train Window* by Robert Finch. The ostentatiously impassive sensibility retails the prosaic:

> The truck holds eleven cakes of ice,
> each cake a different size and shape.
> Some look as though a weight had hit them.
> One, solid glass, has a core of sugar.

Finch's poem is every bit as "poetic" as the world it depicts: the point is, if you are sufficiently attentive to the world, a straight account will suffice. What is poetic is not in the technique, but in the object contemplated. Finch seeks to intensify a deeply felt perception; so does Raymond Souster's *Drunk: On Crutches*, which is boozily lyrical in its hardboiled vernacular:

> Simply being drunk makes it
> Tough enough to get around,
> But a guy hobbling on crutches—
> How does he figure it at all?

There is in the Canadian voice, in this un-English voice that I am noticing, a matter-of-factness which is vocally what imagism is visually. There is a reluctance to make the conventionally poetic sounds and lilts: this is it, says the poet, take it or don't. He isn't going to beguile us with euphony, with rhythms that guide us like banisters, with images that make the new familiar.

Here, he seems to say, is a specimen—like a chunk of newspaper fitted into a collage. And from the nature of the presented object, the "form" and the tone proceed. W. W. E. Ross's *The saws were shrieking* shows this:

> From the revolving
> of the saw
> came slices of clear wood,
> newly sawn,
> white pine and red,
> or spruce and hemlock,
> the sweet spruce,
> and the sweet hemlock.

Wallace Stevens would have turned this into a frenzied baroque on the lines of his *Bantams in Pinewoods*. But Ross's lines could have come from Carlos Williams, with his creed of "No ideas but in things." Take this:

> so much depends
> upon
> a red wheel
> barrow
> glazed with rain
> water
> beside the white
> chickens

That is Williams—the child's innocent and undifferentiating eye, one stage before the elated wonder of Cummings. What we are given, by both Ross and Williams, is an ideogram which celebrates. This is the raw material chopped up into assimilable pieces, each of which is a cause for wonder and a good reason for lingering longer than usual. It is a *sans culotte* mode, seeking to restore us to a sense of primal, unelaborated things. There is a perfectly justified (although perhaps naive) attitude which says: if you want to present unmanipulated specimens, you are more likely to get away with it if you write in the Whitmanish mode; that is, if you compile a collection rather than design a device. And, for me, what is distinctive in modern Canadian poetry is the mode in which the poets equal their French and Modern Greek counterparts, in which they do differently from the Americans (for even Carlos Williams and Pound built their ideograms into a larger fabric), and which is just not attempted in England: the mode of spiritual geography in terms of emblems. The whole process tends toward an attempt at modern epic.

This is why I find nothing specifically different about Jay Macpherson's poems, nothing specifically Canadian; she is a transatlantic Elizabeth Jennings, composing hermetic paradigms that don't really make poetry out of the modern scene. I don't think that is true of Ronald Bates, Fred Cogswell, John Glassco, George Johnston, Alden Nowlan and James Reaney. Miss Macpherson seems nearer to European sophistication and sophistry, and is therefore in greater danger of composing cerebral riddles in the manner of the English "Movement." Her little paradigms are nearer to ballad than to Whitman: she is at once more traditional and more avant-garde than her contemporaries. Their stand is quite often rawness, the unfancy, the unpoeticized. Take, for example, Fred Cogswell's poem about Lefty:

> There was Lefty and there was the hen.
> He had her hung up with a cord
> round her neck too tight for a squawk,
> and he was sawing off her legs
> with a dull jack-knife. Sawing and whistling . . .
>
> He heard me as I walked in
> and turned, standing there,
> and you could almost have heard
> the blood dripping off the end
> of the knife-blade for a minute.
> "You son of a whore", I said.
> "You son of a whore".
> And Lefty broke and cried like a girl,
> And I left.

The logical outcome of this is raw vision in raw form for subtle reasons. But mere use of the speech of everyday cannot ensure the achievement of an illustrious vernacular: only the old tricks of word-juggling can effect that. The poet is a reporter, yes; he is also a verbal artist. And where the sheer magic of the object contemplated fails to enliven the words, the result is likely to be an ordinariness that only verbal magic can redeem. The laconic tone is not enough in itself: it has to be subtly interwoven with other tones and other techniques—as it is in Pound's *Cantos*, James Reaney's *A Suit of Nettles* and Dudek's *Europe*.

After tone, the complete view. Few Canadian poets seem

rounded enough. The new industrial landscape doesn't seem to
have caught at the poets' imaginations, whereas the pastoral in
its literal and literary senses seem ineluctable. Milton Wilson,
writing in *The Canadian Forum* (June, 1959), puts some pertinent questions apropos of John Glassco's *The Deficit Made
Flesh:*

> What are (he asks) the typical images and attitudes of the
> typical Canadian poem? Ralph Gustafson provides us with a
> list in the introduction of his new Penguin anthology. Among
> the things included are the primal sea, a good deal of diving,
> green out of the white of winter, antagonistic hills, and sym-
> bolic eyes and fishes. It's a good list. It fits a few poets from a
> few parts of Canada, and what more can we ask? But there are
> plenty of alternatives. What about a vision of the collapsed
> mine or barn, the soiled and discarded virgin, the ghost town,
> grey snow, roads that peter out or lead to a dead structure,
> fruit gone soft before it ripens, parricide before puberty?

I can't really say how pertinent Mr. Wilson's answers are—they
do seem Audenish, and tempt me to think up an eclecticism of my
own which includes the national prurience, the seedy school-
room on the Indian reservation, Old British Fish and Chips,
sleazy beer-parlors, desolate plains, blue lakes, "plaid" shirts,
the cult of virility and Scottishness, picture-windows, gaudy and
finny cars, galoshes, "homes" rather than houses, dead moose
and pure cold. A slightly fey list, yes; but a list that one should
be able to compile from Mr. Gustafson's anthology. One can't,
however, because many Canadian poets see their country as
idealized pastoral. For every George Johnston, with his *Cruising
Auk*, the publishers provide a dozen vaguer visions.

But there are signs of epic methods, as a careful reader of the
Gustafson and Smith anthologies can see: Pratt's broad historical
vision; Ross's imagistic pungency; blunt Knister and the Scott of
the satirical reportage; Finch's matter-of-factness; Birney's own
Perse-like vision of history and exploration (as in *Pacific Door*);
Layton's concern for the delicious, tart variety of life; Anne
Marriott's feeling for prairie and LePan's invigorating piece-of-
an-epic, *Canoe-trip:*

> What of this fabulous country
> Now that we have reduced it to a few hot hours
> And sunburn on our backs?
> On this south side the countless archipelagos,

> The slipway where titans sent splashing the last great glaciers;
> And then up to foot of the blue pole star
> A wilderness . . . .

One would like to see something such as Neruda has done for Chile. My own guess is that it will have to be done in the Whitmanish, capacious, untidy mode; in the Canadian voice and in visual terms. Life's quality will have to be transferred to poems. Perhaps Canada is the country where young poets might find some use for Eliot, who has had next to no following in England and has exerted most of his influence in Greece, India and France. His method of the disjointed epic is perhaps just what is needed: something comprehensive without the sheer bulk of Pound's *Cantos*. After all, in a country that is more of a myth than of a conurbation, the epic writer is the man most likely to succeed. When history's magic and the modern scene have been brought subtly, grandly and colloquially together, the epic of a "fabulous country" will be a dignified reality, and not—what it may seem at present—another figment of right-minded, chauvinistic humbug.

One young Canadian poet who seems to have epic intentions or an embryonically epic mind is Ronald Bates, whose first volume, *The Wandering World*, appeared recently. Mr. Bates is a conventionally serious poet, examining his world in terms of histories, myths, interiors and landscapes. There are really two poets in him: one is rhetorical, requiring a good deal of elbow-room and long fluent lines; the other seems to arrive by way of Yeats and Auden: a little cramped, a little too self-conscious and rather too dispassionate. But in his rhetorical role Mr. Bates is outstanding: he creates a massiveness of colloquial flux in which everything appears relevant. He thinks in large units—in fact, units which seem appropriate to the wandering world of his title. These units, or deep poetical breaths, are just right for his celebration of the Canadian continent, of the vast hinterland of his own memory, for the flight of gull or goose, the leap of salmon or even of the enthralled watcher's heart. Surely the following is magnificent without being in any way magniloquent:

> And so spring comes, it may be after
> One year, or two, or five,
> But Spring must come at last, and one must hear

> Above the sounds of traffic in a sun-drowsed square,
> The crack of spring-ice breaking on a thousand lakes,
> While, in the blue, behind a Gothic spire,
> A wild goose arrowhead spears north.
> And the pull of the outbound tide at last
> Goes with the sun.

That suggests great things to come. But when Mr. Bates attends
to the paraphernalia of the modern scene, he seems to be forcing
himself: he gets off-hand and takes all kinds of clichés on trust;
many of his combinations are wilful and cerebral. For instance:
"We cannot escape. Blood is thicker than / Transmission oil or
octane gasoline." Yes, it is; but my assent to that is not assent to
a-truth-turned-into-poetry. Or take this stanza from *Overheard
in the Garden:*

> Don't let him in. Your last clue:
> Avoid the garden; shun the dark;
> Shadow the suspect in the park.
> You may find out that he is you.

Most of Mr. Bates's suspenseful paradoxes evoke the glibbest and
emptiest stunts of Auden—which is a pity, for the attempt to
cope with detectives, Palm Beach suits, cocktail bars and high
heels is laudable. It seems to me that Mr. Bates makes this attempt
in much the same spirit as he might take a cold bath; he keeps
slipping back into the elegiac mode. In that mode he is astonish-
ingly good. What he needs now is a texture that will carry all
kinds of mixtures. Somehow, I feel, he hasn't yet found out how
to fuse the trappings of industrial society with the lyricism of the
great outdoors.

   But he is certainly either a signpost or a weathercock. He
encourages us to believe that Canadian poetry may yet handle
a national theme robustly, subtly, vividly and above all in modern terms. If poets such as Mr. Bates keep on looking with their
own eyes instead of those of their predecessors, we might not
have to wait long. It is a measure of Canadian poetry's promise
that the best of the younger English poets—Elizabeth Jennings,
Ted Hughes, Dom Moraes—suggest quite different and less
exciting maturities. Confronted with, involved with Canada, the
coy colossus, poets will have to be ambitious and bold. It is hard
to see how one or two of them, already on the right lines, can
fail to make an epic about a country already (and still) myth-
ologized.

IV

ROBERT L. McDOUGALL

The Dodo and the Cruising Auk: Class in Canadian Literature

This is a paper about our society and our literature, and it assumes a correlation between the kind of society which has evolved in this country and the kind of literature it has produced. It is substantially the paper which I gave almost a year ago to an interdisciplinary seminar sponsored by the Institute of Canadian Studies at Carleton University for the purpose of examining the question of "Class in Canada." Since the paper then took its place in a context of studies made of the same subject by my colleagues in other disciplines, I must reactivate enough of that context now to make clear my point of departure. Before I do this, however, I should like to say that the intervening federal election of April last has shown very plainly the extrapolation of the argument you are about to hear into the field of politics. I was and am concerned, as many were to become concerned in the period leading up to the election, with the negative image presented by many aspects of the life of our nation. Mr. Pearson has offered the electorate his "Sixty Days of Decision" as the way out of the wasteland of Canadian political inertia. My interests for present purposes are literary: I have examined the deficiencies of the literary imagination in Canada and have asked by what means a Dodo can become at least a Cruising Auk.

My point of departure is supplied chiefly by the work of Professor John Porter of our Department of Sociology at Carleton, who has written extensively about social class in Canada and who will publish soon an important book on the power élite in Canadian society. Professor Porter is not happy about our society, and I must now tell you briefly about some of the features of the Canadian social profile which he brings to my notice that are at

Reprinted from *Canadian Literature* 18 (Autumn 1963) by permission of the author.

once unusual and unattractive. At the level of the distribution of economic wealth, for example, he shows me not a pyramid (which, he tells me, is what I should see) but something which, like a space-capsule, is narrow in the up-ended neck and dumpy at the base. The design, good for space travel, does not in this context reflect a free flow of economic opportunity. Other inhibitors darken the picture. The powerful groups are subtly but adamantly exclusive in terms of the training of their members, their ethnic origin, even the religious faith they profess. So subtle are they that they spend a good deal of their time hiding their true colors and are therefore, despite their power, a dull lot. Too few bright birds hatched in other and lower orders of society get in from the outside to liven things up; too many bright birds stay more or less where they are put, and in doing so fail to realize the creative potential that is in them. What is worse, they seem content to stay put; indeed the entire community congratulates itself on the superiority of its social arrangements over those made by neighboring communities. This much, oversimplified, from Professor Porter. His message seems plain: Canadian society is moribund and doesn't know it; it is a flightless bird that preens its vestigial wings.

Now I have asked myself what our literature, and especially our fiction (since fiction is the form of literature most directly concerned with the image of man in society) has to say about this message. And I must tell you immediately, with mixed sadness and elation, that it seems to me to say that the message is true. Professor Porter and I differ on many points, and we are of course looking at different bodies of evidence; but as far as that part of his thesis I have just examined is concerned, we see eye to eye. I shall ask you to detect in our literature a climate of thought and feeling that is frigid and constrained. The air is cold; hostile forces threaten; hope is deferred. In this environment, man's stance is static, his mood introverted, his virtues stoic. More directly, I shall ask you to conclude that our literature shows what can only be described as an abnormal absence of feeling for class and of concern for what the class structure can do in a developing society to make or mar the life of the individual. I shall ask you to regard its silence on the question of class as ominous. I shall say that it is due partly to the existence within our culture of inhibitions so strong as to all but rule out the possibility of a dynamic theory of social mobility, and partly to the fact that most Canadian writers belong to a single social group identifiable with a university-based Establishment.

I have begun to speak metaphorically because metaphor is the language of literature. In my examination of the social implications of our literature, I have thought it wise to avoid the use of direct comments which our writers have made in fiction or in poetry about Canadian society. I could offer you a collection of such comments quite easily. Navel-gazing on a national scale is something our writers do very well. But I believe, as you must, that when writers are being most self-consciously sociological they are being most marginally literary. I see no point in asking our writers to testify as amateur sociologists. Fortunately, poets and novelists have another manner of speaking which is truly their own and which involves the use of language to create a work of art rather than, primarily, a social document. As it happens, since the way in which their imaginations characteristically work within the books or poems they write are themselves social facts, we can listen to them when they speak the language of literature and still remain within a sociological frame of reference.

I have said that metaphor is the language of literature. I mean by this that men and women who write novels or poems discover in doing so what R. W. B. Lewis in *The American Adam* has described as the "representative images" and "stories" for the ideas and attitudes of the society in which they live. Taking a long and broad look at American literature, Mr. Lewis has concluded that "a century ago, the image contrived to embody the most fruitful contemporary ideas was that of the authentic American figure of heroic innocence and vast potentialities, poised at the start of a new history." Hawthorne's description, in a fantasy of 1844 called "Earth's Holocaust," of a huge bonfire built on the western prairies, "upon which was piled all the world's 'outworn' trumpery," becomes in this context the complement of Thoreau's representative image of the "busk," a New England custom which entailed the replacing of old things with new in village homes and the ritual burning of the past on the village green. Such images and stories, says Mr. Lewis, considered in relation to the anti-types which inevitably develop from them, help to define the characteristic debate or dialectic of American society. My only departure from this form of inquiry into the basic metaphor of a body of literature is to insist (in company with Miss Bodkin in her *Archetypal Patterns in Poetry* and Wilson Knight in his Shakespearean criticism) that as much, perhaps even more, validity attaches to the representative image produced by the writer when he is unaware of the implications of what he is doing as to the representative image he produces as a "conscious" literary artist.

As we might expect, neither the subsuming form of the representative image or "story" nor the debate or dialectic which is the sign of its vitality is as apparent this side of the border as it is to the south. No simple myth or ideology is available within whose field the separate symbols can find their orientation. The Americans took over the only ones truly appropriate to this continent some centuries ago: the Adamite myth and the ideology of democratic egalitarianism. Urged partly by our history and partly by sheer perversity, we have been looking fruitlessly for alternatives ever since. Nevertheless, a pattern exists here, even though, as we shall see, its organizing principle is negative.

In 1946, Northrop Frye contributed to the periodical *Gants du Ciel* an article entitled (the piece was translated from the English) "La Tradition Narrative dans la Poésie Canadienne-Anglaise." In this article he pointed out that the Canadian poet, though he might be younger than Eliot or Yeats, wrote in an environment for which it would be difficult to find a counterpart in England without going back to a period prior to the age of Chaucer. Our poets, he said, shared with authors of *The Wanderer* and *The Seafarer* a certain attitude or feeling:

> a feeling [he said] of melancholy inspired by a sparsely settled and northern country, a feeling of the terrible loneliness of the creative spirit in such a country, a feeling of resignation to misery and isolation as the only means of achieving, if not serenity, at least a sort of stoic calm.

He noted a family resemblance between on the one hand the defeat of the English at Maldon and the heroism of the French at Roncesvalles, and, on the other, the archetypes of our national history: the martydom of the Jesuits in Huronia; Dollard's stand against the Iroquois at the Long Sault; the desperate courage of the Indians who died beside Tecumseh and Riel;

the stirring yet abortive winter of our discontent in 1837; the hopeless struggle against gas at St. Julien in World War I; the sacrificial raid on Dieppe in World War II. The images and "stories" of the literature which emerges from this environment, Professor Frye goes on to say, reflect a consistent view of the human situation: man is a beautiful but frail creature encompassed by forces beyond his ability to control which strike out repeatedly and blindly to destroy him. Max, the hero of Isabella Valancy Crawford's *Malcolm's Katie*, at the very moment when he is defending the march of civilization and an idealistic view of human nature, is struck down by a falling tree. In Lampman's *At the Long Sault*, as the image of the defeat of Dollard's band merges with the image of the magnificent bull-moose attacked and destroyed by a pack of wolves, we see the ritual destruction of the higher forms of life by the lower.

Professor Frye's feeling for this part of our literature seems to me so absolutely right (his accounting for what he finds is another matter, for I think he is misleading when he says that the northern environment is the cause) that I have only to go on from where he leaves off. Within the field of the description he has provided lie, and lie all one way, the central themes, certainly the mood and spirit, of the main part of our poetry and fiction. E. J. Pratt is in many ways our most vigorous and affirmative poet. Yet the dominant linear image of Pratt's poetry is the image of the parabola, of the line moving obliquely and curving back upon itself. In his *Come Away, Death*, after the obliterating blast of the bomb, "human speech curved back upon itself/Through Druid runways and Piltdown scarps,/Beyond the stammers of the Java caves." Evolution and reversion are two functions of the same graph. More obviously, the central image of Pratt's long poem on the sinking of the *Titanic* is that of an iceberg whose colossal strength, two-thirds hidden beneath the surface, rips through the bowels of the ship that is man's pride and joy. In D. C. Scott's poetry, which E. K. Brown has called a poetry of "restrained intensity," there is the image of the Indian crone who had once baited her hook with her own flesh to catch fish for her child, but who now, cast off by her tribe to die in the wilderness, sits mantled with snow, her breath a thin meerschaum of vapor in the white silence. Jay Macpherson's Adam is the fallen Adam barred from re-entry into Eden by the Cherubim's flaming sword until the second Adam comes. Even the titles of collections of poems are emblematic: Margaret Avison's *Winter Sun*; Patrick Anderson's *The White Centre*; A. M. Klein's *The Rocking Chair* ("symbol of this static folk"); James Reaney's *A Suit of Nettles*.

Turn to our fiction, which is perhaps more telling in its evidences because it is more dependent in its form on a total human situation, and we find images and "stories" consistent with those of the poetry. The representative figure of Canadian fiction is not the innocent Adam, nor yet the Adam of the fortunate fall who is triumphant even in defeat at the hands of the alien tribe —as, for example, are Melville's Billy Budd or the Joads in Steinbeck's *The Grapes of Wrath*. Nor is he, like Dorothea Brooke in George Eliot's *Middlemarch*, the figure made strong and capable of extended life by voluntary renunciation. These are positive; our archetype is negative. Grove's heroes inhabit the world of the dark tragedies, the world of *Lear* and *Othello*. Morley Callaghan's protracted study of the nature of innocence in a fallen world ends with the identification, in Harry Lane of *The Many Coloured Coat*, of innocence with presumption and guilt. His Father Dowling, in *Such Is My Beloved*, unable to see a solution either in conventionally Christian or in Marxist terms to the problem posed by the two prostitutes he has befriended, steps back over the lintel and the door closes on the dark room of his insanity. In Hugh MacLennan's *Two Solitudes*, two race legends touch but do not join, and Athanase Tallard, at the point of the novel's real climax, dies an immolation to unappeasable gods. Tallard's son Paul, ostensibly the man in whom the two worlds become one, does *not* rise Phoenix-like from the ashes, and we are to be consoled with the image of oil and alcohol in a bottle which, we are told, "had not broken yet." The real hero of MacLennan's earlier novel, *Barometer Rising*, is the chance explosion of 3,000 tons of T.N.T. in Halifax harbor which removes from the scene, in addition to 6,000 Haligonians, Neil MacRae's enemy, Colonel Wain. In Sinclair Ross's *As For Me and My House*, Philip Bentley withdraws so repeatedly behind the slammed door of his study that the image becomes an organizing principle of the action; and, in the same novel, the Puritan-ridden town of Horizon, from which, we feel, the railway lines run out only to other and quite as empty Horizons, is a frontier town which has known no youth but only old age. Milton Wilson reviewing a recent collection of Canadian short stories, writes: "In the end, when the long line of dead birds, animals, and children, of frozen, inarticulate sons and lovers, of crucified hired men and farm boys has filed past, one is both appalled and impressed"; it is a world, he concludes, of "sacrificial chilliness" in which man's responses are "passive and inarticulate."

Can one escape conclusion? This is a negative rather than a positive literature. I was on the point of saying that it is a literature of the Everlasting Nay, but the Everlasting Nay, as Carlyle and Melville testify, is deeply affirmative. In our literature, heroic action remains possible but becomes so deeply tinged with futility that withdrawal becomes a more characteristic response than commitment. The representative images are those of denial and defeat rather than fulfilment and victory.

In the presence of these images it seems superfluous to ask whether our literature embodies a dynamic view of our social arrangements or supports a vigorous debate on the problem of freedom of movement for the individual within the mosaic of the class structure. Still, to round out my argument, the question may be put and an answer given. I shall confine my attention to the fiction.

One has the impression, in reading our fiction, that the social environment is in sharp focus. I presume it was this fact which led M. Falardeau, in the Plaunt lectures for 1960, to attempt a distinction between English-Canadian and French-Canadian literature.

> If one compares the English and French literatures of Canada, one discovers that the former expresses itself along an axis which I would see as horizontal while the latter has a more vertical axis. . . . For most English-Canadian novelists, the novel as artistic expression is more the description and analysis of a social situation than a plunging into the depths of an individual soul. . . . In the French-Canadian novel, with Langevin, Elie, or Charbonneau, the characteristic tension is one between man and himself. More exactly, it is a tension between the individual and his destiny.

I think M. Falardeau is right up to a point: the English-Canadian novel, less lyric and "romantic" than its French-Canadian counterpart, belongs to a tradition of realism in which the horizontal dimension is clearly displayed as part of the requirement for what Henry James called "solidity of specification." Moreover, as I suggested at the beginning of my paper, it is a novel notable for the at least superficial evidence it gives of social awareness. Hugh MacLennan, for example, is most accurately aware of Professor Porter's tight little circle of corporate élite. Huntley McQueen, in *Two Solitudes*, is a modest member of the pack which daily rides the elevator of the Bank Building in St. James Street:

> The elevator continued with McQueen to the top floor. The thought crossed his mind that if an accident had occurred between the first and second floors, half a million men would at that instant have lost their masters. It was an alarming thought. It was also ironic, for these individuals were so remote from the beings they governed, they operated with such cantilevered indirections, that they could all die at once without even ruffling the sleep of the remote employees on the distant end of the chain of cause and effect. The structure of interlocking directorates which governed the nation's finances, subject to an exceptionally discreet parliament, seemed to McQueen so delicate that a puff of breath could make the whole edifice quiver. But no, McQueen smiled at his own thoughts, the structure was quite strong enough. The men who had ridden together in the elevator this morning were so sound they seldom told even their wives what they thought or did or hoped to do. Indeed, Sir Rupert Irons was so careful he had no wife at all. They were Presybterians to a man, they went to church regularly, and Irons was known to believe quite literally in predestination.

Similarly, it would be possible to derive from English-Canadian fiction the material for a demographic map which would show plainly the difference, let us say, between the social environment of Mort, in *The Equations of Love*, who lives on Powell Street in Vancouver, and that of Mr. H. Y. Dunkerley, the lumber magnate, who lives in the British Properties in West Vancouver; or between the social environment of the Carvers, in *The Loved and the Lost*, who live on the Mountain in Montreal, and that of Peggy Sanderson, who frequents the St. Antoine district of the city, just north of the tracks. Is this not to say that M. Falardeau is right, then? And is this not to say that English-Canadian fiction does indeed present a dynamic view of class in Canada?

The fact is that class is not a central issue in any significant part of our fiction. The social awareness of which I have spoken remains almost everywhere a social awareness marginal to the purposes of the novel. Characteristically, it is the awareness of a detached observer who says what he has to say about a social problem in a sequence of mildly ironic comments which leave him, as the device of irony permits, uncommitted. Irony is of course an excellent literary device. But the use of it on a national scale, and the use on a national scale of that particular form of it which conceals position rather than reveals it, seems to me to have disturbing implications. Some years ago, Malcolm Ross was astute enough to identify irony as the Canadian way of doing things in literature. The difference between us is simply that Professor Ross thinks the ironic mode a good basis for a sense of identity while I do not.

I must answer M. Falardeau further by saying that even where the question of class appears to be a central issue in our fiction, in the end almost invariably it is not. Morley Callaghan, for example, who is on the surface a novelist preeminently concerned with the social structure in Canada, on closer examination turns out to be a novelist preeminently concerned with personal values and "inscape." In *They Shall Inherit the Earth*, published in 1935, the conclusion which Michael Aikenhead, on a hunting trip, draws from the spectacle of the apparently wanton slaughter of deer by a pack of wolves virtually kills the debate on social justice which the novel has sponsored. The lesson which nature supplies is ambiguous, it would seem, and in the face of this ambiguity we must, for the sake of unity, suspend judgment on the question of justice in society. It is a defensible position. It is nevertheless a peculiarly static and negative position in the context of the thirties. The effect in the novel is to drive the emphasis squarely back upon what has been its central issue from the beginning, the personal relation between Michael and his father; and this issue is then cautiously resolved in terms of the cautious conclusion of the book's social debate. And *They Shall Inherit the Earth* is perhaps the most "horizontal" of Callaghan's novels. Elsewhere, and especially in the more recent novels such as *The Loved and the Lost* and *The Many Coloured Coat*, the "vertical" is unquestionably the main dimension of the work.

Callaghan is of course not the English-Canadian novel, but since my time is limited I must ask you to believe that what we find and do not find in him is representative of a wide spectrum of Canadian fiction. Ernest Buckler's *The Mountain and the Valley* (1952) is a novel locked in space and time, its theme one of containment, its mood retrospective, its emphasis, as Dr. Bissell has pointed out, "not so much on movement forward as on exploration below." Hugh MacLennan's *The Watch That Ends the Night* (1959), despite its brilliant reconstruction of the ferment of the thirties in Montreal and the presence in it of the rather unrepresentative Life-Force figure of Jerome Martell, is a spiritual odyssey of the search for the meaning of pain and life and death in which the action folds progressively inward upon the private worlds of the narrator and his invalid wife. Consistently, in Sinclair Ross as in such unlikely quarters as Robertson Davies and Mazo de la Roche, the "horizontal" tilts to the "vertical." English-Canadian writers have more in common with French-Canadian writers than M. Falardeau would lead us to believe.

And as the private worlds enlarge, of course, the worlds of social relationship diminish. Nature and puritanism and the illiberal mind are forces to be reckoned with here, and any combination of these can act in a social context to frustrate the individual and nourish his self-doubt. But the class structure itself is not, apparently, a challenge. There are exceptions. I believe some of our minority-group writers, as they might be called, have had (and for obvious reasons) a genuine feeling for the problem of social mobility—John Marlyn, for example, in *Under the Ribs of Death*, and Mordecai Richler in *Son of a Smaller Hero*. I think also of Ethel Wilson's "Lilly's Story," though Ethel Wilson writing "Lilly's Story" is Jane Austen writing *Sister Carrie*. But the exceptions are too few to be significant.

Indeed it is quite simply the monolithic uniformity of the picture that disturbs me. I concede that Morley Callaghan has done well in his inquiry into the problem of faith and guilt in a fallen world, and I can tell you that I was his champion long before Edmund Wilson took him up, and still am. I concede that any novelist worthy of his calling will see any individual as being in a sense in a class by himself, that all good novels are concerned with the inner life, and that the probing of man's consciousness and conscience at the expense of external social reference has been increasingly the mark of fiction in the western world over the past fifty years. But where in our literature, early or late, do we find the infusion of that bold concern for placing the individual's problems in significant relation to the structure of his society which is so clearly to be seen in the literatures of England and the United States? Dickens knew about class in a society well advanced toward industrialization, and Dickens wrote about class in *Hard Times* and *Bleak House* and *Great Expectations*. George Eliot knew the class structure of a town like Middlemarch as well as she knew the palm of her hand and could use this knowledge to illuminate the action and discourse of her characters. Henry James thought the principle of exclusiveness so important to the art of fiction that he went to Europe where he could observe it in its purest form and where he then proceeded to write novel after novel in which (with no sacrifice of inwardness, be it noted) he juxtaposed New World ideas about class with those of the Old. Within a few years of James's departure, the American novelist W. D. Howells had satisfied his own Jamesian concern for the principle of exclusiveness by writing, in *The Rise of Silas Lapham*, a full-length and artistically satisfying study of the issue of class that had risen with the pressure of the new economic élite of industrial America upon the Brahmin class of Boston society. Theodore Dreiser in *Sister Carrie* and Horatio Alger in *Struggling Upward* made a literary image out of the sociological concept of upward mobility. Lady Chatterley's lover is a gamekeeper, and this simple fact stands close to the heart of what Lawrence is trying to say in that novel. Steinbeck in *The Grapes of Wrath* sees the class issue with the hard clarity of a Marxist.

Here in Canada we seem to have had no feeling for this sort of thing—or, if we had a feel for it once, we have lost it. Susanna Moodie looked with a shrewd eye on what she called the "mixed society" growing up along the "front" of the St. Lawrence River in the 1840's and was well aware of the implications of the new kind of class structure she saw taking shape in the new environment. Later, Sara Jeanette Duncan was able, in *The Imperialist*, to do with excellent insight for the small Ontario town of Elgin (her Brantford) what George Eliot had done for Middlemarch. But thereafter the record diminishes. It is true that the thirties produced a spate of socially directed poetry in this country, and I have no wish to question the sincerity of the convictions which led F. R. Scott and Earle Birney and others to write it. But the voice of the poetry of these years is ambiguous, as a glance at the volume *New Provinces* (published in 1936) will show. Above all, I see in it little evidence of what I should call a genuine feeling for class. It is academic. One has the impression that it is a poetry written neither by Brahmins nor by proles. And if we turn to the fiction of the depression years, the essential lack remains. Irene Baird's *Waste Heritage*, whose setting is hobodom in Vancouver during the riots and sitdown strikes of the thirties, is a genuinely proletarian novel, and it is a piece of work that has a good deal of the quality of gusto and authenticity of approach to the social scene that I am looking for. But it is the only one of its kind. In the post-war years, evidence of the feel for class in our literature all but disappears.

The record, I repeat, has been different elsewhere. Scott Fitzgerald hated the privileges of the high "with the smouldering hatred of a peasant," while at the same time coveting the freedom and beauty which, it seemed to him, only wealth provided. "Gatsby," we read in Fitzgerald's famous novel of the twenties, "was overwhelmingly aware of the youth and mystery that wealth imprisons and preserves, of the freshness of many clothes, and of Daisy, gleaming like silver, safe and proud above the hot struggles of the poor." Waiving the question of which of our novelists can write like that, which of them gives us any reason to believe that he can *feel* like that about the ceremonies and attributes of class? None, to my knowledge. And if you think (wrongly, as I would believe) that the social conditions which sparked Fitzgerald in the twenties have no counterpart in Canada today, which of our novelists can answer in kind to the energetic vision of class and of individual problem seen in relation to the class structure which is embodied in Alan Sillitoe's *Saturday Night and Sunday Morning* and John Braine's *Room at the Top?* Again none, to my knowledge.

I do not propose to explore the reasons for this gap in our literature. The reasons are our history and where and how that history has evolved, and if you really want to linger lovingly over how difficult it has all been you can do no better than to take a Great Books course of reading in the Reports of our Royal Commissions of Inquiry. There is, however, one probable reason for the gap which seems to me worth looking into for a moment before I close because it involves the kind of evidence that my friend Professor Porter likes to use in his analysis of Canadian society. It has to do with the question of recruitment to the ranks of authors in this country.

I have said that our poetry of the thirties gives one the feeling of having been written neither by Brahmins nor by proles. I have said that it has an academic flavor. The same observation can be made of poetry written before and after the decade of the thirties and of almost the entire run of Canadian fiction. Had I had time, I might have prepared for you a set of statistics to show that the representative hero of Canadian fiction has a university degree or its equivalent, and that the representative setting for Canadian fiction is one which links the action directly or indirectly to an institution of higher learning. What I have been able to do is to gather a few biographical facts about our authors.

Observe the common denominators in family background and education. Hugh MacLennan, the son of a surgeon, was educated first at Halifax Academy, then at Dalhousie University where he was winner of the Governor-General's Gold Medal and where he took his B.A. in 1929. As a Rhodes Scholar he attended Oriel College, Oxford, where he took his M.A. in 1932. He went next to Princeton, where he became M.A. squared and where he took his Ph.D. in 1935. He was a Guggenheim Fellow in 1943–44 and is currently a Professor of English at McGill University and an Associate Fellow of the Royal Society of Canada. Morley Callaghan took his B.A. at St. Michael's College, Toronto, in 1925 and later attended Law School at Osgoode Hall. E. J. Pratt, the son of a clergyman, is E. J. Pratt, C.M.G., M.A., PH.D., D.LITT., D.C.L., LL.D., F.R.S.C., and Professor Emeritus at Victoria University, Toronto. F. R. Scott, the son of Archdeacon F. G. Scott and the grandson of Professor Scott who for forty years taught anatomy at McGill University, is F. R. Scott, LL.D., B.A., B.LITT., B.C.L., F.R.S.C. He too was a Rhodes Scholar and attended Magdalen College, Oxford. He has been a High School teacher and a teacher at Bishop's and at Lower Canada College. He is currently Macdonald Professor of Law and Dean, McGill University. Robertson Davies, the son of Senator William Rupert Davies, was educated at Upper Canada College, Queen's University, and Balliol College, Oxford, where he took his B.Litt. He is to be the first Master of Massey House, the new graduate center at the University of Toronto. Earl Birney, PH.D., F.R.S.C., pursued higher education at the universities of British Columbia, Toronto, California and London, and has been a scholar and teacher all the days of his working life. Dorothy Livesay, journalist and social worker, attended Glen Mawr school in Toronto and took her B.A. at Trinity College, Toronto, in 1931. She took her Diplome d'études supérieures at the Sorbonne in 1932 and then returned to the University of Toronto to complete her studies in the social sciences in 1934. She is currently a lecturer in creative writing on the staff of the Department of Extension at the University of British Columbia. A. M. Klein took his B.A. at McGill University in 1930, studied for a time to become a rabbi, then took a degree in law at the Université de Montréal in 1933. A. J. M. Smith, M.A., PH.D., D.LITT., has been for many years Professor of English at Michigan State College. I note that besides being a poet, Professor Smith is our foremost anthologist and therefore in a sense the custodian of our poetic tradition. James Reaney holds an M.A. degree from the University of Toronto and has been a university professor all the days of his working life. Mazo de la Roche, the descendant of United Empire Loyalist stock and the daughter of a professor of classics and letters at Baltimore University, was educated at Parkdale Collegiate Institute and at the University of Toronto. Ethel Wilson was educated at private schools in England and Vancouver and attended the provincial Normal School in that city. She was a teacher for some years prior to her marriage in 1920 to Dr. Wilson. There is more of the same, but I think the pattern is plain.

There is no law which says that a university man cannot have, as a writer, a feeling for class. Scott Fitzgerald and many of his fellow writers of the twenties were graduates of one or other of the Ivy League universities. Yet surely there is something unusual and, I think, even alarming in the overwhelming uniformity of the picture I have presented. In most cases the formative years, to say nothing of entire lives, have been spent in academic circles. T. S. Eliot, in his introduction to the Cresset Press edition of *Huckleberry Finn*, has this to say about Mark Twain's grip upon his subject:

> There are, perhaps, only two ways in which a writer can acquire the understanding of environment which he can later turn to account: by having spent his childhood in that environment—that is, living in it at a period of life in which one experiences much more than one is aware of; and by having had to struggle for a livelihood in that environment—a livelihood bearing no direct relation to any intention of writing about it, of *using* it as literary material.

I believe this to be true. For the great bulk of Canadian writers the environments of childhood and of "the struggle for a living" are uniform in kind; professional, relatively well-to-do, "genteel," above all, academic. Is one to expect from these closed, circumspect and intellectually sophisticated ranks a dynamic view of society? It is not surprising that our literature lies all one way, and it is not surprising that within this literature the concepts of class are dim and the response to the problem of individual freedom within the social structure negligible.

If it is not surprising, it is, for me at least, deeply disturbing. The dead cold air, the uniformity of assumptions, the lack of commitment are oppressive. I am not here concerned specifically with the way out of the wasteland, but insofar as the way out is implicit in all that I have said you will see that the path I look to is a different path from the one favored by radical sociologists like Professor Porter. I am not interested in what the sociologists call "class abatement"; we shall always have classes in the broad sense in which I have understood the term, and I am content that this should be so. I think the heart of the matter is the question of individual liberty and of the vital relation which the principle of individual liberty must always bear to the life of a democratic nation. It is not the reinforcing of the class struggle that is wanted, not the triumph of the proletariat nor of John Birch societies, for this would simply be to substitute one form of fixed response for another. It is rather turbulence that is needed—the kind of turbulence that encompasses the whole of the social mosaic and in the end makes possible within it that freedom of choice and of movement for the individual which, from a secular point of view, is the best means open to us of enabling him to realize the creative potential within him. The station to which it has pleased God to call us is not always the station to which it has pleased man to call us. We have an obligation to debate perpetually the credentials of the social plan.

I doubt whether the opening up of the routes to higher education, as we at present conceive of higher education, is the panacea. Professor Porter seems to think it is. Ezra Pound, rallying American writers of the twenties to take a stand against the political and social platitudes of the Old Gang in this period of low ebb in the nation's life, diagnosed the difficulty in plain terms: "Anemia of guts on the one hand," he said, "and anemia of education on the other." I mistrust our universities. I mistrust, from the point of view of literary criticism, the mob they house of gentlemen who write with ease, who are cosmopolitan and urbane to the last drop of sherry that flows in their veins. I mistrust, from the student's point of view, the leveling and debilitating effects of our universities. In their growing role as a fifth estate of the realm, they seem to me to be creating a new and pernicious dimension to the problem of the class structure. I mistrust their hold upon writers and writing in this country. The fault is not of course in the nature of the institutions themselves, but in how we conceive of them. I merely think that aspiring writers, for the time being at least, would be well advised to stay away from them. The present state of our society considered, I think a portion at any rate of those who intend to write in Canada would do better to learn elsewhere what they need to know about life, and, in their spare time, as Whitman demanded, "go freely with powerful uneducated persons."

I shall end as I began, with metaphor. About a year ago I saw a television play based on the death of the Avro-Arrow project, and the title of the play was *The Day of the Dodo*. The Americans have their eagle; our emblem may well be the wingless, flightless Dodo. We, and especially our writers since it is theirs to make as much as it is to reflect the national will, must get off the ground. And the beauty of it is that the kind of wings we need are made at the sole cost of the mind and heart. Energy and a positive thrust to the imagination can accomplish all. We can become at least a cruising auk, the cruising auk that George Johnston's Mr. Murple saw: "a splendid auk/Flying across the sky." Can you not see him?

> Surely his eye belittles our despair,
> Our unheroic mornings, afternoons
> Disconsolate in the echo-laden air—
> Echoes of trumpet noises, horses' hooves.
>
> Splendid, however, we can
> Rejoice in him, cruising there:
> He is our uncle and lo,
> O Mr. Murple, O beloved friends,
> Airborne!

V

WARREN TALLMAN

Wolf in the Snow

PART ONE: FOUR WINDOWS ONTO LANDSCAPES

To enter the fictional house these novels form is to take up place in rooms where windows open out upon scenes in Saskatchewan, Quebec and Nova Scotia: two prairie towns, one farm, a small seacoast city and St. Urbain Street in Montreal. In order to prevent view from jostling view it is convenient to single out the characters Philip Bentley (*As for Me and My House*), Brian O'Connal (*Who Has Seen the Wind*), David Canaan (*The Mountain and the Valley*), Alan MacNeil (*Each Man's Son*) and Duddy Kravitz (*The Apprenticeship of Duddy Kravitz*), letting their lives suggest the details which make up the study. Since these five form into a handful, it is best to enter the fictional house at once and move across rooms to where the windows open out.

From whichever window one chooses to look, at whichever person, the initial impression gained is that of his isolation. Superficially, this isolation traces to the ways in which each is alienated from the natural childhood country of ordinary family life. In *As for Me and My House*, Philip Bentley has this comfort stolen from him even before it is provided when his unmarried father, a divinity student, turned atheist, turned artist, dies before Philip is born. That the son is cast by this deprivation into the

Reprinted from *Canadian Literature* 5 (Summer 1960): 7–20 and *Canadian Literature* 6 (Autumn 1960):41–48, by permission of the author and Oxford University Press.

In this essay Warren Tallman bases a study of modern Canadian fiction on five books which he considers particularly significant as examples of literary attitudes in Canada. They are *As for Me and My House* by Sinclair Ross, *Who Has Seen the Wind* by W. O. Mitchell, *Each Man's Son* by Hugh MacLennan, *The Mountain and the Valley* by Ernest Buckler, and *The Apprenticeship of Duddy Kravitz* by Mordecai Richler.

limbo of an uncreated childhood becomes evident when he emerges into adult life also a divinity student, turned atheist, turned artist, struggling without success to discover the father he did not know while married to a woman who is all too obviously more a mother to him than she is a wife. In *The Mountain and the Valley*, David Canaan is gifted with yet cursed by reactions far too intense ever to mesh except occasionally with the more ordinary responses of his brother, sister, parents and grandmother. When he fails in a school play, his family has no resources with which to meet the violence of humiliation which fairly explodes within him. His childhood and youth are a long succession of such intensities leading to such explosions. Each time the pieces settle back together, he finds himself inched unwillingly away from others onto a precarious plane of solitary being from which he can communicate his extravagant reactions only by other extravagances which further emphasize his growing isolation.

If David's is the most painful face turned toward us, Brian O'Connal's is the most deceptive. Even as *Who Has Seen the Wind* opens, he is shown growing away from his family in order to follow impulses which bring his struggling consciousness into contact with what are described in the preface as "the realities of birth, hunger, satiety, eternity, death." But if Brian appears to discern a deeper than familial ordering of experience in and around the Saskatchewan town where he grows up, the persons and personifications which illustrate his discernment tell, I think, quite another story. They tell of a sensitive boy's attempts to reconcile himself to the human viciousness and natural desolation which characterize the town and the prairie. Of this conflict, more in place. Unlike Philip, David and Brian, Alan MacNeil in *Each Man's Son* is less an individualized child and more simply the naive witness to a stylized pattern of adult conflict. Thus he is the puppet son to each of three disparate fathers: Doctor Ainslee, the type of inhibited intellect; Archie MacNeil, the type of unthinking animal force; and the Gallic Louis Camire, the type of passionate spontaneity. Because the larger human pattern of which these men are parts has been broken, each partial man struggles toward a different solution to his incompletion, one which excludes the others. When their longings for wholeness draw them to Alan and his mother, the pattern will no longer knit. Alan's role as each man's son is to witness the gradual forcing together of these disastrously alienated men.

The kinds of alienation which I have sketched point to a common problem. When the hazards of life reach out to disrupt families and isolate children it is almost certain that such children will respond with attempts to create a self strong enough to endure the added stress and more extreme fluctuations of experience. Yet the very disturbances which create a need for such strength frequently conspire to take away the opportunity. Prematurely conscious of weakness in the face of experience, the timid self stands back from contention. And much of the isolation is in the standing back. Yet to lose out in this way is to gain in another. For so persistent and powerful are the mysterious forces which drive self on its journeys toward some measure of fulfillment that when the journey is interrupted self will either struggle to make the island upon which it finds itself habitable, or—if particularly hard-pressed—may strike out for new islands of its own making. To know experience or novels even cursorily is to realize that such attempts are among the decisive gestures of human experience. The more vital the attempt, the more interesting the discoveries, the more illuminating the journeys. But to say all this and then turn to Philip, David, Brian and Alan is to encounter difficulties.

First Brian. Throughout *Who Has Seen the Wind* we are shown his growing consciousness of the grim passive cruelty of the prairie and of the only somewhat less grim cruelties of the community. The prairie doesn't care and the townspeople care too much, but in all of the wrong ways. Mitchell would have us understand that Brian attains insight into deep permanent forces of man and nature and so becomes reconciled to the problems of his existence. But if the winds and gods of the prairie and the town are shown ministering to the evolution of a troubled boy's consciousness, there are many reasons to question the nature of their influence. For what Brian actually discovers and enters into is somewhat uneasy communication with a hierarchy of odd and withdrawn persons, most of them caught up as he is in attempting to resolve the dilemma of their alienation from the community. At the head of this hierarchy are several disaffected persons whose professional standing gives them precarious half-footing in the community: Hislop, the enlightened minister who is forced to leave; Doctor Svarich, Miss Thompson, the school teacher with whom he has had an unsuccessful love affair else- where, and Digby, the school principal. Because these humane persons are only half accepted by a community which they in turn only half accept, they lead incomplete, almost inert lives.

Brian's more active education begins where their influence leaves off: with his uncle Sean, whose intelligent efforts to cope with the drouth are met by a human inertia so perverse that he is reduced to random cursing; with Milt Palmer, the shoe and harness maker, who eases his discontent with the jug he keeps under the counter in his shop and the copy of Berkeley's phi- losophy he reads and discusses with Digby, presumably to get at the nature of existence, actually to escape the pointlessness of the existence he leads; with Ben, the town ne'er-do-well, who makes his still and his gifts as a raconteur the basis for contact with a community that otherwise despises him; with the son, young Ben, who responds to his father's disgrace by a withdrawal so marked that his human impulses only glimmer at depths of his remote eyes; and with old Sammy, the town idiot, who lives almost totally withdrawn in a self-built insane asylum at the outskirts of town, his intelligence—that light which keeps the human psyche habitable—lost in the nightmare clutter which existence becomes when the light flickers out.

It is all but impossible to accept Mitchell's inference that con- tact with these persons serves to reconcile Brian's consciousness to the "realities of birth, hunger, satiety, eternity, death." What he learns, if anything, is that the kinds of suffering which afflict those who are completely alienated from the community are far more damaging than the kinds of suffering which afflict those who are only partly alienated. It isn't surprising that the two most vivid portraits in the novel are those of young Ben and old Sammy, the two most severely withdrawn of all the persons presented. Young Ben appears to Brian in unexpected places and at unpredictable moments with all of the suddenness of a hallu- cination projected from Brian's unconscious. To be Brian in the kind of community Mitchell represents is to be not far from young Ben. And what is old Sammy in his age and insanity but young Ben later on and farther out on the road leading away from contact with other human beings. What but negative les- sons can Brian learn from such dissociated beings—so grim a school of lives!

Nor is it possible to accept the protective, but not very protective, screen of humor with which Mitchell has softened and attempted to humanize the world Brian experiences. Here contrast is helpful. The mordant western humor of Mark Twain, Ambrose Bierce and Bret Harte derives the tensions which make it effective from these writers' awareness of the overt savagery of the settlement years. In Brian's world the savagery is still there —the gratuitous cruelty of the community drives the Chinese restaurant owner to despair and suicide—but it has become socially organized, hence acceptable. Mrs. Abercrombie, the town assassin, is also the town social leader. However, the intended humor of the scenes in which her control over the school board is finally broken is without animation because it is without true animosity. The firing of the enlightened minister, the exclusion of the Chinese children from the community, the suicide of their father, the sadistic persecution of young Ben, as well as the constant badgering of the school teachers, provide cause enough for any amount of enmity. But far from being a gesture of delight at the downfall of a despicable person, the humor is simply a droll and softening pretense that she never was actually dangerous.

The need for this pretense is not far to seek or at least to suspect. If the town is presided over by Mrs. Abercrombie, an incarnation of community enmity toward personality—let them be citizens instead—the prairie is presided over by old Sammy, an incarnation of the disintegration which is likely to overtake all but the most resourceful personalities when the individual self wanders beyond sphere of human community. These two represent the actual, the most powerful of the gods who preside over Brian's attempt to establish contact with human and natural forces which will sustain his precocious selfhood. And despite her overt hatred of the diversity and freedom that are essential for self-nurture, Mrs. Abercrombie is less fearsome than is old Sammy who presides with his mad, mumbled incantations over psychic chaos and old night. Or let us say that the open emptiness of the prairie is humanly more frightening than the huddled pettiness of the town. Because this is so, the town must be sugar coated with humor so that the lackluster perversity of the place will seem merely droll, hence bearable. But readers who find it impossible to swallow Mrs. Abercrombie under any circumstances at all will feel that the failure of the humor reflects a failure of the novel to confront the actuality which it suggests.

As a place for Brian to discover a community which will foster self-growth, the town in its resourcelessness more nearly resembles the prairie. The humor is scarcely a compensation for such desolation.

To turn to the more severe isolation from which David Canaan suffers in *The Mountain and the Valley* is to encounter a more intense but scarcely a more successful attempt to discover new ground upon which the withdrawn self might stand in its efforts to move into presence. During his childhood and youth David's vivid impulses fascinate his family and friends. Mutual responsiveness brings on that gradual blur of familiarity which can cause us to notice least those persons we know best; but when responsiveness is somehow short-circuited the one who stands apart becomes impressive in his otherness. Throughout childhood and early youth David moves among others with the aura about him of the chosen person, the mysterious Nazarite who is motioned toward an unknowable destiny by unseen gods. But what is an advantage during his early years becomes a disadvantage later when the appealing mystery of his loneliness becomes the oppressive ordeal of his unbreakable solitude. More devastating still, at no point in his life is he capable of actions which might rescue him from the limbo in which he dwells.

He carries on a correspondence and later a friendship with the Halifax boy, Toby, but makes no attempt to visit Toby and explore possibilities for new experience in the city. He is conscious of talents which might open experience out for him so that his self could follow into presence. But he turns his back upon these talents and remains on the farm even though aware that it is his prison rather than his promised land. He quarrels with his parents but seems unable to move past the evident incest barriers which bind him to them even as they shut him away from them. That the male mountain and the female valley of the title loom up so prominently in the novel is surely a sign, here as with Wordsworth, that natural objects have been endowed with all the seeming numinousness of their inaccessible human equivalents. Conversely, other persons in the novel are invested with a deceptive glamor. The breath of life fans the nucleus of David's impulses into a glow, but because these impulses are checked they never achieve the release of communication, much less communion. Unable to know his family in their ordinariness, he must create his own knowledge in the image of his arrested, his childish and childlike psychic. Consequently his parents are perceived as mythical, almost biblical beings and this appearance is sustained as long as David's response is intense enough, the glow white hot. Such intensities are as much the hallmark of the novel as a markedly devitalized humor is the hallmark of Mitchell's. But like Mitchell's humor, the intensity is badly flawed.

For David is trying to sustain an illusion. Whenever the hot impulse cools the glow goes out of the novel and we see David's family and friends for what they are, very unbiblical, unmythical, ordinary human beings. At no time does his friend Toby demonstrate those distinguished qualities with which David invests him. His sister Anna is represented as soul of David's soul, but it is only possible for David to sustain this sublimated conception by overlooking the almost overtly incestuous basis for their relationship. Only the looming mountain can provide adequate expression for the childlike awe with which he regards his father. In his relations with others David is much like one inside a house which he cannot leave looking out at persons he has never known because he has never actually moved among them. As one by one these persons depart, he begins to notice the emptiness, room leading silently to room. The novel is an account of David's attempt to ward off such knowledge. But fathers and mothers die, and brothers, friends and sisters—soul of his soul—depart. Until only the grandmother is left, calling out "Where is that child?" even as the child, unable to endure both an outer and an inner emptiness, goes at last up the snow covered mountain into the final dimension of his solitude. The emptiness, the silence and the snow into which he sinks down at the end of the novel figure forth the constant nothingness against which his bright intensities had beat, thinking it the high shores of this actual world. His life would be pathetic if it were not heroic.

The heroism is in his effort, in the extreme tenacity with which David clings to the sources of his suffering, and it is in the novel, in the record of that suffering. The very intensity which creates those illusions with which David tries to live also creates a distinctive lyric exaltation. Because perception is so consistently at fever pitch, the descriptive surfaces of the novel are exceptionally fine-grained, the communion with nature, with appearances, with actions, so close that many passages read like lyric poems. But paradoxes are endless, and if the unreleased intensity which is a tragedy for David becomes an advantage for the novelist it in turn becomes another kind of disadvantage for the reader. For Buckler has no compositional key except maximum intensity. Sentence after sentence is forced to a descriptive pitch which makes the novel exceptionally wearing to read.

One turns with something like relief from the kind of illusions with which Brian O'Connal and David Canaan seek to escape isolation to the blunt but subtle absence of such illusions in *As for Me and My House*. The bleak assumption of this beautiful novel is that Philip Bentley has no ground whatsoever upon which he might stand, no communion at all through which he might discover saving dimensions of self. The overwhelming desolation which rims Horizon around—the hostile wind, the suffocating dust and sand and the even more suffocating and claustrophobic heat—recurs on the pages of Mrs. Bentley's diary as outward manifestation of the inner desolation felt by her husband. All that Philip can claim or cling to is his maddeningly inarticulate impulse to create. The novel is less like a story than it is like a cumulative picture in which Ross, by a remarkable, almost *tour de force* repetition of detail, grains a central scene upon the reader's consciousness so that all other details and even the action of the novel achieve meaningful focus in relation to the one scene at the center, repeated some thirty times. It is of course that in which Philip is shown retreating to his study where he will sit interminable evening superimposed upon interminable evening, drawing or fiddling at drawing, or staring with baffled intensity at drawings he has in some other time and place tried to draw. Yet, "Even though the drawings are only torn up or put away to fill more boxes when we move, even though no one ever gets a glimpse of them . . . still they're for him the only part of life that's real or genuine." The novel is a projection through the medium of Mrs. Bentley's remarkably responsive consciousness of the despair in which her husband is caught, "some twisted, stumbling power locked up within him . . . so blind and helpless it can't find outlet, so clenched with urgency it can't release itself." And the town itself, with the dust "reeling in the streets," the heat "dry and deadly like a drill" and the wind "like something solid pressed against the face," is simply a place name for the limbo in which Bentley lives, "a wilderness outside of night and sky and prairie with this one little spot of Horizon

WARREN TALLMAN

hung up lost in its immensity" beneath which "he's as lost and alone."

Philip's need to escape from this isolation drives him to art. But just as he can find no terms under which he may act as a self so he can find no terms under which he may act as an artist. His most characteristic drawing is a receding perspective in which a looming false-front building gives way to a diminished next building, and a next, and a next, an endless progression which provides a portrait of the monotony of his own being. The novel is a study of a frustrated artist—actually, a non-artist—one unable to discover a subject which will release him from his oppressive incapacity to create. The excellence of the study traces to the remarkable resourcefulness with which Ross brings into place the day-to-day nuances of Mrs. Bentley's struggling consciousness as he builds up her account of an artist who cannot create because he cannot possess himself and who cannot possess himself because there is no self to possess. Certainly there are more deep-reaching portraits of the artist, for in this novel all is muffled within Philip's inarticulation, but none that I know represents with so steady a pressure of felt truth the pervasive undermining of all vital energies which occurs when the would-be artist's creativity is thwarted. No momentary exuberance survives. The flowers won't grow. The adopted boy, for whom Philip tries to provide that childhood he did not have himself, cannot be kept. Neither can his horse. Neither can his dog. Nothing can drive away the "faint old smell of other lives" from the house. No one and nothing can intercede to shut out the wind, prevent the dust, lessen the heat in which the Bentleys are "imbedded . . . like insects in a fluid that has congealed." Not once in the novel does Philip break through the torment of his constraint to utter a free sentence. Even when his wife confronts him with knowledge of his covert love affair with Judith West his response, beyond the endurance of even an Arthur Dimmesdale, is silence. But if the beauty is in the detailing, it does not trace to the dreariness which is portrayed. It traces to the constant presence in Mrs. Bentley's consciousness of an exuberance which flares up like matches in the wind and struggles to survive, a counter-impulse within her by which life attempts to defeat the defeat. This bravery loses out to the dreariness—the flowers *won't* grow—but in the process of struggling it animates the novel.

240

However, there is no mistaking the meaning which events bring into place during the last distraught days which the diary records when Judith West dies and even the wind rebels, blowing the false-front town flat. When creative power is thwarted, destructive power emerges. "It's hard," Mrs. Bentley tells us, "to stand back watching a whole life go to waste." But the diary is an inch by inch representation along the walls of her resisting consciousness of the relentless crumbling under destructive pressure of her husband's life and hence her own as the undertow of bitter silence about which the portrait is built drags these prairie swimmers under wind, under dust, under heat, to that ocean floor of inner death upon which silence rests, strongest swimmers most deeply drowned.

There is a superb scene in which the Bentleys walk during an April snow storm to the outskirts of town:

> The snow spun round us thick and slow like feathers till it seemed we were walking on and through a cloud. The little town loomed up and fell away. On the outskirts we took the railroad track, where the telegraph poles and double line of fence looked like a drawing from which all the horizontal strokes had been erased. The spongy flakes kept melting and trickling down our cheeks, and we took off our gloves sometimes to feel their coolness on our hands. We were silent most of the way. There was a hush in the snow like a finger raised.
>
> We came at last to a sudden deep ravine. There was a hoarse little torrent at the bottom, with a shaggy, tumbling swiftness that we listened to a while, then went down the slippery bank to watch. We brushed off a stone and sat with our backs against the trestle of the railway bridge. The flakes came whirling out of the whiteness, spun against the stream a moment, vanished at its touch. On our shoulders and knees and hats again they piled up little drifts of silence.
>
> Then the bridge over us picked up the coming of a train. It was there even while the silence was still intact. At last we heard a distant whistle-blade, then a single point of sound, like one drop of water in a whole sky. It dilated, spread. The sky and silence began imperceptibly to fill with it. We steeled ourselves a little, feeling the pounding onrush in the trestle of the bridge. It quickened, gathered, shook the earth, then swept in an iron roar above us, thundering and dark.
>
> We emerged from it slowly, while the trestle a moment or two sustained the clang and din. I glanced at Philip, then quickly back to the water. A train still makes him wince sometimes. At

night, when the whistle's loneliest, he'll toss a moment, then lie still and tense. In the daytime I've seen his eyes take on a quick half eager look, just for a second or two, and then sink flat and cold again.

The hushed, almost sealed, inner silence which is the price Philip Bentley pays for his failure to summon self into presence is not broken but poured momentarily full of the "iron roar . . . thundering and dark" which in times past had signaled to him an escape from the desolation of his childhood. Even on this forsaken April day it echoes into lost realms of self to those times when his eyes took on a "quick half-eager look" until the weight of silence reasserts itself and they turn "flat and cold" like the day. When an artist in fact discovers that close correspondence to life which he is always seeking, life takes over and the details of representation become inexhaustibly suggestive. D. H. Lawrence's unhappy lovers have wandered through Sherwood Forest to just such sudden "deep ravines" and have half glimpsed the "shaggy tumbling swiftness" which they, like the Bentleys, have lost from their lives. And James Joyce's depressed Dubliners have had the same universal angel of silence shake snow into drifts upon "shoulders and knees and hats" as the pounding onrush of the train, thunder in the blood, dwindles and disappears, leaving the scene, "distorted, intensified, alive with thin, cold bitter life." It is not surprising that the departing train draws Mrs. Bentley's thoughts—it is one pathos of the novel that we never learn her first name—back in the longest retrospective passage of the diary to her husband's childhood in search of the bitterness, constantly emphasized, which gradually seals him in, seals her out. Nor is it surprising that later when she becomes aware of the force of mute passion with which Judith West breaks through Philip's constraint she is at once reminded of the April day she and her husband "sat in the snowstorm watching the water rush through the stones"—the silence, the snow, the water and the stones—the story of their lives in a profound moment, a magnificent scene.

If knowledge of Philip Bentley's uncreated childhood comes mostly through the indirection of his adult life, our knowledge of Alan MacNeil's isolation and insecurity comes through the indirection of the adult conflicts he witnesses. And most of the adults in *Each Man's Son* can be known only through the additional indirection of the assigned part each plays in the general scheme of conflict which MacLennan has devised. They are like those persons in actual life whose roles become masks concealing self from access. Such arrangements are as unsatisfactory in novels as they are in actuality. Self is the center of being, the source of our most vital impulses, and when those fictional persons who enact the artist's vision of life are not directly related to the artist's self, they will inevitably speak and act mechanically, without true animation. This is so decidedly the case in *Each Man's Son*—as in MacLennan's fiction as a whole—that any attempt to understand Alan MacNeil's plight must be an attempt to move past the masks MacLennan has created in order to reach what is vital, the source rather than the surfaces of his vision.

The mask in *Each Man's Son*—as, again, in all of MacLennan's novels—is made up of the pseudo-sophistication, the surface civilization in terms of which the portrait of Doctor Ainslee is built. MacLennan never wearies of extolling his surgical prowess and yet his human *savoir faire* and yet his intellectual probity. He is the fastest man in North America with an appendectomy and other doctors stand by, not to help, but to hold the watch on his performance, noting afterward with knowing glance that Ainslee has done it again. If I seem to be suggesting that Doctor Ainslee is Walter Mitty played straight, this is less an accusation than it is an identification. For it is not, as MacLennan would have us believe, residual effects of Calvinistic sin which constantly unsettle the doctor's composure. It is the all but impossible facade he seeks to maintain, so false that MacLennan is incapable of animating it because it has so little to do with the profound naiveté and relative crudity of response in which MacLennan's true force as an artist is rooted.

If all the world were true there would be no place in fiction for falsity. But, notoriously, the world is far from true, and Doctor Ainslee's cultural veneer is all too accurate in its patent falsity—true of Ainslee, true of a good half of MacLennan's protagonists, true—above all—of most North Americans, who also adopt European disguises having little or nothing to do with the self beneath, the source of vital energy. Constant anxiety is the price Ainslee pays in order to maintain his facade. But if MacLennan would have us believe that the reason for the anxiety is the Calvinism, a more apt explanation for both the anxiety and the mask comes to us from the other, the vital side of the novel.

The night that Ainslee operates upon Alan he flees to the harborside from the strain of both a professional and a personal involvement—cutting the child he hopes to adopt—and experiences a partial breakdown in which "his mind was pounding with its own rhythms and his body was out of control." To escape the panic that grips him, he runs up the wharf.

> Before he realized that his feet had caught in something soft he plunged forward, an explosion of light burst in his head and his right temple hit the boards. For a moment he lay half stunned, trying to understand what had happened. He rolled to get up, and as he did so, the hair on the nape of his neck prickled. He had stumbled over something alive, and now this living thing was rising beside him. He could smell, feel and hear it, and as he jerked his head around he saw the outline of a broken-peaked cap appear against the residual light from the sea. It rose on a pair of huge shoulders and stood over Ainslee like a tower.

The tower is Red Willie MacIsaac, and Ainslee in his fear, repugnance and anger shouts out, "You drunken swine, MacIsaac —don't you know who I am?" This outcry under these circumstances does much to illuminate the novel.

For the drunken swine, Red Willie, is one of the group of incredibly naive and endlessly quarrelsome displaced Highlanders whose portraits in their really superb clarity and exuberance make up much the most vital part of the novel. These Highlanders, doomed to wear their vitality away in the dreary Cape Breton Island mines, rebel like the profound children they are by recourse to the only political action of which they are capable, their endless evening brawls. The sum of their whimsical and powerful impulses is crystallized into the portrait of their downfallen hero, Archie MacNeil, the finest single portrait in MacLennan's novels.

Now the main use to which Doctor Ainslee's mask—his civilized facade—is put is to hold these impulses in check. A word from him and the miners back away, chagrined. When he cries out, Red Willie becomes contrite. But the identification is surely much closer. When the rhythms of Ainslee's mind and body become separated and he trips over and becomes mingled with Red Willie there is reason to believe that "this living thing . . . beside him" is simply the self behind the mask, the vital, violent being held in check by the civilized surface. That Ainslee can and does check Red Willie is an obvious victory for Ainslee and it is a tragedy for Alan's actual father, Archie. For Ainslee stumbles over Red Willie immediately after Archie has been ruinously defeated in Trenton. And the voice that emerges when he lies tangled with Red Willie mutters, "There was dirty tricks in the States last Friday and by chesus I am going to kick them up your ass." The blame is, if dubiously aimed, properly assigned. The conflict at the heart of the novel is between the civilized facade maintained by Ainslee and the naive violence of the place represented by Archie MacNeil.

Alan is caught between the violent needs which drive his father away on the forlorn prize fighter's Odyssey in which his one-time physical magnificence becomes the dupe of unscrupulous promoters and the counter needs which drive Ainslee to fill in the chinks of his cultural facade by inching his way through the alien Greek of the classical Odyssey. Both men want to save Alan from the mines, those holes in the ground which give nothing and take everything away, but each tries to do so in ways which rule out the other. At the conclusion of the novel, when Archie prevails and smashes down his wife and her lover and he and Ainslee confront each other, it is the civilized surface confronting the violent self among the ruins created by their tragic alienation.

PART TWO: THE HOUSE REPOSSESSED

To read novels is to gain impressions and these are what I tried to document in the first part of this essay. Now let the four windows of the fictional house become as one view and let the four occupants (Alan MacNeil from *Each Man's Son*, Philip Bentley from *As for Me and My House*, David Canaan from *The Mountain and the Valley* and Brian O'Connal from *Who Has Seen the Wind*) be re-grouped in a scene where the intangibles which I have been calling Self look toward other intangibles which most decisively influence its efforts to come into presence. At the back depth of this scene an immeasurable extent of snow is falling in a downward motion that is without force through a silence that is without contrasts to an earth that is "distorted, intensified, alive with thin, cold, bitter life." How bitter can best be shown by lifting the snow shroud to let the sun shine momentarily as Morley Callaghan's three hunters (*They Shall Inherit the Earth*) move across "rocky ridges and the desolate bush" to where a herd of deer whose hooves had become caught in the snow crust now lie in bloody heaps, abandoned where they have been destroyed by a pack of thin, cold, bitter wolves. As the hunters watch, the sun sets, and "a vast shadow fell over the earth, over the rocky ridges and the desolate bush and over the frozen carcasses." The night shadows mingle with the wolf shadows and cover the dark blood of the deer as the wavering shroud of snow again begins to fall through the "dreadful silence and coldness" felt everywhere at the back depth of the scene.

Move now to the middle depth where from the left a bleak expanse of prairie gives way at the center to forests and mountains which merge on the right with the seacoast looking toward Europe where Alan stands with his mother as he did the day his novel began. That day, Alan emulated Yeats's sad shepherd from the opposite Irish shore, but in Alan's shell the "inarticulate moan" which the shepherd heard becomes that "oldest sound in the world," the remote waterfall roaring of his own salt blood. When Yeats's shepherd grew and changed into an ominous older man the sound in the shell darkened and strengthened into the beating of a prophetic "frenzied drum" which later still became a "blood-dimmed tide" carrying to the Europe of his imagination as to the Europe of succeeding years "the fury and mire of human veins." But in Alan's less tutored ear on his side of the Atlantic, the blood sea sounds a more innocent summons as his thoughts follow along those unseen paths wandered by his bright and battered highland father. All Alan knows is that this father is the "strongest man in the world." All that this strongest man knows is the inner thrust of a ceaseless mindless desire to prevail so powerful that even as he stumbles from defeat to defeat he follows this path down as though it were a way up to the championship, that mountain peak in the mind from which no opposing force could ever banish him. And so powerful is the son's consciousness of his father's destiny that even at the last when "the pack of muscles under the cloth of his jacket shifted" and the "poker shot up," Alan's immediate thought, far off from the murder at hand, is. "So that was what it meant to be the strongest man in the world!"

The desire to prevail. Move to where David Canaan is standing in a field beside the tracks as the train taking his friend Toby back to Halifax "came in sight thundering nearer and nearer." But Toby, whom David had expected to wave as the train drew past, "didn't glance once, not once, toward the house or the field." And as the thundering on the tracks diminishes, the thunder in David's blood takes over and "a blind hatred of Toby went through him. It seemed as if that were part of his own life he was seeing—his life stolen before his eyes." His protest at being canceled out rises from hatred to rage and he "slashed at the pulpy turnips blindly wherever the hack fell," until he slashes his way through the rage and discovers a deeper depth where "in his mind there was only a stillness like the stillness of snow sifting through the spokes of wagon wheels or moonlight on the frozen road or the dark brook at night."

At the far left, the prairies slope away like Shelley's "lone and level sands." But there is no fallen Ozymandias here where no Ozymandias has ever stood. Instead there are the false-front stores of Horizon, warped by the heat, sand-blasted by the drouth dust, and blown askew by the prairie wind. Here, Mrs. Bentley walks once more—as in her diary she so often mentions —along the tracks to the outskirts of town where five grain elevators stand "aloof and imperturbable, like ancient obelisques," as dust clouds "darkening and thinning and swaying" in the ominous upper prairie of the sky seem "like a quivering backdrop before which was about to be enacted some grim, primeval tragedy." The swaying dust clouds above, the darkening prairie beneath, the ancient-seeming elevators she huddles against, as well as her mournful sense of the grim, the primeval, the tragic—these details speak for the entire scene which I have been sketching. They speak of a tragedy in which the desire to prevail that drives self on its strange journeys toward fulfillment is brought to an impasse on northern fields of a continent which has remained profoundly indifferent to its inhabitant, transplanted European man. The continent itself—the gray wolf whose shadow is underneath the snow—has resisted the culture, the cultivation, the civilization which is indigenous to Europe but alien to North America even though it is dominant in North America.

If Alan, Philip, Brian and David are notably to discover alternatives to the isolation from which they suffer, this is not because they are resourceless persons but because the isolation is in-grained, inherent, indwelling. One alternative is much like the next when all the rooms are equally empty in the vast space-haunted house they occupy. And those gods who over-rule the house toward whom self quickens in its need to prevail are such as preside over forests and open fields, mountains, prairies and plains: snow gods, dust gods, drouth gods, wind gods, wolf gods —native to the place and to the empty manner born. These divinities speak, if at all, to such as lone it toward the mountain pass and the hidden lake, the rushing river and the open empty road. And the experiential emptiness of the place shows on the faces of such loners as that weathered yet naive expressionlessness, the stamp of the man to whom little or nothing has happened in a place where the story reads, not here, not much, not yet. Underneath the European disguises North American man assumes, self too is such a loner. And the angel at his shoulder, met everywhere in the weave of these novels because it is everywhere and omnipresent in the vast house we occupy, is silence. Out of the weave of the silence emerges the shroud of snow. But underneath the snow, the dark blood brightens.

For self does not readily accept separation, isolation and silence. These are conditions of non-being, and whether one assumes that the ground toward which self struggles in its search for completion is divine and eternal or only individual and temporal, either alternative supposes rebellion against no being at all. It is from this fate that Brian O'Connal flees in panic the night he walks from his uncle's farm to town. "It was as though he listened to the drearing wind and in the spread darkness of the prairie night was being drained of his very self." It is against this same fate that Alan MacNeil's father beats with his fists, seeking some eminence from which the physical strength that is his measure of self cannot be pulled down to defeat. It is against this fate that Philip Bentley struggles those evenings in his study, seeking to liberate "some twisted stumbling" creative power locked up within him even though all he can create is sketches which reveal how pervasively non-being has invaded his life. And it is against this fate that David Canaan slashes in the field beside the tracks before yielding when he lies down against the flank of the mountain under a blanket of snow upon a bed of silence.

But it is not here that the scene dims out. For the last sound that David hears is that North American lullaby which sings the sleeping self awake as a train "whistled beyond the valley" then "thundered along the rails and was gone." Had Alan MacNeil turned his back upon Europe, the blood sound in the shell would have been that rising up from the railroad earth, those train sounds hooting all loners home to where, up front in the scene, the dark silence breaks up into the gushing of the neon and the noise.

But along St. Urbain Street in Montreal, the marvelous, the splendid and the amazing have given way to the common-place, the shabby and the unspeakable. And even before think-ing of anything so portentous as a new self, Mordecai Richler has been engaged in the much more onerous task of clearing away the debris which has accumulated in a world where all disguises have been put in doubt. His first three novels are studies of ruined lives: André, the guilt-haunted Canadian artist, who is eventually murdered by the Nazi, Kraus, whose sister Theresa then commits suicide; the guilt-ridden homosexual, Derek, his equally guilty sister, Jessie, and her equally guilty husband, the alcoholic, Barney; the Wellington College professor, Theo Hall, and his wife, Miriam; Norman, the American Fifth Amend-ment expatriate, whose brother is murdered by Ernst, the German youth whom Sally, the Toronto girl, ruins her life trying to save. All of these persons reach out, cry out, for any masks other than the ones they have.

And they testify to Richler's affinity with that side of modern life where the misbegotten wander through ruined Spains of self-pity, poisoned to the point of near and at times actual mad-ness by self-loathing. However, Richler does not seek out these persons in order to demonstrate several times over that we are wrapped up like so many sweating sardines in world misery, world guilt, world sorrow. Like André, Norman and Noah, the protaganists of these novels, he is inside the misery looking for a way out. What looks out is a courageous intelligence struggling to realize that the tormented sleep of self loathing which he explores is just that—a sleep, a dream, a nightmare: but not the reality.

In his fourth novel, *The Apprenticeship of Duddy Kravitz*, the sleeper begins to come awake. The nightmare is still there, but it is not the same nightmare. In *The Acrobats* and *A Choice of Enemies*, Richler chooses areas of world guilt as the basis for dream terror. The Spanish war, the second world war, the victims of these wars and of their ideologies make up the mani-fest content, the general human failure which images and invites the latent personal failures represented. People whose lives have gone smash drift into areas where life has gone smash and consort with the ghosts who have survived. In *Duddy Kravitz* the scope contracts. Both the ghosts who make up the nightmare and the ideologies through which they wander have faded from mind. Duddy's father, his brother Lenny, his uncle and aunt, his teacher MacPherson, his friend Virgil, his enemy Dingleman, and his shiksa Yvette all live tangled lives in a world where they do not know themselves. But they are caught up by personal disorders rather than world disorder, family strife rather than international strife, individual conflict rather than ideological conflict. And within the localized dream we meet an entirely different dreamer. We meet the direct intelligence and colloquial exuberance that is Duddy's style—and Richler's.

T. S. Eliot has said that poetry in our time is a mug's game. So fiction, and Richler is one of the mugs. Duddy has ceased to care for appearances and this insouciance releases him from the nightmare. All of the other people in the novel cannot possess themselves because their vital energies are devoted full-time to maintaining the false appearances in terms of which they identify themselves. These appearances—the cultural, ethical, communal pretensions to which they cling—mask over but scarcely conceal the distinctly uncultured, unethical, isolated actuality in which they participate. Hence the importance in their lives of Dingleman, the Boy Wonder, who is a projection of their actual longings to be at ease in Zion in a Cadillac at the same time as he is a projection of the limitation of these longings, being hopelessly crippled. But Duddy, who has ceased to care for appearances, sees people for what they are, himself included. And what he sees, he accepts—himself included. In an acquisitive world he is exuberantly acquisitive. When he is tricked, he weeps. When threatened, he becomes dangerous. When attacked, he bites back. When befriended, he is generous. When hard-pressed he becomes frantic. When denied, he is filled with wrath. From the weave of this erratic shuttling, a self struggles into presence, a naive yet shrewd latter-day Huck Finn, floating on a battered money raft down a sleazy neon river through a drift of lives, wanting to light out for somewhere, wanting somewhere to light out for.

Plato tells us that when a new music is heard the walls of the city tremble. The music in Duddy Kravitz is where in novels it always is, in the style. The groove in which the style runs is that of an exuberance, shifting into exaggeration, shifting into those distortions by which Richler achieves his comic vision of Montreal. The finest parts of the novel are those in which Richler most freely indulges the distortions: the sequence in which the documentary film director Friar produces a wedding ceremony masterpiece which views like the stream of consciousness of a lunatic, a fantasia of the contemporary mind; the entire portrait of Virgil who wants to organize the epileptics of the world and be "their Sister Kenny," as well as the more somber portraits of Dingleman and Duddy's aunt Ida. Because Duddy has ceased to care for appearances, he moves past all of the genteel surfaces of the city and encounters an actuality in which all that is characteristically human has retreated to small corners of consciousness and life becomes a grotesque game played by bewildered grotesques. The persons who make up this gallery not only fail to invoke self but can scarcely recognize what it is to be a human being. They are like uncertain creatures in a fabulous but confusing zoo, not sure why they are there, not even sure what human forest they once inhabited.

They testify in the language of the sometimes comic, sometimes grim, distortions Richler has created to the oppressive weight of doubt, guilt, remorse, shame, and regret that history has imposed upon modern man, particularly upon man in the city, where the effects of history, most closely organized, are most acutely felt. The greater the system of threats to self, the more extensive the system of appearances needed to ward off those threats, the more marked the distortions of characteristic human need and desire. And the more marked the distortions, the more difficult the artist's task. For sensibility, that active sum of the artist's self, never does exist in relation to itself alone. It exists in relation to what *is*—actual persons, an actual city, actual lives. When the impact of accomplished history imposes distortions upon that actuality, sensibility must adjust itself to the distortions. The story of these adjustments is, I think, the most significant feature of North American fiction in our time. Long ago and far away, before World War One o'clock, Theodore Dreiser could look at the world with direct eyes. Characteristic human impulses of love, sorrow, hope, fear, existed in the actual world as love, sorrow, hope, fear; and Dreiser could direct his powerful sensibility into representation which was, as they say, "like life." But after World War One, in *The Great Gatsby*, possibly the most significant of the between-wars novels, there is open recognition of a distorted actuality necessitating a re-ordering of sensibility, one which both Gatsby and Fitzgerald fail to achieve.

Since World War Two the need for adjustment has become even more marked, simply because the distortions have become more pronounced. In *Duddy Kravitz*, Richler follows closely in the groove of Duddy's exuberance and on out into the exaggerations and distortions which make up his adjustment to actual Montreal. By doing so he is able to achieve an authentic relationship to life in that city—Duddy's dream of Caliban along the drear streets of Zoo. In this Richler is at one with the considerable group of contemporary writers—call them mugs, call them angry, call them beat—who all are seeking in their art those re-adjustments which will permit them to relate their sensibilities to what actually is. History has had and continues to have her say. These writers are trying to answer back. If the vision which Richler achieves in answer to history jars upon our sensibilities, that is because we have all heard of Prospero's cloud capped towers and gorgeous palaces. Yet, if the style which conveys the vision twangles from glib to brash, from colloquial to obscene, that is because the true North American tone, at long past World War Two o'clock, is much closer to that of Caliban than ever it has been to that of Prospero whose magic was a European magic, long sunk from sight, and whose daughter and her beau and their world are out of fashion like old tunes or like the lovers on Keats's urn, maybe forever but address unknown. The brave new world toward which Duddy's self quickens is like the lake property he covets throughout the novel and finally possesses. When he dives in, seeking a rebirth, he scrapes bottom. But he doesn't care, he doesn't care, he doesn't care. Which is why the mug can make with the music.

D. H. Lawrence contended that in the visions of art a relatively finer vision is substituted for the relatively cruder visions extant. But in North America, as I hope this restricted study at least partially confirms, finer is relatively crude, because frequently untrue, and crude can be relatively fine. All too often, in fiction as in life, those pretensions which we seek out because they make us fine provide false furnishings for the actual house in which we live. This fine is crude. Duddy, who would not know a pretension if he met one, wanders for this reason by accident and mostly unaware into the actual house. His crude is relatively fine. True, there are no gods hovering over Duddy's lake, no grandiose hotel, no summer camp for children. There is only old mother North America with her snow hair, her mountain forehead, her prairie eyes, and her wolf teeth, her wind song and her vague head of old Indian memories. And what has she to do with Duddy Kravitz? A lot, I think. For when the house is repossessed the gods come back—snow gods, dust gods, wind gods, wolf gods—but life gods too. And life is the value. When history conspires against life, ruining the house, life will fight back in the only way it can, by not caring. Heavy, heavy doesn't hang over Duddy's head. And that is his value.

Snow melts away. Mountains can be very beautiful. Wheat is growing on the prairies. And in the dark forest beside the hidden lakes the deer are standing, waiting. So turn off the neon, tune out the noise, place Duddy in the foreground of the scene. Since life is the value, let blood melt snow, and place David Caanan beside him. Strike a match to light Mrs. Bentley a path through the wolf-wind night with its dust-grit teeth until she appears standing beside Duddy and David. Smooth over that bashed-in face, those cauliflowered ears, and let Highland Archie MacNeil, strongest man in the world, appear. For this reader it is these four who emerge from the novels considered as crude with the true crudeness of the place, and by this token most fine, most worth close consideration by those who take the visions of fiction as a decisive mode of relatedness to the actual house in which we live. And of these four, it is Mrs. Bentley in her utter absence of pretentiousness and Duddy in his utter absence of pretentiousness who most effectively and convincingly come forward and take their awkward North American bows. At which point, close out the scene.

VI

HENRY KREISEL

The Prairie: A State of Mind

Soon after I first arrived in Alberta, now over twenty years ago, there appeared in the *Edmonton Journal* a letter in which the writer, replying to some article which appeared sometime earlier, asserted with passionate conviction that the earth was flat. Now in itself that would have been quite unremarkable, the expression merely of some cranky and eccentric old man. Normally, then, one would not have been likely to pay very much attention to such a letter, and one would have passed it over with an amused smile. Nothing pleases us more than to be able to feel superior to pre-scientific man, secure behind the fortress of our own knowledge. I am no different in this respect from most other people. But there was something in the tone of that letter that would not allow me that kind of response. Far from feeling superior, I felt awed. Even as I write these lines, the emotion evoked in me by that letter that appeared in a newspaper more than twenty years ago comes back to me, tangible and palpable.

The tone of the letter was imperious. Surveying his vast domains, a giant with feet firmly rooted in the earth, a lord of the land asserted what his eyes saw, what his heart felt, and what his mind perceived. I cut the letter out and for some time carried it about with me in my wallet. I don't really know why I did that. I do know that in my travels round the prairie in those early years of my life in the Canadian west I looked at the great landscape through the eyes of that unknown man. At last I threw the clipping away, but the imagined figure of that giant remained to haunt my mind.

Years later I finally came to terms with that vision in a story that I called "The Broken Globe." This story deals with the clash between a father and his young son. The son, who is

Reprinted from *Transactions of the Royal Society of Canada*, vol 6: series 4, June 1968, copyright © Royal Society of Canada, by permission of the author and the Royal Society of Canada.

eventually to become a scientist, comes home from school one day and tells his father that the earth moves. The father, a Ukrainian settler, secure in something very like a medieval faith, asserts passionately that it does not and that his son is being tempted and corrupted by the devil. The story is told by a narrator, an academic who goes to visit the father, now an old man, to bring him greetings from his estranged scientist-son. At the end of the story, after the narrator has heard from the father about the conflict that alienated him from his son, the narrator rises to leave:

> Together we walked out of the house. When I was about to get into my car, he touched me lightly on the arm. I turned. His eyes surveyed the vast expanse of sky and land, stretching far into the distance, reddish clouds in the sky and blue shadows on the land. With a gesture of great dignity and power he lifted his arm and stood pointing into the distance, at the flat land and the low-hanging sky.
>
> "Look," he said, very slowly and very quietly, "she is flat and she stands still."
>
> It was impossible not to feel a kind of admiration for the old man. There was something heroic about him. I held out my hand and he took it. He looked at me steadily, then averted his eyes and said, "Send greetings to my son."
>
> I drove off quickly, but had to stop again in order to open the wooden gate. I looked back at the house, and saw him still standing there, still looking at his beloved land, a lonely, towering figure framed against the darkening evening sky.[1]

You will have noticed that the images I used to describe my imagined man seem extravagant—"a lord of the land," "a giant." These were in fact the images that came to me and I should myself have regarded them as purely subjective, if I had not afterward in my reading encountered similar images in the work of other writers who write about the appearances of men on the prairie at certain times. Thus in Martha Ostenso's *Wild Geese* a young school teacher sees "against the strange pearly distance . . . the giant figure of a man beside his horse," and when he comes closer she recognizes Fusi Aronson, "the great Icelander. . . . He was grand in his demeanor, and somehow lonely,

[1] Henry Kreisel, "The Broken Globe," in *The Best American Short Stories 1966*, edited by Martha Foley and David Burnett (Boston: Houghton Mifflin Co., 1966), p. 165.

as a towering mountain is lonely, or as a solitary oak on the prairie" (31).[2] On the very first page of *Settlers of the Marsh*, Philip Grove, describing two men "fighting their way through the gathering dusk," calls one of them, Lars Nelson, "a giant, of three years' standing in the country" (11).[3] And in his autobiography, *In Search of Myself*, Grove, recalling the origin of *Fruits of the Earth* and his first encounter with the figure who was to become Abe Spalding, describes the arresting and startling sight of a man plowing land generally thought to be unfit for farming. "Outlined as he was against a tilted and spoked sunset in the western sky," he writes, "he looked like a giant. Never before had I seen, between farm and town, a human being in all my drives." Grove goes on to tell how he stopped his horses and learned that this man had only that very afternoon arrived from Ontario, after a train journey of two thousand miles, had at once filed a claim for a homestead of a hundred and sixty acres, had unloaded his horses from the freight-car, and was now plowing his first field. And when Grove expresses his surprise at the speed with which this newcomer set to work, the man replies, "Nothing else to do" (259).[4]

I set the image of the giant in the landscape over against the more familiar one of man pitted against a vast and frequently hostile natural environment that tends to dwarf him, at the mercy of what Grove calls, in *Settlers of the Marsh*, "a dumb shifting of forces" (152). Man, the giant-conqueror, and man, the insignificant dwarf always threatened by defeat, form the two polarities of the state of mind produced by the sheer physical fact of the prairie.

There are moments when the two images coalesce. So the observant Mrs. Bentley, whose diary forms the substance of Sinclair Ross's novel *As for Me and My House*, records the response of a prairie congregation during the bleak and drought-haunted 1930s:

[2] Martha Ostenso, *Wild Geese* (originally published 1925). References in parentheses are to the New Canadian Library edition, published by McClelland and Stewart, Toronto, 1961.

[3] Frederick Philip Grove, *Settlers of the Marsh*. References in parentheses are to the first edition, published by the Ryerson Press, Toronto, 1925.

[4] Frederick Philip Grove, *In Search of Myself*. References in parentheses are to the first edition, published by the Macmillan Co. of Canada, Toronto, 1946.

The last hymn was staidly orthodox, but through it there seemed to mount something primitive, something that was less a response to Philip's sermon and scripture reading than to the grim futility of their own lives. Five years in succession now they've been blown out, dried out, hailed out; and it was as if in the face of so blind and uncaring a universe they were trying to assert themselves, to insist upon their own meaning and importance. (19)[5]

All discussion of the literature produced in the Canadian west must of necessity begin with the impact of the landscape upon the mind. "Only a great artist," records Mrs. Bentley, "could ever paint the prairie, the vacancy and stillness of it, the bare essentials of a landscape, sky and earth" (59). W. O. Mitchell, in the opening sentences of *Who Has Seen the Wind*, speaks of the "least common denominator of nature, the skeleton requirements simply, of land and sky" (3).[6] He goes on to describe the impact of the landscape on Brian O'Connal, a four-year-old boy, living in a little prairie town and venturing for the first time to the edge of town:

He looked up to find that the street had stopped. Ahead lay the sudden emptiness of the prairie. For the first time in his four years of life he was alone on the prairie.

He had seen it often, from the veranda of his uncle's farmhouse, or at the end of a long street, but till now he had never heard it. The hum of telephone wires along the road, the ring of hidden crickets, the stitching sound of grasshoppers, the sudden relief of a meadow lark's song, were deliciously strange to him. . . .

A gopher squeaked questioningly as Brian sat down upon a rock warm to the back of his thigh. . . . The gopher squeaked again, and he saw it a few yards away, sitting up, and watching him from his pulpit hole. A suave-winged hawk chose that moment to slip its shadow over the face of the prairie.

And all about him was the wind now, a pervasive sighing through great emptiness, unhampered by the buildings of the town, warm and living against his face and in his hair. (11)

[5] Sinclair Ross, *As for Me and My House* (originally published 1947). References in parentheses are to the New Canadian Library edition, published by McClelland and Stewart, Toronto, 1957.

[6] W. O. Mitchell, *Who Has Seen the Wind* (originally published 1947). References in parentheses are to a new edition, published by Macmillan of Canada, Toronto, 1960.

Only one other kind of landscape gives us the same skeleton requirements, the same vacancy and stillness, the same movement of wind through space—and that is the sea. So when Mrs. Bentley records in her diary that "there's a high, rocking wind that rattles the window and creaks the walls. It's strong and steady like a great tide after the winter pouring north again, and I have a queer, helpless sense of being lost miles out in the middle of it" (35), she might well be tossing in heavy seas, protected only by a small and fragile little bark. In Grove's *Over Prairie Trails*, that remarkable book of impressionistic essays describing seven trips that Grove made in 1917 and 1918 between Gladstone and Falmouth near the western shore of Lake Manitoba, the prairie as sea becomes one of the controlling patterns shaping the imagination of the observer. On one of these trips—in the dead of winter—Grove prepares his horse-drawn cutter as if it were a boat being readied for a fairly long and possibly dangerous journey:

> Not a bolt but I tested it with a wrench; and before the stores were closed, I bought myself enough canned goods to feed me for a week should through any untoward accident the need arise. I always carried a little alcohol stove, and with my tarpaulin I could convert my cutter within three minutes into a windproof tent. Cramped quarters, to be sure, but better than being given over to the wind at thirty below. (60-61)[7]

Soon the cutter, the horses, and the man meet the first test— very like a Conradian crew coming to grips with a storm at sea. A mountainous snowdrift bars the way. The horses, Dan and Peter, who become wonderful characters in their own right, panic. They plunge wildly, rear on their hind legs, pull apart, try to turn and retrace their steps. "And meanwhile the cutter went sharply up at first, as if on the vast crest of a wave, then toppled over into a hole made by Dan, and altogether behaved like a boat tossed on a stormy sea. Then order returned into the chaos. . . . I spoke to the horses in a soft, quiet, purring voice; and at last I pulled in" (69).

He becomes aware of the sun, cold and high in the sky, a relentless, inexorable force, and suddenly two Greek words come

---

[7] Frederick Philip Grove, *Over Prairie Trails* (originally published 1922). References in parentheses are to the New Canadian Library edition, published by McClelland and Stewart, Toronto, 1957.

into his mind: Homer's *pontos airygetos*—the barren sea. A half
hour later he understands why:

> This was indeed like nothing so much as like being out in rough
> waters and in a troubled sea, with nothing to brace the storm
> with but a wind-tossed nutshell of a one-man sailing craft. . . .
> When the snow reached its extreme depth, it gave you the feel-
> ing which a drowning man may have when fighting his des-
> perate fight with the salty waves. But more impressive than that
> was the frequent outer resemblance. The waves of the ocean
> rise up and reach out and batter against the rocks and battle-
> ments of the shore, retreating again and ever returning to the
> assault. . . . And if such a high crest wave had suddenly been
> frozen into solidity, its outline would have mimicked to per-
> fection many a one of the snow shapes that I saw around. (77)

And when, at the end of another journey, the narrator reaches
home, he is like a sailor reaching harbor after a long voyage:

> there was the signal put out for me. A lamp in one of the
> windows of the school. . . . And in the most friendly and wel-
> coming way it looked with its single eye across at the nocturnal
> guest.
>   I could not see the cottage, but I knew that my little girl lay
> sleeping in her cosy bed, and that a young woman was sitting
> there in the dark, her face glued to the window-pane, to be
> ready with a lantern which burned in the kitchen whenever I
> might pull up between school and house. And there, no doubt,
> she had been sitting for a long while already; and there she was
> destined to sit during the winter that came, on Friday nights—
> full often for many and many an hour—full often till midnight—
> and sometimes longer. (18)

The prairie, like the sea, thus often produces an extraordinary
sensation of confinement within a vast and seemingly unlimited
space. The isolated farm-houses, the towns and settlements, even
the great cities that eventually sprang up on the prairies, become
islands in that land-sea, areas of relatively safe refuge from the
great and lonely spaces. In *Wild Geese* Martha Ostenso describes
a moment when the sensation of safety and of abandonment are
felt to be evenly balanced:

> Fine wisps of rain lashed about the little house, and the wind
> whistled in the birch trees outside, bleak as a lost bird. These
> sounds defined the feelings of enclosed warmth and safety. . . .
> But they did also the opposed thing. They stirred the fear of

loneliness, the ancient dread of abandonment in the wilderness in the profounder natures of these two who found shelter here. For an imponderable moment they sought beyond each other's eyes, sought for understanding, for communion under the vast terrestrial influence that bound them, an inevitable part and form of the earth, inseparable one from the other. (64)

At the same time the knowledge of the vast space outside brings to the surface anxieties that have their roots elsewhere and thus sharpens and crystallizes a state of mind. In *As for Me and My House* Mrs. Bentley uses the prairie constantly as a mirror of her own fears, frustrations, and helplessness:

> It's an immense night out there, wheeling and windy. The lights on the street and in the houses are helpless against the black wetness, little unilluminating glints that might be painted on it. The town seemed huddled together, cowering on a high, tiny perch, afraid to move lest it topple into the wind. Close to the parsonage is the church, black even against the darkness, towering ominously up through the night and merging with it. There's a soft steady swish of rain on the roof, and a gurgle of eave troughs running over. Above, in the high cold night, the wind goes swinging past, indifferent, liplessly mournful. It frightens me, makes me feel lost, dropped on this little perch of town and abandoned. I wish Philip would waken. (5)

That, however, is not the only, perhaps not even the most significant response to the challenge of lonely and forbidden spaces. It is easy to see Mrs. Bentley's reaction as prototypical of the state of mind induced by the prairie, but it would not be altogether accurate. It is one kind of response, but set over against it there is the response typified in Grove's *Settlers of the Marsh* by Niels Lindstedt, who, like a Conradian adventurer, a Lord Jim or a Stein, is driven to follow a dream. It expresses itself in "a longing to leave and go to the very margin of civilization, there to clear a new place; and when it is cleared and people began to settle about it, to move on once more, again to the very edge of pioneerdom, to start it all over anew. . . . That way his enormous strength would still have a meaning" (180).

To conquer a piece of the continent, to put one's imprint upon virgin land, to say, "Here I am, for that I came," is as much a way of defining oneself, of proving one's existence, as is Descartes's *cogito, ergo sum*. That is surely why that man whom Grove saw plowing a field barely two hours after his arrival was driven to do it. He had to prove to himself that he was in some way master of his destiny, that he was fully alive, and that his strength had meaning. When he told Grove that he was doing what he was doing because there was nothing else to do, he was telling him the simple truth, but leaving a more complex truth unspoken, and probably even unperceived.

The conquest of territory is by definition a violent process. In the Canadian west, as elsewhere on this continent, it involved the displacement of the indigenous population by often scandalous means, and then the taming of the land itself. The displacement, the conquest of the Indians, and later the rising of the Métis under Louis Riel, are events significantly absent from the literature I am discussing. Occasionally Riel breaks into the consciousness of one or another of the characters, usually an old man or an old woman remembering troubled times; occasionally the figure of an Indian appears briefly, but is soon gone. No doubt that is how things appeared to the European settlers on the prairie; no doubt our writers did not really make themselves too familiar with the indigenous people of the prairie, seeing them either as noble savages or not seeing them at all, but it is likely that a conscious or subconscious process of suppression is also at work here.

The conquest of the land itself is by contrast a dominant theme, and the price paid for the conquest by the conqueror or the would-be conqueror is clearly and memorably established. The attempt to conquer the land is a huge gamble. Many lose, and there are everywhere mute emblems testifying to defeat. "Once I passed the skeleton of a stable," Grove records in *Over Prairie Trails*, "the remnant of the buildings put up by a pioneer settler who had to give in after having wasted effort and substance and worn his knuckles to the bone. The wilderness uses human material up" (11). But into the attempted conquest, whether ultimately successful or not, men pour an awesome, concentrated passion. The breaking of the land becomes a kind of rape, a passionate seduction. The earth is at once a willing and unwilling mistress, accepting and rejecting her seducer, the cause of his frustration and fulfilment, and either way the shaper and controller of his mind, exacting servitude.

The most powerful statement of that condition in the literature of the Canadian west is, I think, to be found in Martha Ostenso's *Wild Geese*, the story of Caleb Gare, a tyrannical man who, himself enslaved to the land, in turn enslaves his whole family to serve his own obsession. Characteristically, Ostenso sees him as a gigantic figure. "His tremendous shoulders and massive head, which loomed forward from the rest of his body like a rough projection of rock from the edge of a cliff," she writes, "gave him a towering appearance" (13). He is conceived in a way which makes it difficult to speak of him in conventional terms of human virtue or human vice, for he is conceived as "a spiritual counterpart of the land, as harsh, as demanding, as tyrannical as the very soil from which he drew his existence" (33). He can only define himself in terms of the land, and paradoxically it is the land and not his children that bears testimony to his potency and manhood. As he supervises his sons and daughters, grown up, but still only extensions of himself, working in the fields, he is gratified by the knowledge that what they are producing is the product of *his* land, the result of *his* industry, "as undeniably his as his right hand, testifying to the outer world that Caleb Gare was a successful owner and user of the soil" (171). At night he frequently goes out with a lantern swinging low along the earth. No one knows where he goes or why he goes, and no one dares to ask him, but his daughter Judith once remarks scornfully "that it was to assure himself that his land was still all there" (18). Only the land can ultimately give him the assurance that he is alive: "Before him glimmered the silver grey sheet of the flax—rich, beautiful, strong. All unto itself, complete, demanding everything, and in turn yielding everything—growth of the earth, the only thing on the earth worthy of respect, of homage" (126–27).

Being so possessed by the prairie, his mind and body as it were an extension of it, he cannot give himself to anyone else. Since he is incapable of loving another human being, he can receive no love in return. He marries his wife knowing that she has had a child born out of wedlock because this gives him the power of blackmail over her and, in a stern and puritan society, chains her forever to him and to his land. He knows that she once gave herself to another man in a way in which she can never give herself to him, but he cannot see that he chose her because he wanted someone who could not demand from him a love he is incapable of giving. Having committed his mind and his body to the land, greedily acquiring more and more, he can only use other human beings as instruments to help feed an appetite that can never be satisfied. His human feelings must therefore be suppressed, and the passion of his blood must remain forever frustrated, sublimated in his passion for the acquisition of more and more land. Man, the would-be conqueror, is thus also man, the supreme egoist, subordinating everything to the flow of a powerful ambition. "Caleb Gare—he does not feel," says Fusi Aronson, the Icelander. "I shall kill him one day. But even that he will not feel" (31).

He does feel for his land. But the land is a fickle mistress, and he must live in perpetual fear, for he can never be sure that this mistress will remain faithful. She may, and indeed she does, with hail and fire destroy in minutes all that he has labored to build.

Caleb Gare's obsession may be extreme, and yet a measure of egocentricity, though more often found in less virulent form, is perhaps necessary if the huge task of taming a continent is to be successfully accomplished. At the same time the necessity of survival dictates cooperative undertakings. So it is not surprising that the prairie has produced the most right-wing as well as the most left-wing provincial governments in Canada. But whether conservative or radical, these governments have always been puritan in outlook, a true reflection of their constituencies.

The prairie settlements, insecure islands in that vast land-sea, have been austere, intensely puritan societies. Not that puritanism in Canada is confined to the prairie, of course, but on the prairie it has been more solidly entrenched than even in rural Ontario, and can be observed in something very like a distilled form.

It can be argued that in order to tame the land and begin the building, however tentatively, of something approaching a civilization, the men and women who settled on the prairie had to tame themselves, had to curb their passions and contain them within a tight neo-Calvinist framework. But it is not surprising that there should be sudden eruptions and that the passions, long suppressed, should burst violently into the open and threaten the framework that was meant to contain them. In the literature with which I am dealing this violence often takes the form of melodrama, and though this sudden eruption of violence sometimes seems contrived for the sake of a novel's plot, it is also clearly inherent in the life the novelists observed. It is natural that novelists should exploit the tensions which invariably arise when a rigid moral code attempts to set strict limits on the instinctual life, if not indeed to suppress it altogether. Thus illicit love affairs, conducted furtively, without much joy, quickly begun and quickly ended, and sometimes complicated by the birth of illegitimate children, can be used as a perhaps obvious but nevertheless effective center for a novel's structure, as for example in Stead's *Grain*, in Ostenso's *Wild Geese*, in Laurence's *A Jest of God*, in Ross's *As for Me and My House*.

It is because *As for Me and My House* contains the most uncompromising rendering of the puritan state of mind produced on the prairie that the novel has been accorded a central place in prairie literature. In the figure of Philip Bentley, a Presbyterian minister and artist *manqué*, we have—at least as he emerges from the diary of his wife—an embodiment of the puritan temperament, the product of his environment and much more a part of it than he would ever admit, angry not really because the communities in which he serves are puritan, but because they are not puritan enough, because they expect him to purvey a genteel kind of piety that will serve as a respectable front to hide a shallow morality. But his own emotions remain frozen within the puritan framework from which he cannot free his spirit. So he draws more and more into himself, becomes aloof and unknowable, not in the end so different from Caleb Gare, though in temperament and sensibility they seem at first glance to move in totally different worlds. Philip's wife is certain that "there's some twisted, stumbling power locked up within him, so blind and helpless still it can't find outlet, so clenched with urgency it can't release itself" (80). His drawing and painting reflect an inner paralysis. He draws endless prairie scenes that mirror his own frustration—the false fronts on the stores, doors and windows that are crooked and pinched, a little schoolhouse standing lonely and defiant in a landscape that is like a desert, "almost a lunar desert, with queer, fantastic pits and drifts of sand encroaching right to the doorstep" (80). Philip Bentley's emotional paralysis affects of course his relationship with his wife. Thus she describes in her diary how he lies beside her, his muscles rigid, and she presses closer to him, pretending to stir in her sleep, "but when I put my hand on his arm there was a sharp little contraction against my touch, and after a minute I shifted again, and went back to my own pillow" (116).

Only once does the twisted power that's locked up within him find some kind of outlet—and then disastrously, when he seduces the young girl Judith who has come to help in the house during his wife's illness.

Prairie puritanism is one result of the conquest of the land, part part of the price exacted for the conquest. Like the theme of the conquest of the land, the theme of the imprisoned spirit dominates serious prairie writing, and is connected with it. We find this theme developed not only in Ross's novel, where it is seen at its bleakest and most uncompromising, not only in Grove's and Ostenso's work, but also in more recent novels, such as Margaret Laurence's two novels, *The Stone Angel* and *A Jest of God*, and in George Ryga's *Ballad of a Stone Picker*, and, surprisingly perhaps, in W. O. Mitchell's *Who Has Seen the Wind*, which is conceived as a celebration and lyrical evocation of a prairie childhood. Brian O'Connal is initiated into the mysteries of God and nature, of life and death, but he is also brought face to face with the strange figure of the young Ben, a curious amalgam of noble savage and Wordsworthian child of nature. Again and again he appears, seemingly out of nowhere, soundlessly, the embodiment of a kind of free prairie spirit. His hair is "bleached as the dead prairie grass itself" (12), his trousers are always torn, he never wears shoes. He has "about as much moral conscience as the prairie wind that lifted over the edge of the prairie world to sing mortality to every living thing" (31). He does not play with other children, takes no part in organized school games. Though he can run "with the swiftness of a prairie chicken," and jump like an antelope, he refuses to have anything to do with athletic competitions. School itself is "an intolerable incarceration for him, made bearable only by flights of freedom which totaled up to almost the same number as the days he attended" (147). The solid burghers of the town, strait-laced and proper, try desperately to tame him, for his wild spirit represents a danger to them. But they cannot control him any more than they can control the wind. Brian O'Connal is drawn to the young Ben, and though they rarely speak to each other, there grows up between them a strong bond, what Mitchell calls "an extra-sensory brothership" (89). The young Ben is Brian's double, the free spirit Brian would like to be, but dare not be. For Brian, one feels, will ultimately conform to the demands of his society and he will subdue the young Ben within himself.

Most of the works that I have dealt with were conceived and written more than a quarter of a century ago. There have been social and industrial changes on the prairie since then, and the tempo of these changes has been rapidly accelerating in the past ten years or so. Yet it is surprising that such novels as Adele Wiseman's *The Sacrifice* and John Marlyn's *Under the Ribs of Death*, published in the 1950s, and Margaret Laurence's *The Stone Angel* and *A Jest of God* and George Ryga's *Ballad of a Stone Picker*, published in the 1960s, should still adhere to the general pattern of the earlier works. The Winnipeg of Wiseman and Marlyn is the city of the 1920s and 1930s, a city of newly arrived immigrants, and the small towns of the Laurence and Ryga novels are clearly the small towns Ross and Ostenso knew.

For though much has changed in the west, much also still remains unchanged. Prairie puritanism is now somewhat beleaguered and shows signs of crumbling, but it remains a potent force still, and the vast land itself has not yet been finally subdued and altered. On a hot summer day it does not take long before, having left the paved streets of the great cities where hundreds of thousands of people now live, one can still see, outlined against the sky, the lonely, giant-appearing figures of men like Caleb Gare or the Ukrainian farmer in my story. And on a winter day one can turn off the great superhighways that now cross the prairies and drive along narrow, snow-covered roads, and there it still lies, the great, vast land-sea, and it is not difficult to imagine Philip Grove in his fragile cutter, speaking softly to Dan and Peter, his gentle, faithful horses, and preparing them to hurl themselves once more against that barren sea, those drifts of snow.

VII

DOROTHY LIVESAY

The Documentary Poem: A Canadian Genre

The documentary, whether in film, radio, or television, has been much with us during the past thirty years. John Grierson began the trend in the forties when he used film to document the immediacy of peoples' lives, be it in the Arran Islands or the London Post Office. Later Dylan Thomas used the same techniques on radio, in *Under Milk Wood*. But Canadian poets, in my view, have been using this approach for a very considerable time. Today we find, linked with the use of documentary material as the basis for poetry, the employment of the actual data itself, rearranged for eye and ear. J. R. Colombo's and F. R. Scott's "found" poems are of this order. The former has, for instance, used the speeches of William Lyon Mackenzie King as the basis for a printed poem; the latter has set down lines from native Indian historical documents with ironic intent, as in *Trouvailles*. An extension of this method can be found in the *locus* poems of Frank Davey, in which he seeks to portray the city of Victoria through immediate mood pictures linked with historical flashbacks. George Bowering attempts the same effect in his recent book *Rocky Mountain Foot*.

What interests me in these developments is the evidence they present of a conscious attempt to create a dialectic between the objective facts and the subjective feelings of the poet. The effect is often ironic; it is always intensely personal (as in Purdy's *The Cariboo Horses*). The more the pattern is studied, the more clearly it seems that such poems are not isolated events in Canadian poetry. Rather, they are part of a tradition which has enlivened our English-Canadian literature for a hundred and fifty years. Although this tradition has been somewhat loosely termed "narrative," I propose to show that in our literary context it is more than that: it is a new genre, neither epic nor narrative, but *documentary*.

Paper presented to A.C.U.T.E. at the Learned Societies, York University, 12 June 1969.

To analyze the long poem in Canada is not easy because so much of the material that would be of interest has not been made available throught republication. And Canadian anthologists, with one notable exception, have tended to put such emphasis on our lyric, satirical, and mythopoeic poetry that it is perhaps unfashionable, if not actually daring, to suggest that our most significant body of poetry exists in the longer poem. Yet as far back as 1946, Northrop Frye made an ardent plea for attention to this genre. In an article published, rather surprisingly, in French, he wrote:

> In looking over the best poems of our best poets, we are sur-
> prised to find how often the narrative poem has been attempted,
> and attempted with uneven but remarkable success. ... We tend
> to form our canons of criticism on carefully polished poetry,
> but such standards do not always apply to the narrative, for
> the test of the great narrative is ability to give the flat prose
> statement a poetic value.[1]

As his first example Frye uses Heavysege's "Jephthah's Daughter," where:

> In this poem Heavysege has put together certain essential ideas:
> the contrast of human and civilized values with nature's dis-
> regard of them in a civilized country, the tendency in the re-
> ligion of such a country for God to disappear behind the mask
> of nature, and the symbolic significance when that happens,
> of human sacrifice and the mutilation of the body.

But after laying down this fruitful area of inquiry, Frye seems to have lost his concern for it. In an article written ten years later he says almost the opposite:

> But the poet who tries to make content the informing principle
> of the poetry can write only versified rhetoric, and versified
> rhetoric has a moral but not an imaginative significance: its
> place is on the social periphery of poetry, and not in its articulate
> centre.[2]

What Frye means, presumably, is that such "social poetry" can be dismissed as "cold-blooded carpentry" (to use Professor

[1] Northrop Frye, "La tradition narrative dans la póesie canadienne-anglaise," *Gants du Ciel* (Spring 1946).
[2] Northrop Frye, "Preface to an Uncollected Anthology," in *Studia Varia*, ed. E. G. D. Murray (Toronto: University of Toronto Press, 1957).

Whalley's term). This is precisely the point on which I mean to take issue. For in my view the long storytelling poem with a theme may indeed be the most interesting *poetically*, as well as being deeply representative of the Canadian character.

In pursuit of this argument I will ask several questions. First, how closely have our poets been following the strict narrative pattern in a Browningesque or Tennysonian manner? To what degree are our narratives epic, concerned with an idealized "hero" as in *Beowulf?* Or do they deal rather with the development of individualized characters, as in Chaucer? Further, I would ask: Do our long poems follow the same pattern as the great American epics: *Leaves of Grass, The Columbiad, Conquistador, John Brown's Body, The Bridge,* and *Patterson,* where the emphasis is on historical perspective and the creation of a national myth?

I would deny that our storytelling in verse is concerned with any single one of these approaches. My premise is indeed that the Canadian longer poem is not truly a narrative at all—and certainly not a historical epic. It is, rather, a *documentary* poem, based on topical data but held together by descriptive, lyrical, and didactic elements. Our narratives, in other words, are not told for the tale's sake or for the myth's sake: the story is a frame on which to hang a theme. Furthermore, our narratives are told not from the point of view of one protagonist, but rather to illustrate a precept. Where there is conflict, as of course there must be, it is conflict between man and everyman; between man and nature. Moreover, our narratives reflect our environment profoundly; they are subtly used to cast light on the landscape, the topography, the flora and fauna as well as on the social structure of the country. Last, it could be proved that since the 1930s our narratives have followed the experimentations originally made by Grierson in film: they are documentaries to be heard aloud, often specifically for radio. Examples come quickly to mind: Marriott's *The Wind Our Enemy,* my own *Call My People Home,* Birney's *Trial of a City,* Pratt's *The Titanic.*

Such then, is my thesis. I know it can only be substantiated by a very close analysis of literature in this genre, a task beyond the scope of this paper. But I hope, by dealing here with a few representative examples, to give enough evidence at least to create discussion.

Isabella Valancy Crawford's *Malcolm's Katie* was published

in 1884. It purports to be "a love story." On the surface it
seems to have as model a Victorian type of domestic narrative
such as *Michael*—or more particularly, Tennyson's *Enoch
Arden*. In the latter poem we have two men circling around a
girl, Annie. One, the rough proletarian sailor, is her choice; but
in order to make a living he must leave her and sail across the
world. Instead of returning as promised, he is shipwrecked.
After a ten-year wait Annie chooses the other suitor; but the
rescued Enoch comes back to the village to die. Tennyson's
story is extremely simple and straightforward, making use of
some dialogue to carry the narrative. There is only one lyrical
descriptive passage—and that a most memorable one—where man
is pitted against nature: a kind of tropical Eden from which he
cannot escape:

> but what he fain had seen
> He could not see, the kindly human face,
> Nor ever hear a kindly voice, but heard
> The myriad shriek of wheeling ocean-fowl,
> The league long roller thundering on the reef
>
> . . . .
>
> As down the shore he ranged, or all day long
> Sat often in the seaward-gazing gorge,
> A shipwrecked sailor, waiting for a sail.

Compare Tennyson's passage now with the description of
Max, from *Malcolm's Katie*, not shipwrecked, but willingly
exiled in order to claim the land:

> The mighty Morn strode laughing up the land,
> And Max, the lab'rer and the lover, stood
> Within the forest's edge beside a tree—
> The mossy king of all the woody tribes—
> Whose clattering branches rattled, shuddering
> As the bright axe cleaved moon-like thro' the air
> Waking strange thunders, rousing echoes linked,
> From the full lion-throated roar to sighs
> Stealing on dove-wings through the distant aisles.

The language is the same mid-Victorian language (*Enoch
Arden* was published in 1864, time enough for Crawford to
have come upon it before she wrote *Malcolm's Katie*). But
in the Canadian poem there is a sense of vigor and fight rather
than lassitude. Max is determined to conquer nature:

> "O king of Desolation, art thou dead?"
> Cried Max, and laughing, heart and lips, leaped on
> The vast prone trunk, "And have I slain a king?
> Above his ashes I will build my house
> No slave beneath its pillars . . . but—a king!"

Crawford, moreover, in this seeming narrative has not wholly centered her attention on the human beings and their three-cornered struggle (for Max, like Enoch Arden, also has a rival); Crawford creates another dimension altogether by her animism, her description of primeval nature as seen through native Indian imagery. She must indeed have read Longfellow as well as Tennyson, and in the language and meters we find echoes also of Hiawatha. But compare those langorous lines:

> This is the forest primeval; the murmuring pines
> and the hemlocks. . . .

with

> The South Wind laid his moccasins aside,
> Broke his gay calumet of flowers, and cast
> His useless wampum, beaded with cool dews,
> Far from him Northward; his long, ruddy spear
> Flung sunward, whence it came, and his soft locks
> Of warm, fine haze grew silvery as the birch.
> His wigwam of green leaves began to shake:
> The crackling rice-beds scolded harsh like squaws:
> The small ponds pouted up their silver lips;
> The great lakes eyed the mountains, whispered "Ugh!
> Are ye so tall, O chiefs? Not taller than
> Our plumes can reach," and rose a little way
> As panthers stretch to try their velvet limbs
> And then retreat to purr and bide their time.

Malcolm's Katie is a poem over forty pages long, in seven parts. It begins with a straight love story, and a pattern is set that calls to mind the drama of Romeo and Juliet, with the young lovers conniving against a stern, powerful father. Part 2 contains five pages of animated nature description, and by animated I mean nature strongly personified. Not a Christian God, but spirits of wind, water, sun, moon, and night guard the secrets of the forest from Max, who like a young giant fearless and free enters the picture determined to work with nature and conquer it. Two most memorable stanzas must be quoted to illustrate the passionate force with which Crawford conceived this land-clearing scene:

> Soon the great heaps of brush were builded high,
> And, like a victor, Max made pause to clear
> His battle-field high strewn with tangled dead.
> Then roared the crackling mountains, and their fires
> Met in high heaven, clasping flame with flame:
> The thin winds swept a cosmos of red sparks
> Across the bleak midnight sky; and the sun
> Walked pale behind the resinous black smoke.
>
> And Max cared little for the blotted sun,
> And nothing for the startled, outshone stars;
> For love, once set within a lover's breast,
> Has its own sun, its own peculiar sky,
> All one great daffodil, on which do lie
> The sun, the moon, the stars, all seen at once
> And never setting, but all shining straight
> Into the faces of the trinity—
> The one beloved, the lover, and sweet love.

The final passages glow with belief and hope for the thousands of immigrants "upheaved by throbs of angry poverty." The documentation is exact:

> So shanties grew
> Other than his amid the blackened stumps
>
> . . . .
>
> The pallid clerk looked at his blistered palms
> And sighed and smiled, and girded up his loins
> And found new vigour as he felt new hope.
> The laborer with trained muscles, grim and grave,
> Looked at the ground and wondered in his soul
> What joyous anguish stirred his darkened heart
> At the mere look of the familiar soil,
> And found his answer in the words, "Mine own!"

And while in the midst of all this hum Max is king, we are reminded that his actions are motivated by love:

> O love builds on the azure sea
> And love builds on the golden sand.

In part 3 we return to the great farmhouse where Katie waits for Max to return and claim her, but where the other suitor, Alfred, begins his scheming. Whereas Max is a poet, a young

David, Alfred is a cultured intellectual. We do not know his exact calling, but we never see him with the plough or the ax in his hands! Rather, he scorns the whole pioneer philosophy: "But now another passion calls me forth . . . and makes me lover, not of Katie's face, but of her father's riches."

Alfred is a realist, scorning treasure built up in heaven. He wants what he wants when he wants it, and will go to Mephistophelian lengths of deception and intrigue to achieve it. At first, however, he lays his plans with caution. Chance comes to his aid: he rescues Katie from drowning. He hopes to win her then and there, but no:

> But Katie's mind was like a plain, broad shield
> Of a table diamond, nor had a score of sides.
> And in its shield, so precious and so plain
> Was cut through all its clear depths Max's name.

Part 4 initiates the denouement. It combines arresting descriptions of nature "From his far wigwam sprang the strong North Wind" with those of the laborer, Max, still wielding his ax, still singing:

> My axe and I, we do immortal tasks;
> We build up nations—this my axe and I!

But into this pioneer scene Alfred suddenly appears, and pours scorn on all the hero's efforts:

> "Oh," said the other with a cold, short smile,
> "Nations are not immortal. Is there now
> One nation throned upon the sphere of earth
> That walked with the first gods and with them saw
> The budding world unfold in slow-leafed flower?"

Alfred's long passages are eloquent. His argument is so strong that he throws Max off his stride, telling him: "Naught is immortal save immortal—death." But Max replies:

> "O preach such gospel friend
> To all but lovers who most truly love."

He swears by Katie's love, but Alfred ruthlessly seeks to destroy his vision. In a dramatic climax, "the bright axe faltered," the tree swayed

> In a death-throe, and beat him to the earth
> And the dead tree upon its slayer lay.

Alfred, true to his villainy, makes no attempt to rescue Max, but leaves him for dead.

> "Well, Max, thy god or mine
> Blind Chance, here played the butcher—'twas not I."

At this point in the poem we have all the elements leading to a Romeo and Juliet type of tragedy. Perhaps, dramatically speaking, it would have been effective to end the story by having Katie, hearing of Max's death, throw herself into the river! But this was not the poet's intent. Crawford was not merely concerned with telling a story: hers was a saga of pioneers. They came and conquered. It was the poet's purpose to show the triumph of love and hard work, working in unison. Hence Max *had* to be rescued from near death, *had* to return and claim his love.

So much for the story and its theme. What is remarkable throughout is the interplay of the characters with the natural world they set out to dominate. The real power of the lovers' relationship comes into being precisely because they are in harmony with nature—they are not fallen angels being driven from the garden! Katie's final words are significant, after she has reconciled her father, her husband Max, and her child to living together on the new farm wrested from the wilderness:

> "Oh Adam had not Max's soul," she said
>
> . . . .
>
> I would not change these wild and rocking woods,
> Dotted by little homes of unbarked trees,
> Where dwell the fleers from the waves of want,
> For the smooth sward of selfish Eden Bowers."

Here a mythological pattern is set of deep significance to Canadian literature. By deposing the old myths a new myth is asserted: the Canadian frontier, it is suggested, will create the conditions for a new Eden. Neither a Golden Age nor a millennium, neither a paradisal garden nor an apocalyptic city, but a harmonious community, here and now. That idea occurs again and again in our poetry and fiction. So also do the two symbolic characters: Max, the builder and singer; Alfred, the isolated intellectual.

Today a new version of the myth seems to be emerging in a way which makes Crawford's words seem prophetic. For today the pattern of pioneer life is being repeated and many "fleers from the world of want" to the south of us, and many young people from our cities are returning to the Canadian wilderness; often simply to learn to live off the land, impervious to materialistic desires. The theme is both a Canadian one and a true one for our time. As Vico remarked centuries ago, "Human truth is historical." Central to that view is the passionate desire to prove that life can be changed, here and now.

Let us return then to the poem *Malcolm's Katie*. It is not mere narrative. It is documentary and a prophecy, interspersed with some of the loveliest lyrics in our English-Canadian poetry. I will conclude this description with one of these:

> Doth true Love lonely grow?
>   Ah, no! ah, no!
> Ah, were it only so,
> That it alone might show
>   Its ruddy rose upon its sapful tree,
>   Then, then in dewy morn
>   Joy might his brow adorn
>   With Love's young rose as fair and glad as he.
>
> But with Love's rose doth blow,
>   Ah, woe! ah, woe!
> Truth, with its leaves of snow,
> And Pain and Pity grow
>   With Love's sweet roses on its sapful tree!
>   Love's rose buds not alone,
>   But still, but still doth own
>   A thousand blossoms cypress-hued to see!

I. V. Crawford, the firstborn of the group known as the Confederation Poets, herself lived through the period of pioneer construction and expansion. As a child of eight she came with her parents from Ireland to that same Rice Lake country in Ontario where other pioneer women were already living and reporting—the Strickland sisters. In consequence the documentary side of Crawford's narrative was not "researched" in the contemporary sense of the term. She lived in a narrow world which she was able to explore with intensity: the world of the British settler vis-à-vis the native Indian culture and myth.

The case is somewhat different with the Ottawa poets, Duncan Campbell Scott and Archibald Lampman. They knew firsthand the sophistication of town life. For knowledge of the wilderness

they had to go north on long canoe trips; they had also to study
the documents of fur traders, missionaries, and Indian agents.
Without that early documentation it is doubtful whether literature could have flourished at all—in Canada, or for that matter, in
America. Knowledge of historical and topical background enabled the poets to reorganize their material imaginatively. The
critic E. K. Brown has presented a pertinent comment on this
point in his introduction to Lampman's *At the Long Sault*. After
describing the historical event on which the poem is based,
the defense of the faraway village of Hochelaga (Montreal) by
a holding maneuver higher up the St. Lawrence, accomplished
by Daulac and a small body of men beleaguered by the Iroquois,
Brown comments:

> The issue was of epic significance; the background heroic in
> quality. The subject might well have been treated in a long
> narrative, but Lampman preferred to concentrate tightly upon
> the climactic action and to despatch the whole in just short of
> a hundred lines. Again and again he shows his power in pre-
> senting men and their fate with dramatic intensity and ripe
> understanding. The comparison of the individual hero with a
> desperately enduring moose is one instance.[3]

Perhaps it would be well to recall those lines, in which the
themes of courage and sacrifice are developed through metaphor:

> like a tired bull moose
> Whom scores of sleepless wolves, a ravening pack,
> Have chased all night, all day
> Through the snow-laden woods, like famine let loose;
> And he turns at last in his track
> Against a wall of rock and stands at bay;
> Round him with terrible sinews and teeth of steel
> They charge and re-charge; but with many a furious
> plunge and wheel,
> Hither and thither over the trampled snow,
> He tosses them bleeding and torn;
> Till, driven, and ever to and fro
> Harried, wounded and weary grown,
> His mighty strength gives way
> And all together they fasten upon him and drag him down.

[3] E. K. Brown, introduction to *At the Long Sault*, by Archibald Lampman (Toronto: Ryerson Press, 1943).

The Documentary Poem: A Canadian Genre

Lampman was working in this genre at the time of his death. He believed this was the way Canadian poetry might well go: not into straight narrative, but into the use of facts as the basis for interpretation of a theme. Lampman's great friend D. C. Scott had encouraged him in this direction, for he also had been experimenting with the form for several years. Scott had a head start, for as a civil servant in the Department of Indian Affairs he had a firsthand knowledge of the terrain and of Indian history, folklore, and culture. Out of this factual background he was able to create narratives strongly dramatic, often bound together by the theme explored long before by Heavysege: the theme of sacrifice. Perhaps his two most famous poems in this genre are *The Forsaken* and *At Gull Lake*. It is notable that the latter poem contains many elements not strictly narrative. The opening lyric, like Lampman's, sets the scene:

> Gull Lake set in the rolling prairie—
> Still there are reeds on the shore.

These long undulant lines take on a different stance when the Indian heroine is being described:

> In the close dark of the teepee,
> Flutterings of colour
> Along the flow of the prairies,
> . . . .
> Star she was named for
> Keejigo, star of the morning,

Scott's theme here, as throughout all his work, is "the beauty of terror, the beauty of peace." But he, like all these poets, is concerned with the theme of sacrifice: for love's sake, for humanity's sake. We shall see that this theme becomes the central column in E. J. Pratt's architecture.

Almost any one of Pratt's long satiric or serious pieces would illustrate his importance as a documentarian. He spent weeks of research on *The Cachelot*, *The Titanic*, *Towards the Last Spike*, *Brébeuf and His Brethren*, before he set pen to paper. But the strongest evidence of this is available if we consider the poem *The Roosevelt and the Antinoe* (1930). At first glance this poem is straight narrative: a story based on an act of heroism, of life-saving, during the great Atlantic storm of 1926. Pratt undoubtedly was drawn to write of it because he, of all Canadian

poets, really knew the sea. Sights and sounds of shipwrecks were
a part of his growing up in Newfoundland. But the poem owes
its creation to the fact that mere intuitive knowledge was not
enough, in Pratt's view. He has described, very movingly[4] how
he went to New York with a letter from his publishers to the
manager of the United States Steamship Lines, seeking permission to go aboard the Roosevelt for a few days and to examine
the ship's log recording the great sea disaster. Ostensibly Pratt
chooses as his "hero" Captain Fried of the *Roosevelt*, a man who
controls the rescue operation with a masterful hand and uncanny intuitive sense, his enemy being the crudest, fiercest
power of nature, a hurricane at sea. But even though Fried is
indeed the master hand, we never feel or see him as more than a
type. He is Captain Everyman, representative of "the breed,"
man; related to the animals but able to rise above them through
the power of his intelligence. He hurls himself not against God,
Evil, or Fate, but against Chance itself—the vagaries of wind and
wave.

A great deal of this long poem is descriptive of raw nature.
And here Pratt's power over language is compelling. He has
lived through such storms, he has been aboard fishing boats and
trawlers, he has documented the ship's log. Thus his poetry is
forearmed, invulnerable. Here, for instance, is the description of
the lowering of a first lifeboat:

> The crew holding suspended lines that ran
> Along the spring-stay, freeboards from the stern
> To bow were jacked to gunwales; at a turn
> Of the quadrant screw both boat and davit swung
> Outboard. The oars and boat-hooks kept her free.
> With painters taut at fore and aft, she hung
> For her sixty feet of journey to the sea.
> Below, like creatures of a gabled past,
> From their deep hidings in unlighted caves,
> The long processions of great-bellied waves
> Cast forth their monstrous births which with gray fangs
> Appeared upon the leeward side, ran fast
> Along the broken crests, then coiled and sprang

[4] E. J. Pratt, "The Roosevelt and the Antinoe," in *The Collected
Poems of E. J. Pratt*, 2d ed., edited by Northrop Frye (Toronto: Macmillan, 1962).

> For the boat impatient of its slow descent
> Into their own inviolate element.
>
> (*The Roosevelt and the Antinoe*, p. 195)

Documentation combined with raw experience; direct, plain, accurate language; sudden leaps into metaphor—these elements provide a setting for action. Added to this is the sense of "cliff-hanging" which Pratt knows so well how to handle. We *know* that the *Roosevelt* won through, or else the poet would not have attempted to record the rescue; but climax after climax leaves us breathless. Yet we have still to ask, Why trouble to tell a tale in verse that could be written down in prose, as a heroic adventure story? Why put it into verse at all, unless there lies in it a lesson of human significance, a myth larger than life? Here is how Pratt himself has commented on the theme (in a statement I believe to be unpublished):

> A job was done just in time. A call well-answered—a call of the instruments joined with the hail of human voice; and the sacrificial blood beating on the pulses. Science in league with goodwill; individual courage and humanity behind the machine. It's that sort of thing that's the hope of the world.
>
> And when the *Roosevelt* arrived in Plymouth with her brood of castaways all England was on its knees acknowledging a great deed.[5]

What is the poetic truth Pratt is reaching for here? In a time of crisis men of all races work together as a communal unit—"the breed" against implacable nature. "The frontier" means crisis and this crisis creates heroes. Pratt's relation to Crawford is manifest! The myth is being restated.

After Pratt, Earle Birney tried his hand at the narrative poem. But he also sought to adapt it to documentary patterns; *David* conforms closely to the narrative style. The particular interest for us is how the characters in the poem are related to the natural background (the Rocky Mountains). As in Pratt's work, the landscape is a key element in the drama. And always it is

---

[5] E. J. Pratt, unpublished tape recording, "A Poetry Reading," at U.N.B., Fredericton.

formidable, almost menacing, and yet indifferent. It is in league only with Chance.

Birney's most interesting documentary is *Trial of a City*. Note that it was designed to be heard as a radio documentary. It has no story line, but develops as *argument*. The scene is a trial scene and the city of Vancouver is being condemned to damnation unless enough witnesses, past and present, can defend its existence. The courtroom setting has a medieval air and the characters are people out of Everyman: "Minister of History," "P. S. Legion," "Gabriel Powers." It is intentional that the "Counsel for the Office of the Future" should speak in a spooneristic jargon linguistically akin to Anglo-Saxon. But the fun and games in this poem seem somehow to detract from the hearer's attention. One truly moving scene, charged with dramatic irony, is that in which the tribal chief of the Sechelts describes the devastation the white man has wrought on his culture and his tranquillity:

> *Chief*—Before the tall ships tossed their shining tools
> to us, my uncle was our carpenter.
> With saw of flame he laid the great cedars low,
> split the sweet-smelling planks with axe of slate,
> bowed them his way with steam and thong,
> shaped the long wind-silvered house
> where thirty of my kin and I lived as bear and lusty.
> He made it tight against the rain's long fingers,
> yet panelled to let in the red-faced sun.
> He hollowed the great canoes we rode the gulf safe as gulls.
> My uncle knew the high song of the cedar tree;
> he had a Guarding Power with Brother Wood.
>
> *Leg*— You got along somehow—that's all you really mean.

All of this scene deserves to be recorded and anthologized. It truly contains the elements of a documentary: topical data, historical and geographic, based on research; no single protagonist; man versus nature which must be dominated if man wants "progress"; and a view of nature itself as brooding, implacable, but not sinister (Isabella again!). Significantly, in *Trial of a City* it is a woman who reveals the theme. For does she not say at the end of the poem:

The Documentary Poem: A Canadian Genre

> *Woman*—I am mistress over you My Master Powers—
> The only future's what I make each hour.
>
> .   .   .   .
>
> Each day discovery delights me
> My child's quick thought, old music newly heard;
> The friend emerging from the stranger lights me
> Along the ever-branching lanes of human search.

And she concludes:

> It's my defiant fear keeps green my whirling world.

If space permitted I could give a wide variety of examples showing the growth and development of the documentary poem in
Canada. I think of Anne Marriott's picture of prairie drought,
The Wind Our Enemy, or my own poem of the frontier
versus industrialism, *The Outrider*, or the more recent subjective interpretations mentioned at the beginning of this paper.
Anyone curious enough to seek will find this work as authentic
as a Filmboard "short." Such poems record immediate or past
history in terms of the human story, in a poetic language that is
vigorous, direct, and rendered emotionally powerful by the intensity of its imagery. Thus we have built up a body of literature in a genre which is valid as lyrical expression but whose
impact is topical-historical, theoretical and moral. For we are a
curious breed, we Canadians, who somehow or other imagine
we can save man from self-destruction. A myth? Likely! But one
in which our poets continually challenge us to believe.

BIBLIOGRAPHY

The bibliography lists general rather than specialized studies of
Canadian society and Canadian writing. For critical accounts of
particular writers, the reader is referred to three new series:
McClelland and Stewart's "Canadian Writers," Copp Clark's
"Studies in Canadian Literature," and Forum House's "Canadian
Writers and their Works." The introductions to the individual
volumes of McClelland and Stewart's New Canadian Library series
also provide valuable material, as does Ryerson's "Critical Views on
Canadian Writers," which collects in separate volumes critical essays
on major writers or movements in Canadian writing. *The Literary
History of Canada*, edited by Carl F. Klinck, remains, of course, the
standard history; extensive discussions of contemporary developments may be found in the collected essays of George Woodcock,
Odysseus Ever Returning, in Desmond Pacey's *Essays in Canadian
Criticism*, and in D. G. Jones's cultural history, *Butterfly on Rock*.

GENERAL

Bell, Inglis F., and Port, Susan W. *Canadian Literature, littérature
canadienne 1959–1963: A checklist of creative and critical writings*. Vancouver: University of British Columbia Publications
Centre, 1966.

Brown, Mary Markham. *An Index to the Literary Garland (Montreal (1838–1851)*. Toronto: Bibliographical Society of Canada,
1962.

Canadiana. A List of Publications of Canadian Interest. Ottawa:
National Library of Canada, 1951–.

*Canadian Catalogue of Books Published in Canada, about Canada,
as well as Those Written by Canadians*. 2 vols. with cumulated
author index. Toronto Public Libraries, 1959.

Canadian Periodical Index, 1929–1932; 1938–(Windsor, Public Library, 1928–32; Toronto Public Libraries, 1938–).

Horning, Lewis E., and Burpee, Lawrence J. *A Bibliography of
Canadian Fiction (English)*. Toronto: Briggs, 1904.

James, Charles C. *A Bibliography of Canadian Poetry (English)*.
Toronto: Briggs, 1899.

Milne, W. S. *Canadian Full-Length Plays in English*. [Ottawa]:
Dominion Drama Festival, [1964].

Morse, W. Inglis. *The Canadian Collection at Harvard University*.
6 vols. Cambridge, Mass.: The University, 1944–49.

Tanghe, Raymond, comp. *Bibliography of Canadian Bibliographies*.

Toronto: University of Toronto Press, 1960. *Supplement 1962 and 1963*, compiled by Madeline Pellerin. Toronto: Bibliographical Society of Canada, 1964.

Thomas, Clara. *Canadian Novelists, 1920–1945*. Toronto: Longmans, 1946.

Tod, Dorothea D., and Cordingley, Audrey M. *A Bibliography of Canadian Literary Periodicals*. Ottawa: Royal Society of Canada, 1932.

Watters, Reginald Eyre. *A Check List of Canadian Literature and Background Materials, 1628–1950*. Toronto: University of Toronto: University of Toronto Press, 1959.

Watters, Reginald Eyre, and Bell, Inglis F. *On Canadian Literature, 1806–1960: A Checklist of Articles, Books, and Theses on English-Canadian Literature, Its Authors, and Language*. Toronto: University of Toronto Press, 1966.

CANADIAN LITERATURE: GENERAL

Bailey, A. G. "Literature and Nationalism after Confederation." *University of Toronto Quarterly* 25 (July 1956): 409–24.

———. "Creative Moments in the Culture of the Maritime Provinces." *Dalhousie Review* 29 (October 1949): 231–44.

Baker, R. P. *A History of English-Canadian Literature to the Confederation: Its Relation to the Literature of Great Britain and the United States*. Cambridge, Mass.: Harvard University Press, 1920.

Bissell, Claude. "A Common Ancestry: Literature in Australia and Canada." *University of Toronto Quarterly* 25 (January 1956): 131–42.

———. "Literary Taste in Central Canada during the Late Nineteenth Century." *Canadian Historical Review* 31 (September 1950): 237–51.

———, ed. *Our Living Tradition*. First Series. Toronto: University of Toronto Press, 1957.

Bourinot, John George. *The Intellectual Development of the Canadian People*. Toronto: Hunter Rose, 1881.

———. "Our Intellectual Strength and Weakness." *Royal Society of Canada Proceedings and Transactions*, First Series, 2 (1893): 3–54.

———. "Literary Culture in Canada." *Scottish Review* 30 (July 1897): 143–63.

———. "Literature and Art in Canada." *Anglo-American Review* 3 (February 1900): 99–110.

Brown, E. K. *Canadian Literature Today*. Toronto: University of Toronto Press, 1938.

———. "The Development of Poetry in Canada 1880–1940." *Poetry* 58 (April 1941): 34–37.

————. "The Immediate Present in Canadian Literature." *Sewanee Review* 41 (October 1933): 430–42.

Burpee, Lawrence J. *A Little Book of Canadian Essays*. Toronto: Musson, 1909.

Bush, Douglas. "Is There a Canadian Literature?" *Commonweal* 11 (6 November 1929): 12–14.

"Canadian Conference of the Arts." *Canadian Art* 18 (September–October 1961): 286–310.

Canadian Literature. Tenth Anniversary Issue. 41 (Summer 1969). Vancouver: University of British Columbia.

Collin, W. E. *The White Savannahs*. Toronto: Macmillan, 1936.

Colombo, John Robert."A Conference on Creative Writing." *Canadian Forum* 42 (April 1962): 13–15.

Cook, Eleanor, and Cook, Ramsay. "Writing in English." In *The Canadian Annual Review for 1961*, ed. John T. Saywell. pp. 356–70. Toronto: University of Toronto Press, 1962.

————. "Writing in English." In *The Canadian Annual Review for 1962*, ed. John T. Saywell, pp. 361–77. Toronto: University of Toronto Press, 1963.

Davies, Robertson. *A Voice from the Attic*. Toronto: McClelland and Stewart, 1960.

Edgar, Pelham. "English-Canadian Literature." In *Cambridge History of English Literature*, 14: 380–400. Cambridge: Cambridge University Press, 1917.

Eggleston, Wilfrid. "Canadian Geography and National Culture." *Canadian Geographical Journal* 43 (December 1951): 254–73.

————. "Canadians and Canadian Books." *Queen's Quarterly* 52 (Summer 1945): 208–13.

————. *The Frontier and Canadian Letters*. Toronto: Ryerson Press, 1957.

Frye, Northrop. "English Canadian Literature, 1929–1954." *Canadian Library Association Bulletin* 13 (December 1956): 107–12.

Gustafson, Ralph. "Writing and Canada." *Northern Review* 3 (February–March 1950): 17–22.

Harlow, Robert. "Bastard Bohemia: Creative Writing in the Universities." *Canadian Literature* 27 (Winter 1966): 32–43.

Jones, D. G. *Butterfly on Rock*. Toronto: University of Toronto Press, 1970.

King, Carlyle. "Literature [in English]." *Food for Thought* 10 (May 1950: 1–8.

Klinck, Carl F. et al. *Literary History of Canada: Canadian Literature in English*. Toronto: University of Toronto Press, 1965.

Logan, J. D., and French, Donald G. *Highways of Canadian Literature*. Toronto: McClelland, 1924.

Lower, Arthur R. M. "Canadian Values and Canadian Writing." *Mosaic* 1 (October 1967): 79–83.

Luchkovich, Michael. "Racial Integration and Canadian Literature." *Canadian Author and Bookman* 36 (Summer 1960): 14–16.

McCormack, Thelma. "Writers and the Mass Media." *Canadian Literature* 20 (Spring 1964): 27–40.

McDougall, Robert L., ed. *Our Living Tradition*. Toronto: University of Toronto Press in association with Carleton University, 1959, 1962, 1965.

MacLennan, Hugh. "Culture, Canadian Style." *Saturday Review of Literature* 28 March 1942.

MacMechan, Archibald M. *Head-Waters of Canadian Literature*. Toronto: McClelland, 1924.

MacMurchy, Archibald M. *Handbook of Canadian Literature (English)*. Toronto: Briggs, 1906.

McPherson, Hugo. "Canadian Writing, Present Declarative." *English* 15 (Autumn 1965): 212–16.

Marquis, Thomas G. *English-Canadian Literature*. Toronto: Glasgow Brook, 1913.

Matthews, John P. "The Inner Logic of a People: Canadian Writing and Canadian Values." *Mosaic* 1 (April 1968): 40–50.

———. *Tradition in Exile*. Toronto: University of Toronto Press, 1962.

New, William H. "A Wellspring of Magma: Modern Canadian Writing." *Twentieth Century Literature* 14 (October 1968): 123–32.

Pacey, Desmond. "Areas of Research in Canadian Literature." *University of Toronto Quarterly* 23 (October 1953): 58–63.

———. "The Canadian Writer and His Public, 1882–1952." *Studia Varia: Royal Society of Canada Literary and Scientific Papers*, ed. E. G. D. Murray, pp. 10–20. Toronto: University of Toronto Press, 1957.

———. *Creative Writing in Canada*. Rev. ed. Toronto: Ryerson Press, 1961.

———. "The Outlook for Canadian Literature." *Canadian Literature* 36 (Spring 1968): 14–25.

———. "The Young Writer and the Canadian Milieu." *Queen's Quarterly* 69 (Autumn 1962): 73–80.

Park, Julian, ed. *The Culture of Contemporary Canada*. Ithaca: Cornell University Press, 1957.

Phelps, A. L. "Canadian Literature and Canadian Society." *Northern Review* 3 (April–May 1950): 23–35.

———. *Canadian Writers*. Toronto: McClelland and Stewart, 1951.

Pierce, L. *An Outline of Canadian Literature (French and English)*. Toronto: Ryerson Press, 1927.

Bibliography

————. *Unexplored Fields of Canadian Literature.* Toronto: Ryerson Press, 1932.

Reaney, James. "A Hut in the Global Village." *Royal Society of Canada Proceedings,* ninth series, 5 (June 1967): 51–56.

Rhodenizer, V. B. *A Handbook of Canadian Literature.* Ottawa: Graphic, 1930.

Ross, M. *Our Sense of Identity.* Toronto: Ryerson Press, 1954.

Ross, Malcolm M., ed. *The Arts in Canada.* Toronto: Macmillan, 1958.

Royal Commission on National Development in the Arts, Letters, and Sciences, *Report.* Ottawa: King's Printer, 1951.

————. *Royal Commission Studies: A Selection of Essays.* Ottawa: King's Printer, 1951.

Smith, A. J. M. "Canadian Literature: The First Ten Years." *Canadian Literature* 41 (Summer 1969): 97–103.

Stevenson, Lionel. *Appraisals of Canadian Literature.* Toronto: Macmillan, 1926.

Story, Norah. *The Oxford Companion to Canadian History and Literature.* Toronto: Oxford University Press, 1967.

Sutherland, Ronald. "The Body-Odour of Race." *Canadian Literature* 37 (Summer 1968): 46–67.

Sylvestre, Guy; Conron, Brandon; and Klinck, Carl F., eds. *Canadian Writers: A Biographical Dictionary.* Toronto: Ryerson Press, 1966.

Tougas, Gerard. *History of French-Canadian Literature.* Translated by Alta Lind Cook. Toronto: Ryerson Press, 1966.

University of Toronto Quarterly. Letters in Canada. Toronto: University of Toronto Press. Annual surveys since 1936.

Watt, Frank. "The Growth of Proletarian Literature in Canada, 1872–1920." *Dalhousie Review* 40 (Summer 1960): 157–73.

Weaver, Robert L. "Notes on Canadian Literature." *Nation* 162 (February 1946): 198–200.

————, ed. *"The First Five Years: A Selection from "The Tamarack Review."* Toronto: Oxford, 1962.

West, Paul. "Canadian Attitudes: Pastoral with Ostriches and Mockingbirds." *Canadian Literature* 16 (Spring 1963): 19–27.

Whalley, George, ed. *Writing in Canada.* Toronto: Macmillan, 1956.

Wilson, Edmund. *O Canada: An American's Notes on Canadian Culture.* New York: Farrar, Strauss and Giroux, 1964, 1965. Montreal: Ambassador Books, 1965.

Wilson, Milton. "Literature in English." In *The Canadian Annual Review for 1960,* ed. John T. Saywell. Toronto: University of Toronto Press, 1961.

Wiseman, Adele. "English Writing in Canada: The Future." *Royal*

Society of Canada Proceedings, fourth series, 5 (June 1967): 45–51.

Woodcock, George. *Odysseus Ever Returning.* Toronto: McClelland and Stewart, 1970.

Zilber, J. "On Canadian Literature." *Delta* 26 (October 1966): 42.

DRAMA AND THEATER

Ball, J. L. "Theatre in Canada: A Bibliography." *Canadian Literature* 14 (Autumn 1962): 85–100.

Cohen, Nathan. "Theatre To-day: English Canada." *Tamarack Review* 13 (Autumn 1959): 24–37.

Davies, Robertson. *Renown at Stratford: A Record of the Shakespeare Festival in Canada 1953.* Toronto: Clarke Irwin, 1953.

———. "The Theatre." In *Royal Commission Studies,* pp. 369–92. Ottawa: King's Printer, 1951.

———. *Thrice the Brinded Cat Hath Mew'd: A Record of the Stratford Shakespearean Festival in Canada, 1955.* Toronto: Clarke Irwin, 1955.

———. *Twice Have the Trumpets Sounded: A Record of the Stratford Shakespearean Festival in Canada, 1954.* Toronto: Clarke Irwin, 1954.

Edwards, Murray. *A Stage in Our Past.* Toronto: University of Toronto Press, 1968.

Granville-Barker, Harvey. "Canadian Theatre." *Queen's Quarterly* 43 (Autumn 1936): 256–68.

Michener, Wendy. "Towards a Popular Theatre." *Tamarack Review* 13 (Autumn 1959): 63–79.

Moore, Mavor. "The Canadian Theatre." *Canadian Forum* 30 (August 1950): 108–10.

Phelps, A. L. "Canadian Drama." *University of Toronto Quarterly* 9 (October 1939): 82–94.

Stratford, Philip. "Theatre Criticism To-day." *Canadian Forum* 39 (February 1960): 258–59.

FICTION

Callaghan, Morley. "The Plight of Canadian Fiction." *University of Toronto Quarterly* 7 (January 1938): 152–61.

Dooley, D. J. "The Satiric Novel in Canada Today." *Queen's Quarterly* 64 (Winter 1958): 576–90.

Grove, Frederick Philip. "The Plight of Canadian Fiction? A Reply." *University of Toronto Quarterly* 7 (July 1938): 451–67.

Hicks, Granville. "Novelists in the Fifties." *Saturday Review* 42 (24 October 1959): 18–20.

McCourt, Edward A. *The Canadian West in Fiction.* Toronto: Ryerson Press, 1949.

Bibliography

New, W. H. "The Novel in English." *Canadian Literature* 41 (Summer 1969): 121–25.

Pacey, Desmond. "The Novel in Canada." *Queen's Quarterly* 52 (Autumn 1945): 322–31.

Smith, A. J. M., ed. *Masks of Fiction: Canadian Critics on Canadian Prose.* Toronto: McClelland and Stewart, 1961.

Weaver, R. L. "On the Novel: A Sociological Approach to Canadian Fiction." *Here and Now* 2 (June 1949): 12–15.

West, Paul. "Canadian Fiction and Its Critics." *Canadian Forum* 41 (March 1962): 265–66.

Whalley, George. "The Great Canadian Novel." *Queen's Quarterly* 55 (Autumn 1948): 318–26.

POETRY

Avison, Margaret. "Poets in Canada." *Poetry (Chicago)* 94 (June 1959): 182–85.

Bowering, George. "Poets in Their Twenties." *Canadian Literature* 20 (Spring 1964): 54–64.

Brown, E. K. *On Canadian Poetry.* Rev. ed. Toronto: Ryerson Press, 1944.

Cogswell, Fred. "Eros or Narcissus? The Male Canadian Poet." *Mosaic* 1 (January 1968): 103–12.

Dehler, C. R. "Canada's English Poetry since 1939." *Culture* 14 (Summer 1953) 247–55.

Dudek, Louis. "The Montreal Poets." *Culture* 18 (June 1957): 149–54.

——. "Nationalism in Canadian Poetry." *Queen's Quarterly* 75 Spring 1968): 557–67.

——. "Patterns of Recent Canadian Poetry." *Culture* 19 (Winter 1958): 399–415.

——. "Poetry in English." *Canadian Literature* 41 (Summer 1969): 111–20.

Dudek, Louis, and Gnarowski, Michael. *The Making of Modern Poetry in Canada.* Toronto: Ryerson Press, 1967.

Francis, Wynne. "Montreal Poets of the Forties." *Canadian Literature* 14 (Autumn 1962): 21–34.

Frye, Northrop. "Canada and Its Poetry." *Canadian Forum* 23 (December 1943): 207–10.

Glassco, John, ed. *English Poetry in Quebec.* Montreal: McGill University Press, 1965.

Gnarowski, Michael. "Canadian Poetry To-day, 1964–1966." *Culture* 27 (Winter 1966): 74–80.

Gustafson, Ralph. "New Wave in Canadian Poetry." *Canadian Literature* 32 (Spring 1967): 6–14.

289

Jones, D. G. "The Sleeping Giant." *Canadian Literature* 26 (Autumn 1965): 3–21.

Livesay, Dorothy. "This Canadian Poetry." *Canadian Forum* 24 (April 1944): 20–21.

Mandel, Eli. "A Lack of Ghosts: Canadian Poets and Poetry." *Humanities Association Bulletin* 16 (Spring 1965): 59–67.

———. "Poetry Chronicle: Giants, Beasts and Men in Recent Canadian Poetry." *Queen's Quarterly* 67 (Summer 1960): 285–93.

McCormack, Robert. "Unspeakable Verse." *Canadian Literature* 12 (Spring 1962): 28–36.

Pacey, Desmond. "English-Canadian Poetry, 1944–1954." *Culture* 15 (Summer 1954): 255–65.

———. *Ten Canadian Poets: A Group of Biographical and Critical Essays.* Toronto: Ryerson Press, 1966.

Park, M. G. "Canadian Poetry." *Meanjin* 78 (1959): 350–52.

Percival, W. P. *Leading Canadian Poets.* Toronto: Ryerson Press, 1948.

Pratt, E. J. "Canadian Poetry Past and Present." *University of Toronto Quarterly* 8 (October 1938): 1–10.

Purdy, A. W. "Canadian Poetry in English since 1867." *Journal of Commonwealth Literature* 3 (July 1967): 19–33.

Rashley, R. E. *Poetry in Canada: The First Three Steps.* Toronto: Ryerson Press, 1958.

Reaney, James. "The Canadian Imagination." *Poetry (Chicago)* 94 (June 1959): 186–88.

Rosenberger, Coleman. "On Canadian Poetry." *Poetry (Chicago)* 64 (February 1944): 281–87.

Roskolenko, Harry. "On Poetry: Post-War Poetry in Canada." *Here and Now* 2 (June 1949): 23–31.

Skelton, Robin. "Canadian Poetry?" *Tamarack Review* 29 (Autumn 1963: 71—82.

Smith, A. J. M. "The Canadian Poet: Part I. To Confederation." *Canadian Literature* 37 (Summer 1968): 6–14.

———. "The Canadian Poet: Part II. After Confederation." *Canadian Literature* 38 (Autumn 1968): 41–49.

———. "Eclectic Detachment: Aspects of Identity in Canadian Poetry." *Canadian Literature* 9 (Summer 1961): 6–14.

———. "Nationalism and Canadian Poetry." *Northern Review* 1 (December-January 1945–46): 33–42.

———., ed. *Masks of Poetry: Canadian Critics on Canadian Verse.* Toronto: McClelland and Stewart, 1962.

Stanley, A. "Our Canadian Poets." *London Mercury* 26 (October 1932): 537–42.

Stephen, A. M. "Canadian Poets and Critics." *New Frontier* 1 (September 1936): 20–23.

Bibliography

Woodcock, George. "Recent Canadian Poetry." *Queen's Quarterly* 62 (Spring 1955): 111–15.

LITERARY CRITICISM

Birney, Earle. *The Creative Writer*. Toronto: C.B.C. Publications, 1966.

Dudek, Louis. *The First Person in Literature*. Toronto: C.B.C. Publications, 1967.

Emery, Tony. " 'Critically Speaking' Criticized." *Canadian Literature* 4 (Spring 1960): 69–71.

Frye, Northrop. *Anatomy of Criticism*. Princeton: Princeton University Press, 1957.

——. *The Educated Imagination*. Toronto: C.B.C. Publications, 1963.

——. *Fables of Identity: Studies in Poetic Mythology*. New York: Harcourt, Brace, 1963.

——. *The Well-Tempered Critic*. Bloomington: Indiana University Press, 1963.

Mandel, Eli. *Criticism: The Silent-Speaking Words*. Toronto: C.B.C. Publications, 1967.

Pacey, Desmond. *Essays in Canadian Criticism, 1938–1968*. Toronto: Ryerson Press, 1969.

——. "Literary Criticism in Canada." *University of Toronto Quarterly* 19 (January 1950): 113–19.

Sparshott, F. E. *The Concept of Criticism*. Toronto: Oxford University Press, 1967.

——. *The Structure of Aesthetics*. Toronto: University of Toronto Press, 1963.

Stainsby, Donald. "Literary Criticism in Canadian Newspapers." *Canadian Author and Bookman* 38 (Winter 1962): 4–5.

Stevens, Peter. "Criticism." *Canadian Literature* 41 (Summer 1969): 131–39.

Sutherland, John. "Critics on the Defensive." *Northern Review* 2 (October–November 1947): 18–23.

Whalley, George. *Poetic Process*. London: Routledge and Kegan Paul, 1953.

Woodcock, George. "A View of Canadian Criticism." *Dalhousie Review* 35 (1955): 216–23.

——, ed. *"A Choice of Critics: Selections from Canadian Literature*. Toronto: Oxford University Press, 1966.

CANADIAN SOCIAL AND HISTORICAL BACKGROUND

Berger, Carl, ed. *Approaches to Canadian History*. Canadian Historical Readings. Toronto: University of Toronto Press, 1968.

Blishen, Bernard R. et al., eds. *Canadian Society: Sociological Perspectives*. Toronto: Macmillan, 1961.

Brady, Alexander. *Democracy in the Dominions*. Toronto: University of Toronto Press, 1958.

Careless, J. M. S. *Canada: A Story of Challenge*. Toronto: Macmillan, 1965.

Clarke, S. D. *The Developing Canadian Community*. Toronto: University of Toronto Press, 1968.

Cook, Ramsay. *Canada and the French-Canadian Question*. Toronto: Macmillan, 1968.

Creighton, D. G. *Canada's First Century, 1867–1967*. Toronto: Macmillan of Canada, 1970.

———. *Dominion of the North*. Boston: Houghton Mifflin, 1944; new edition, Toronto: Macmillan, 1957.

Dawson, R. M. *The Government of Canada*. Toronto: University of Toronto Press, 1963.

Fraser, Blair. *The Search for Identity: Canada, 1945–1967*. Garden City, New York: Doubleday, 1967.

Frye, Northrop. "Culture and the National Will." Convocation address at Carleton University. Carleton: Carleton University, 17 May 1957.

———. *The Modern Century*. Toronto: Oxford University Press, 1967.

Fulford, Robert. *Crisis at the Victory Burlesk: Culture, Politics and Other Diversions*. Toronto: Oxford University Press, 1968.

Grant, George. *Lament for a Nation: The Defeat of Canadian Nationalism*. Toronto: McClelland and Stewart, 1965.

———. *Technology and Empire*. Toronto: House of Anansi, 1969.

Hutchison, Bruce. *Mr. Prime-Minister*. Toronto: Longmans, 1967.

———. *The Unknown Country*. New York: Coward-McCann, 1942.

Innis, H. A. *The Bias of Communication*. Toronto: University of Toronto Press, 1964.

———. *Changing Concepts of Time*. Toronto: University of Toronto Press, 1952.

———. *The Strategy of Culture, With Special Reference to Canadian Literature: A Footnote to the Massey Report*. Toronto: University of Toronto Press, 1952.

Leach, R. H., ed. *Contemporary Canada*. Toronto: University of Toronto Press, 1968.

Lower, A. R. M. *Canadians in the Making*. Toronto: Longmans, 1958.

MacInnes, Edgar. *Canada: A Political and Social History*. New York: Rinehart, 1959.

Bibliography

McLuhan, Marshall. *Counterblast.* Toronto: McClelland and Stewart, 1969.

―――. *The Gutenberg Galaxy: The Making of Typological Man.* Toronto: University of Toronto Press, 1962.

―――. *The Mechanical Bride: Folklore of Industrial Man.* Boston: Beacon Press, 1967.

―――. *The Medium Is the Message.* New York: Random House, 1967.

―――. *Understanding Media: The Extensions of Man.* New York: McGraw-Hill, 1964.

―――. *War and Peace in the Global Village.* New York: McGraw-Hill, 1968.

McLuhan, Marshall, and Parker, Hayley. *Through the Vanishing Point: Space in Poetry and Painting.* New York: Harper and Row, 1968.

McLuhan, Marshall, et al. *Verbi-voco-visual Explorations.* New York: Something Else Press, 1967.

McNaught, Kenneth. *The Pelican History of Canada.* London: Penguin Books, 1969.

Morton, W. L. *The Canadian Identity.* Madison: University of Wisconsin Press, 1961.

―――. *The Shield of Achilles.* Toronto: McClelland and Stewart, 1968.

Porter, John. *The Vertical Mosaic.* Toronto: University of Toronto Press, 1965.

―――. *Canadian Social Structure.* Toronto: McClelland and Stewart, 1967.

Report of the Royal Commission on Bilingualism and Biculturalism. Vols. 1–4. Ottawa: Queen's Printer, 1967–70.

Rotstein, Abraham. *The Prospect of Change: Proposals for Canada's Future.* Toronto: McGraw-Hill, 1965.

Russell, Peter, ed. *Nationalism in Canada.* Toronto: McGraw-Hill, 1966.

Schwartz, Mildred A. *Public Opinion and Canadian Identity.* Berkeley: University of California Press, 1967.

Seeley, John R., et al. *Crestwood Heights.* Toronto: University of Toronto Press, 1956.

Underhill, F. H. *In Search of Canadian Liberalism.* Toronto: Macmillan, 1961.

―――. *The Image of Confederation.* Toronto: C.B.C. Publications, 1967.

Wade, Mason. *The French-Canadians, 1760–1967.* Toronto: Macmillan, 1968.

INDEX

Index

Index